FAITH AND PRACTICE

A GUIDE TO REFORM JUDAISM TODAY

Jonathan A. Romain

Faith and Practice:
A Guide to Reform Judaism Today
by Rabbi Dr Jonathan A Romain

Published by:
The Reform Synagogues of Great Britain
80 East End Road
London N3 2SY

Published 1991
Reprinted 1993

Copyright: RSGB, 1991

British Library Cataloguing-in-Publication Data:
A catalogue record for this book is available from the British Library

ISBN: 0 947884 08 4

All rights reserved. No part of this publication may be reproduced, stored in a retrieval system or transmitted in any form or by any means, electronic, mechanical, photocopying, recording or otherwise, without the prior permission of the publishers.

Cover designed by Marc Michaels
Book designed by Peter Dolton
Indexer: Sarah Ereira

Design and production in association with
Book Production Consultants, 25–27 High Street, Chesterton, Cambridge CB4 1ND

Printed in Great Britain by Redwood Books, Trowbridge, Wiltshire

Jonathan A Romain

Born in 1954, Jonathan Romain graduated from University College, London in Jewish History and Hebrew Literature, and then studied for the Rabbinate at the Leo Baeck College. Since 1980 he has been the Rabbi of Maidenhead Synagogue and recently gained his PhD in Anglo-Jewish History. Previous publications have included *Signs and Wonders* (a Hebrew primer) and *The Jews of England*. Together with Bernard Kops he produced *In A Strange Land*. He contributes articles to a variety of journals and broadcasts regularly on the radio. He is married to Sybil Sheridan and they have four sons.

This book is for Sybil
(with memories of sunshine and little boys in Jerusalem).

CONTENTS

INTRODUCTION	viii
NOTES ON THE TEXT	x
I REFORM JUDAISM	1
1. What is Reform Judaism?	2
2. Why did the Reform Movement start, and what impact has it had on British Jewry and on Orthodoxy?	5
3. What is the Reform attitude to *halachah*?	8
4. What is the difference between the Reform and Liberal Movements?	12
5. What is the role and authority of a Reform Rabbi?	16
6. How has Reform Judaism changed?	19
7. Is Reform Judaism 'true Judaism' or a branch of Judaism or a separate religion?	22
II BELIEFS	27
1. What are Reform beliefs concerning God?	28
2. What is the Reform understanding of the concept of the Messiah?	31
3. Is there a specific approach to suffering in Reform thinking?	33
4. What is the Reform attitude to the after-life, spiritualism and astrology?	36
III CYCLE OF LIFE	39
1. What special ceremonies take place on the birth of a child in Reform synagogues?	40
2. What does a *barmitzvah* involve in Reform synagogues and what is a *batmitzvah*?	43
3. What are the distinctive procedures of a Reform wedding?	47
4. Are Reform marriages recognised by other Jewish authorities?	52
5. What is the Reform attitude to hospices?	54
6. What happens at the time of death, and what is the Reform attitude to autopsies and organ transplants?	56
7. How are Reform funerals conducted?	58
8. What mourning customs are practised by Reform?	62

9. Why is cremation permitted by Reform?   67
10. What happens in special cases such as stillbirths, miscarriages, and suicides?   69
11. Can non-Jewish relatives participate in any of the cycle of life ceremonies?   72

IV SERVICES   77
1. What is different about the structure of the Reform prayer book?   78
2. What is distinctive about the Reform High Holy Day prayer book?   84
3. What is the reason for having English prayers in the services, and how does inclusive language affect the translations?   86
4. What is the role of women in Reform services, and what has been its effect?   89
5. What expectation is there concerning the ritual wear of men and women in synagogue, and of clothing in general?   92
6. What is the practice concerning the *Torah* and *Haftarah* readings in Reform synagogues?   97
7. What is the Reform attitude to having music during synagogue services?   100
8. Is the presence of a *minyan* still regarded as necessary in Reform synagogues?   102
9. Are videos or photographs allowed at a wedding or *bar/batmitzvah* in Reform synagogues?   104

V DAILY AFFAIRS   107
1. What happens in the ordinary day of a Reform Jew?   108
2. What is the Reform attitude to *kashrut*?   111
3. Are women expected to go to the *mikveh* every month?   115
4. What distinctive Jewish characteristics should one's home have?   117
5. How does Reform view the changes in Jewish family life?   120
6. What relationship should Jews have with general society?   123

VI THE SABBATH   129
1. How does one keep the Sabbath 'holy'?   130
2. What activities does Reform consider forbidden on the Sabbath?   133
3. When should the Sabbath begin and end?   138
4. How does one celebrate the Sabbath if one is without a family or finds no support amongst one's family?   139

VII FESTIVALS AND FAST DAYS — **141**
1. What variations are there in Reform observance of the festivals? **142**
2. What is the Reform policy on the 'second days' of festivals? **147**
3. Why are some of the fast days no longer observed in Reform synagogues? **149**
4. How is the Holocaust commemorated in Reform synagogues? **151**

VIII SYNAGOGUE LIFE — **155**
1. What are the requirements for membership of Reform synagogues? **156**
2. Why can women now be ordained as Reform Rabbis? **158**
3. Are synagogue fund-raising activities involving gambling permitted? **160**
4. Is it appropriate to hold appeals in synagogue on *Kol Nidrei*? **161**
5. What is the Reform attitude to Jewish education? **163**
6. What is the Reform policy on mixed-faith marriage? **167**
7. Are 'Jews for Jesus' considered Jewish? **170**

IX STATUS ISSUES — **173**
1. How does the Reform *Beth Din* operate? **174**
2. What is the Reform attitude to conversion? **176**
3. What happens in the conversion of minors and in cases of adoption? **181**
4. What is the procedure for a Jewish divorce in Reform synagogues, and what happens if one partner is unable to obtain a *get* from the other partner? **184**
5. Are Reform conversions and divorces recognised by other Jewish authorities? **187**
6. Why has the category of a *mamzer* been abolished in Reform synagogues? **189**
7. Why has the position of a *cohen* been abolished in Reform synagogues? **191**
8. Is Reform causing a split in the Jewish world by its status policies? **193**

X ISRAEL — 199
1. What is the Reform attitude to Zionism? — 200
2. In what ways should one support the State of Israel? — 203

XI MEDICAL ETHICS — 207
1. What is the Reform view of new methods of human fertilisation and experimentation? — 208
2. What is the Reform attitude to abortion and birth control? — 211
3. Is there a Reform policy concerning smoking? — 214
4. What is the Reform response to AIDS? — 216
5. What is the Reform attitude to euthanasia? — 218

XII CONTEMPORARY ISSUES — 221
1. To what extent should dialogue with other faiths be encouraged? — 222
2. What is the Reform position on business ethics? — 224
3. What is the Reform attitude to homosexuality? — 227
4. Is there a Reform policy on ecology? — 230
5. Should synagogues be involved in political or social action? — 232
6. May Jews become Freemasons? — 238
7. What is the Reform attitude to yoga, New Age and other modern trends? — 240

THIS IS REFORM — 243

APPENDICES — 247

BIBLIOGRAPHY — 251

GLOSSARY — 255

INDEX — 267

INTRODUCTION

What does Reform Judaism say? It is a question that is asked concerning countless topics, ranging from ancient rituals to contemporary issues. It is posed by Jews of all persuasions as well as by many non-Jews. The interest reflects the way in which the Reform Movement has acquired a reputation for being deeply committed to the traditions of Judaism yet willing to make certain changes in the light of modern understanding and new conditions. The result is to keep Judaism as dynamic in the twentieth century as it was in previous generations, with a clear message of faith and values for today.

Not surprisingly there has been a remarkable expansion of the Reform community in recent years, despite the fact that British Jewry as a whole is declining numerically. A variety of excellent pamphlets and essays has been produced on the Reform attitude to particular subjects but there has been no general guide to Reform Jewish practice in Britain. This book is an attempt to provide such a guide. It is not intended as a scholarly work, but to give plain and direct answers to the questions people ask. Nevertheless, references to both traditional and modern sources have been given for those who wish to pursue issues further. For reasons of space some subjects have been covered briefly even though they merit much greater attention. The Bibliography lists works that examine various topics in greater depth.

Whilst it may seem obvious that such a book is needed, two caveats have to be borne in mind. The first is that Reform Judaism believes in 'Progressive Revelation': a process by which the will of God is in a state of constant revelation, and which each generation seeks to understand for its own time. Thus changes may occur, and what may be normal Reform practice now may alter in future years. Although such developments are unlikely to affect the fundamental position of Reform, they will make differences in particular areas. What is more, they will doubtless consist of moves in both more traditional and more radical directions. This has happened in recent years: an example of the former is the introduction of *tevilah* for converts; an example of the latter is the use of inclusive language in the translation of the prayer book.

The second caveat is that Reform allows individual choice in matters of personal ritual. Thus ways of observing the Sabbath and levels of *kashrut* may vary in different households, albeit within certain parameters. Moreover, each synagogue is autonomous and so, although there is a similarity of practice between them, specific details may differ. Thus all have men and women sitting together in the services, with a mixture of Hebrew and English prayers, but some use an organ whilst others do not. This guide seeks to reflect both the general character of Reform and individual or local variations. If any of the latter have been omitted, it is accidental.

The proposal is occasionally made that there should be a 'Reform *Shulchan Aruch*' – a detailed code that commits Reform to definite practices. In the light of the above it is clear that this would not be possible, while many would deem it undesirable in principle and contrary to the thesis upon which Reform Judaism is based. It is very deliberate, therefore, that this publication is described as a guide so that there is no intention that it becomes a rule book. It offers a record of Reform today and provides suggestions for individual consideration.

Thanks are due to members of the Assembly of Rabbis who gave advice on a variety of areas – Rabbis Jeremy Collick, Colin Eimer, Albert Friedlander, Henry Goldstein, Michael Hilton, Steven Katz, Sidney Kay, Walter Rothschild, George Ruben (z.l.), and William Wolff. Particularly appreciated is the help of Rabbi Tony Bayfield, Rabbi Amanda Golby, Raymond Goldman, Maurice Michaels and Professor Ben Segal who read over the manuscript and made invaluable comments, corrections and suggestions. David Walsh was responsible for nurturing the book through its initial production stages while Ruth Cohen oversaw subsequent arrangements. Harry Philipps (z.l.) and Rabbi Sammy Rodrigues-Pereira assisted greatly with the proofreading while Sylvia Morris was extremely patient typing numerous redrafts. I am indebted also to the Hebrew Union College, Jerusalem, in the peaceful atmosphere of whose library most of this was written whilst on sabbatical from Maidenhead.

J.A.R.
December 1991

NOTES ON THE TEXT

Where procedures derive from specific decisions, the source has been given. Unfortunately, some of the earliest records from the West London Synagogue – the first Reform synagogue in Britain – and from the Assembly of Rabbis have been lost. In some instances, therefore, the original reference for a ruling is not known; in these cases the earliest reference available is given instead, prefaced by the abbreviation 'eg'. In many other instances no sources can be pinpointed, as procedures have arisen as the *minhag* (general custom) of communities and lack any formal documentation. Indeed it is one of the purposes of this book to record them for the first time.

Many people will choose to read this book in chronological order. However, the different sections have been written as self-contained units so as to facilitate those readers who wish to consult a particular one independently. Occasionally this necessitates brief mention of things examined more fully elsewhere. Those who wish to pursue different aspects of the topic will find detailed references in the index.

All Hebrew terms are explained in the Glossary.

For the sake of brevity, 'Reform' has been used as a noun and refers to the Reform interpretation of Judaism.

Abbreviations

BCE   Before the Common Era, the Jewish equivalent of BC
CE   Common Era, the Jewish equivalent of AD
RSGB Reform Synagogues of Great Britain
ULPS Union of Liberal and Progressive Synagogues

CHAPTER ONE

REFORM JUDAISM

It is not with you alone that I make this covenant and this oath, with those who are standing with us here today before the Lord our God, but also with those who are not present this day.

Deuteronomy 29.13-14

1. WHAT IS REFORM JUDAISM?

Reform Judaism is a dynamic expression of Jewish life today. It provides a way of comprehending the mystery of Creation, communing with God, relating to fellow human beings, making sense of life and death, and living according to ethical criteria. It sees Judaism as all-inclusive, a guiding force for every aspect of one's life, which colours one's outlook and actions. It is an heir to nearly four thousand years of Jewish tradition and religious experience, and seeks both to preserve it and develop it, harmonising the wisdom of the past with the realities of the present. It has a vision of a Judaism that is not only rich in history but which also appeals to Jews today and responds to modern needs. It regards other expressions of Judaism as equally valid attempts to achieve the same goals, albeit in different ways.

The defining characteristic of Reform Judaism is its attitude to the Revelation at Mount Sinai. Something very special occurred, not just to Moses but to the whole community of Israel. Its impact was such as to propel the Children of Israel from then until today, driving them not just to establish a land of their own but to develop a unique moral code and influence the rest of the world; it also enabled them to maintain their identity even when scattered and persecuted to an extent unknown by any other people. Poetic language is probably better able to portray what happened at Sinai, and we may talk of a marriage between heaven and earth in which a covenant was established between God and Israel. The book describing that event is held by the Orthodox to have been dictated by God, and to contain the exact and unchanging words of God. Its laws are considered immutable, and decisions relating to new situations at any time in the future must conform to it. In the Reform view, the *Torah* was inspired by God but written down by humans according to their understanding of God's will. The *Torah* is the testimony of a formative experience and the religious message derived from it by that and subsequent generations. Its sanctity lies in what it witnessed, not in the way in which it was recorded.

The *Torah* is therefore a continual source book, filled with inspirational passages and practical guidelines, worthy of being delved into and examined for every possible nuance and insight. However, it is still a human book and liable to errors and mis-spellings, open to challenge and revision, and subject to becoming outdated in parts. One can admit that certain sections have less merit than others. Thus the sections advising stoning a rebellious child (Deuteronomy 21.18-21) or subjecting a woman accused of adultery to trial by ordeal (Numbers 5.11-31) can be criticised as misguided, or at least inappropriate for today. Thus details of sacrifices can be regarded as a more primitive form of worship by earlier generations, now relegated to history; the altar offerings are no longer a subject to be studied in depth and for whose restoration we should pray. There is no need to defend passages that repeat or contradict one another, or seek to justify them by searching for hidden meanings in the text. Instead they can be accepted as the natural consequences of a work that has been produced by many hands over several periods. None of this is to lessen the overwhelming role of the *Torah* in Jewish life throughout the ages and still today, but rather to set it in perspective. It is an authoritative text, but does not have final authority. It demands serious attention but, having given it that, we may depart from it. This is because the process of revelation is an ongoing one, with human beings constantly striving to understand the will of God. No generation has a monopoly on the will of God, though each has insights that succeeding generations can refine and extend. In the same spirit as the injunction in the Passover *Haggadah* to consider oneself as directly involved in the redemption from Egypt, Reform emphasises that all Jews should regard the events described in the Book of Exodus not as past chronology but as a living experience, so that we too came out of Egypt (Exodus 13.8) and that we too stood at Mount Sinai (Deuteronomy 29.13-14). It is therefore incumbent on every Jew to seek to understand the demands of God and relate them to the world in which we live today, as did the biblical writers in their time. In the classic formulation of the relationship between past and present, "tradition has a vote but not a veto". Reform believes in 'Progressive Revelation' and the notion that the will of God is constantly unfolding and may be interpreted differently from the past.

This willingness to respect tradition yet be open to re-evaluation has meant that changes in beliefs and practices have become possible, whilst maintaining total loyalty to Judaism. Reform has made a distinction between those parts of Judaism that have eternal significance and absolute value, and those that are temporary and relative. The former apply for all time and include the Sabbath, the pursuit of justice, the sanctity of life; the latter are limited to past eras and include the sacrifices, the power of a husband to negate a wife's vow, the ban on clothes containing a mixture of wool and linen. Orthodoxy regards them all as having equal importance and still binding on Jews today. Reform distinguishes between a form of Judaism suitable for those living two thousand years ago in a nomadic or agrarian society, and that suitable for modern Jews in a sophisticated scientific age.

4 FAITH AND PRACTICE

There is a powerful chain of tradition connecting the one to the other, but the two forms of Judaism cannot be identical. Thus Reform has no hesitation in making changes where necessary. Certain practices are dropped, such as laws of the priesthood or obscure fast days; certain customs are amended, such as including reciprocal vows in the marriage ceremony or permitting the blowing of the *shofar* if *Rosh Hashanah* falls on the Sabbath; certain innovations are introduced such as *batmitzvah* and mourning rites for stillbirths.

Reform has also given prominence to the moral commands over the ritual observances. This is not to devalue or abandon rituals but to emphasise that by themselves they are insufficient; they must be accompanied by, or lead to, moral conduct if they are to maintain their significance. Being scrupulously honest in business or caring for the downtrodden are as much Jewish commands as lighting Sabbath candles or separating milk from meat. Observing the moral implications is crucial to one's Jewish commitment. This is not a novel view but a re-affirmation of a part of Judaism that has sometimes suffered from neglect. It is expressed as early as in the Bible itself, for even then it was necessary to assert the priorities of Judaism and not to let outer forms be confused with inner values. Thus Isaiah makes a ringing denunciation of those who fulfil the ritual commands but act immorally: "To what purpose is the multitude of your sacrifices to Me?" says the Lord; "I am sated with the burnt-offerings of rams ... and I delight not in the blood of bullocks or of lambs or of he-goats ... I cannot endure iniquity along with the solemn assembly ... when you make many prayers, I will not hear; your hands are full of blood ... cease to do evil, learn to do well." (Isaiah 1.11-17).

Another characteristic of Reform is its attitude to modern life. Instead of seeing it as something evil, to be feared and resisted, as some do, it regards it as the natural habitat of Jews today. Whilst there are many unpleasant features of modernity, it also contains much that is good. Judaism has to react positively to it rather than shy away from it. The new opportunities and insights on offer must be harnessed to the enduring values and practices of Judaism. Thus car travel can assist those who live too far, or who are too weak, to walk to synagogue. Thus women are regarded as the religious equal of men, entitled to the same privileges and liable for the same responsibilities, whether at synagogue, at home or in public. Reform Judaism therefore attempts the daunting task of bringing modern conditions and perceptions within the parameters of Jewish life, so that one can be both religious and realistic.

2. WHY DID THE REFORM MOVEMENT START, AND WHAT IMPACT HAS IT HAD ON BRITISH JEWRY AND ON ORTHODOXY?

The Reform Movement began in Germany at the beginning of the nineteenth century. It was a reaction to the new conditions brought about by the emancipation of Jews in the wake of the French Revolution. The ghettos were abolished, Jews were no longer treated as a corporate group but as individuals; they were welcomed into European society; they were exposed to the social and cultural milieu around them. The result was a mass defection of Jews from Jewish life, whilst many of those who remained found that the traditional pattern of worship compared unfavourably to the aesthetic and decorous nature of Christian services. In order to halt the flight from Judaism and to improve the quality of Jewish rituals, various reforms were introduced: prayers in the vernacular, use of the organ and shortening the length of the service. There was also the impact of modern biblical research which had undermined many Jewish tenets. It asserted that the *Torah* was the result of human authorship and it demonstrated the religious development that had occurred within the Bible itself. The effect was to challenge the sanctity and authority of the Bible, and to question its position as the ultimate source for all subsequent Jewish legislation. It also denied the notion that there had always been one unchanging form of Judaism that must continue to be maintained. A radical re-evaluation of Jewish beliefs and practice was necessary to respond to such findings.

In Britain the Reform Movement started for entirely different reasons, although it later developed in the same direction as its German counterpart. Members of the *Sephardi* congregation in the City of London, Bevis Marks, requested for several years that a branch be established in the West End for the wealthier families who had moved there and found the Sabbath walk to the synagogue an arduous journey. Permission was refused on the grounds that this might lessen the influence of the Synagogue Elders, while there were also fears that the wealthy members in the West End would cease to support the poorer members in the main congregation. An impasse was reached and several members broke away from Bevis Marks to form an independent congregation in 1840. They were joined by some *Ashkenazi* families and formed a community free of partisan divisions, entitled the West London Synagogue of British Jews. Thus the congregation began for logistical reasons rather than theological ones. Having achieved independence, it took the opportunity to make minor reforms in the service. More radical changes were introduced by the first minister, Reverend D W Marks, who declared that only the Written Law (the *Torah*) was binding, whereas the Oral Law (the *Mishnah*, *Talmud* and subsequent Rabbinic Literature) lacked authority. Thus the extra days of the festivals, additional to those specifically commanded in the Bible, were abrogated.

Marks' theology was amended by later Reform Rabbis, who regarded parts of the Bible as obsolete and aspects of Rabbinic Literature as enduring. However, his basic premise was accepted, namely that Jewish Law was in need of re-assessment and should be reformed where necessary. It was clear that Judaism had changed and developed in every age, adapting the faith of the Patriarchs to the legislation of Mount Sinai, to the idealism of the prophets, to the practical details of the Rabbis; it had also taken account of the social conditions of the different ages and interacted with, although not necessarily imitated, contemporary lifestyles and attitudes. This is particularly evident in the *talmudic* period when *halachic* principles were debated vigorously and scrutinised critically. Practices felt to be no longer applicable were effectively abolished through hermeneutical devices, and a process of interpretation which gave a different meaning to the plain text of the *Torah*. Thus the death penalty, which was widespread in biblical literature, was hedged with so many conditions that it became impossible to administer. Similarly the phrase "an eye for an eye, a tooth for a tooth" (Exodus 21.24) was divested of any sense of physical retribution and interpreted to mean financial compensation. Later on, Rabbinic decrees were employed to suspend laws that were found to have harmful effects. Thus Hillel's *prosbul* permitted loans to be repaid during the Sabbatical year rather than be negated as the Bible commands. For further evidence of how much traditional Judaism sanctioned changes in the past, it may be noted that at Sabbath services in the second century the service would last an hour, the *Torah* portion would be translated into the vernacular, the prayers would vary from community to community, men would not wear a head-covering, they would be allowed to have more than one wife and they may have sat together with the women.

The dynamic, reforming process that had been characteristic of Judaism suffered from the demise of the *Sanhedrin* in the fifth century and the lack of a central Rabbinic authority with the power to effect major changes in Jewish Law. Thereafter some leading scholars did bring about certain modifications, but there was a reticence to reverse any ruling that had been made by Rabbis of previous centuries. It was always assumed that preceding generations had more merit than they themselves and that it was presumptuous to deviate from the established tradition. The end of the sixteenth century saw the publication of the *Shulchan Aruch*, which was such a precise codification of the practical laws of Judaism that its effect was to stultify future development. It coincided with the rapid development of Hebrew printing and became widely available, dominating both *Ashkenazi* and *Sephardi* Jewry. Conformity to the *Shulchan Aruch* became the test of Jewish authenticity. Rabbinic commentaries continued thereafter but lacked the ability to tackle new situations adventurously and preferred to preserve the status quo. The result was an increasingly wide gulf between Jewish Law and everyday realities. Thus in an age which has witnessed women Prime Ministers of both Israel and Britain, the *halachah* still declares a woman legally incompetent and unfit to act even as a witness (*Shevuot* 4.1). Another example is that it is forbidden to open an umbrella if it is raining on the Sabbath, as it is considered to be akin to erecting a tent, a creative act which is prohibited on the Sabbath. Similarly, a disabled person cannot be pushed in a wheelchair on the Sabbath because the marks on the ground created by the wheels is considered to be akin to writing, another forbidden activity (*Shabbat* 7.2, 49b). Both cases typify the arrested development of Jewish Law and indicate how it has become divorced from reality. Failure to implement any changes was an abrogation of Rabbinic responsibility. Many Jews believed in both the value of tradition and the need for change. Eventually it led to a departure from the stifled world of Orthodox *halachah* in the shape of Reform Judaism.

The impact of the Reform Movement can be measured both in organisational terms and in its influence religiously. The first ninety years of Reform in Britain saw little attempt to spread its ideas to the wider community, and less than a handful of synagogues existed. However, in the 1930s a combination of the energy of West London Synagogue's new minister, Rabbi Harold Reinhart, the influx of refugee Jews from the Continent, and the growing disillusion with Orthodoxy led to a rapid increase in Reform membership, culminating in the establishment of a Reform Movement in 1942. Since then the Movement has grown to forty-one congregations which encompass 42,000 members, and it comprises one in six of all synagogue-affiliated Jews in Britain. In recent years it has been the only national synagogue movement to show an increase in members despite an overall decline in Anglo-Jewry[1]. It has its own *Beth Din*, cemeteries, a Jewish day

---

1 Waterman and Kosmin, *British Jewry in the Eighties*, p.31

8 FAITH AND PRACTICE

school and a major cultural centre in North London. It has become the acknowledged leader in the general Jewish community in a variety of fields such as the Soviet Jewry campaign, youth activities, communal relations, inter-faith dialogue and religious broadcasting. Members of Reform synagogues are prominently represented in the leadership of many communal bodies, such as the Board of Deputies, Joint Israel Appeal, Jewish Welfare Board and Bnai Brith. The Reform Movement has even greater prominence in the United States, although American and British Reform are independent of each other and differ in a variety of areas. In world terms, Reform and other non-Orthodox movements are much larger in size than Orthodoxy.

On a religious level, several of the practices introduced in Reform synagogues and originally condemned by Orthodox authorities have now been adopted by Orthodox synagogues. They include a weekly sermon in the vernacular, use of an organ for weddings, and the institution of a communal *seder*. The enormous success of the *batmitzvah* in Reform synagogues has led to a parallel ceremony for Orthodox girls: the *bat chayil*, albeit performed in a group on a Sunday and without reading from the *Torah*. Also imitated has been the concept of the synagogue as not just a place of prayer and study but as a communal centre with groups for mothers and toddlers, the youth, young marrieds and senior citizens. Moreover, to a certain extent the role of the Orthodox Rabbinate has changed. Pastoral work was not a priority for the European-born and *yeshivah*-trained Rabbis that dominated after the war. Their responsibilities were limited primarily to giving *halachic* decisions and conducting religious ceremonies. Yet Orthodox Rabbis are now expected to emulate many of the pastoral duties that Reform Rabbis have emphasised as part of their role as congregational ministers and that has contributed to community spirit (and membership growth) of many Reform synagogues. As a result many Orthodox Rabbis are judged by their care for the bereaved, lonely and sick as much as by their learning. Both in terms of numbers and impact, it is clear that Reform has become an established part of British Jewry and wields considerable influence in communal life.

3. WHAT IS THE REFORM ATTITUDE TO *HALACHAH*?

The term *halachah* refers to the legal aspects of Judaism and governs both ethics and practices. Theoretically it is a non-partisan term and it could be used to refer to Reform legal practices as much as Orthodox ones. However, the term is so much associated with the way in which Jewish Law has developed according to Orthodox interpretation, both historically and in the popular mind, that the '*halachah*' is generally understood as 'the *halachah* of Orthodox Judaism'. In this sense Reform is non-*halachic* for it does not accept the theory, methodology or practice of Orthodox interpretations of Judaism: the *Torah* is not regarded as the literal word of God; subsequent Rabbinic rulings are not accepted as binding; and many centuries-old practices have been abolished. Even if many observances are the same, the reasons behind them are often different from the *halachic* ones. Thus *mikveh* was re-introduced for Reform conversion procedures, not because the *Talmud* is regarded as sacrosanct, but for the sake of *k'lal Yisrael*, in order to harmonise status procedures with that of other Jewries. Similarly, those Reform Jews who prefer to walk to synagogue on the Sabbath often do so not because they consider starting a car creates a spark and is akin to lighting a fire, and thereby comes under the *halachic* definition of work forbidden on the Sabbath; instead it is because it can be more peaceful than going by car and becoming riled by traffic jams, bad drivers and roadworks. Orthodox and Reform may be concerned with the same issues and practices, but they operate according to very different principles – like two people engaged in a game of draughts who share the same board and use the same pieces but play by a different set of rules.

A more positive description of the Reform approach is that it parallels the *halachah*. Its policies cover all areas of Jewish life and mirror the *halachic* process, but do not necessarily conform to its conclusions. Reform always takes account of the *halachah* and regards it as the starting point for all decisions, but it does not feel bound by it. Reform allows other criteria to play an equal role in formulating a modern Jewish response: conscience, common sense, ethical values, present day knowledge, and the demands of changing circumstances. These, too, determine whether the effect of the law is in keeping with the spirit of Judaism and whether the law enhances or detracts from a life of holiness. It is because of this that Reform abolished the laws concerning the consequences of being a *mamzer*, revised the antiquarian definition of Sabbath work, freed women from the limitations under which they had been placed, deleted prayers for the restoration of sacrifices, and introduced many other changes. Despite the common assumption that such reforms are designed to bring Judaism 'up to date', there is a deeper purpose: to restore the situation whereby Jewish Law serves the Jewish people, answers their needs and guides them through everyday life. Thus while the *halachah* may influence Reform thinking, it does not control it; it acts as an important guide rather than a final authority. Reform is Progressive Judaism rather than *Halachic* Judaism, developing ancient traditions and adapting new insights for the Jews of today.

It is in the nature of this attempt to combine the voice of the past with the demands of the present that one cannot simply replace one system of set rules with another rigid system. Reform Judaism means being constantly open to new situations and perceptions. One example is the general awareness that arose in the 1980s that burying a stillborn child without any mourning rituals can result in damaging effects for the parents, and hence the introduction of burial rites by Reform synagogues. Flexibility is therefore a hallmark of Reform Judaism. Selectivity is also a characteristic, for Reform Judaism is based on the belief that the *Torah* contains the word of God, albeit expressed in the words of human beings. It is therefore inevitable that one has to sift through the *Torah* to discover that which bears the divine imprimatur and which speaks to us today. Failure to distinguish between, say, the command to be compassionate towards strangers (Leviticus 19.34) and the law to stone to death a bride who proved not to be a virgin (Deuteronomy 22.20-21) would be unthinkable. There is, of course, a disadvantage to every system and selectivity can lead to subjectivity. (Nevertheless, even within the Orthodox world there is great selectivity – ranging from which *kashrut* authorities one accepts and rejects, to whether the separation of women from men in synagogue requires that they be in a different room or merely seated separately.) To prevent choice leading to division there are defined procedures in public matters, such as status issues and forms of services, which have been established by the Assembly of Rabbis and adopted by the RSGB. They assure a similarity of practice in Reform communities throughout Britain, although always open to revisions when a general consensus arises. In private matters such as personal observance of *kashrut* or *Shabbat*, guidance is provided by Rabbis but the final decision is left to the individual concerned[1]. This is not so much because compliance is impossible to enforce, but because ultimately religious responsibility rests with each person. It is their duty to conduct themselves based upon knowledge of Jewish tradition, personal integrity and cohesion with the community. This might lead to certain variations in personal practice, but providing it is within a recognised Jewish

---

1 Charles Berg, 'Revelation, Halachah and Mitzvah', *Reform Judaism* (ed Dow Marmur) p.110

structure, there is no reason why the religious response of every individual has to be exactly the same. There is no Reform *Shulchan Aruch* to be meticulously followed, but a fluid relationship between individual freedom and communal identity. Each Jew has both the right to religious self-expression and the duty to help maintain the overall framework.

Of course, it has to be admitted that not all Reform Jews are committed, and some disregard ritual and even ethical guidelines. This is much to be regretted – although it is perhaps inevitable for the same can be said of members of all other Jewish groups, and no approach can be judged by those who follow it in name only. For those who take it seriously, however, Reform brings Jewish values and practice into every aspect of their life, in a way that is morally demanding and spiritually fulfilling.

The decisions and policies adopted by Reform until now have largely been *ad hoc*, reacting to particular issues as they arose, rather than being a systematic process of re-assessing Jewish beliefs and practices. Moreover these were not based upon the application of established principles, but on a general theological approach, the right to change tradition in the name of Progressive Revelation. An evaluation of Reform procedures reveals the history of case law. In recent years a desire has been expressed for a more methodical approach to the whole of Jewish Law and for established criteria by which decisions can be made. These would be different from the hermeneutical rules of Orthodoxy but parallel to them and fulfilling a similar function. A series of guidelines has been suggested which has met with broad approval[1]. The guidelines propose that first consideration should always be given to the traditional view, although one may differ from it if it does not correspond to contemporary situations, a matter which today's Rabbis have the authority to decide. Additional criteria are discretion and common sense, so that individual needs can be catered for and so that one can avoid a generally good law causing harm in particular situations. A hierarchical approach should also operate so that principles of major significance can outweigh lesser ones; thus using the telephone to keep in touch with family can override the traditional ban on using electricity on the Sabbath. Synagogue policy can be used to keep open traditional options that individuals may not be familiar with, although it is regarded as legitimate for individual observances to vary within a certain overall framework; thus the synagogue

---

1 A M Bayfield, *God's Demands and Israel's Needs*; the guidelines are summarised with examples in Appendix I

12 FAITH AND PRACTICE

might observe *kashrut* fully even if that is not necessarily the practice of most members. These guidelines are often employed in decisions on local issues made by individual Rabbis or on larger questions faced by the Assembly of Rabbis, although they have not yet been applied to the totality of Reform Jewish practice. In the meantime Reform continues its policy of marrying tradition and modernity as new circumstances are encountered. It is fully aware of the difficulties in understanding the will of God today, but regards striving to do so as a sacred task that has to be tackled to the best of one's ability.

4. WHAT IS THE DIFFERENCE BETWEEN THE REFORM AND LIBERAL MOVEMENTS?

The Liberal Movement began in 1902 with the formation of the Jewish Religious Union by Lily Montagu, Claude Montefiore and others. It was intended as a supplement to existing Orthodox and Reform services in London. This was at a time when the West London Synagogue was very much more conservative than it is today. Apart from some changes it had made to the Orthodox liturgy, it had not altered the character of the service substantially. Montagu and others were alarmed at the many Jews drifting away from synagogue life, and felt that a more adventurous approach to Judaism was necessary to reclaim them. Initially it was supported by both Orthodox and Reform ministers who backed the attempt to appeal to disaffected Jews. The first Liberal service saw men and women sitting together, a considerable amount of the prayers being in English, and the use of an organ – all of which were lacking elsewhere. However, the quest for religious innovation resulted in it developing into a separate movement, becoming known as the Union of Liberal and Progressive Synagogues. Like the RSGB, the ULPS today is a national network of autonomous synagogues, subscribing to common principles, sharing the same Liberal prayer book, and having its own set of Rabbinic procedures in status matters.

For several decades Liberal synagogues were characterised by radicalism, in which rituals were considered relatively unimportant and sincerity of heart was all-important. Many Liberal Jews abandoned the wearing of headcoverings and the *tallit*. Maintaining Hebrew was regarded as secondary to comprehending the prayers, and so the majority of the service was conducted in English. Certain aspects of the calendar were considered to be inappropriate to the higher ethics of Judaism, and so *Purim* was deleted from the calendar, while parading the scrolls and dancing at *Simchat Torah* were omitted. There was still a great respect for tradition, but it was subject to much more critical scrutiny than in Reform synagogues, and there was less hesitation in rejecting rituals and concepts that were felt to be outdated or counterproductive. Reform also subscribed to the principles of intellectual honesty and the need to take account of modern circumstances, but the Liberals were often much more consistent and thorough in applying it. Thus, since they disagreed with some of Maimonides' *Thirteen Principles of Faith*, the *Yigdal* (the song version of it) was reduced to nine verses, while a tenth was included with a revised wording. Reform had similar reservations, but preferred to maintain the traditional format. Another example, of small consequence in itself but highlighting the contrast, was that the Liberal prayer book opened from left to right in accordance with the way congregants opened every other book, whereas the Reform *siddur* followed the traditional direction dictated by the Hebrew text and opened from right to left.

At root, both Movements shared the same principles of a progressive approach to Judaism, believing that the will of God is revealed in every generation, and therefore both assert the right to institute changes and recognise the integrity of individuals to make their own religious decisions. The differences were more a matter of emphasis and the extent to which such changes were made. Attacks on the Liberals by the Orthodox authorities were often much more severe and sometimes made it appear that the Reform were more acceptable to them. Being inbetween the religious position of Orthodoxy and Liberalism, Reform was wrongly seen as a 'halfway house', whereas both Reform and Liberal were non-*halachic* and much closer to each other than to Orthodoxy. The oft-expressed popular view that "at least they are not as bad as the Liberals" reflected the greater surface traditionalism of the Reform but ignored the underlying approach common to both.

In recent decades the two Movements have changed considerably. The Liberals have re-introduced many traditions previously jettisoned. Head coverings have made a substantial return, Hebrew is valued more highly, and *Purim* is celebrated again. The Reform Movement has also become more traditional in certain areas, although in other respects it has led the way in several radical developments such as the employment of female Rabbis and the use of inclusive language in the liturgy. At the same time, the more rigid form of Orthodoxy that has emerged since the Second World War has led to an increasing gulf with Reform.

In effect the differences between the Reform and Liberals have lessened and the fundamental similarities have come to the fore. Moreover, because of the religious autonomy of each congregation, it is sometimes the case that the type of service at a particular Reform and Liberal synagogue has more in common than between two Reform or two Liberal synagogues. This closeness was both recognised and strengthened in 1964 when the ULPS became a co-sponsor of the Leo Baeck College, the Rabbinical College established eight years earlier by the RSGB, which thereafter trained Rabbis for the two Movements. Rabbis serving Reform and Liberal congregations today have had exactly the same training, while some of them have held pulpits in each Movement. Both Movements belong to the World Union for Progressive Judaism, whilst they are also linked by a variety of organisations established jointly by them: Pro Zion engages in Zionist political activity to promote the cause of the Progressive Movement in Israel, and in particular its struggle for equal rights. The Friends of Progressive Judaism in Israel raises funds for projects launched by the Movement there and in support of its communities. The Council of Reform and Liberal Rabbis co-ordinates Rabbinic activities when a united response to external events is appropriate. The Association of Reform and Liberal *Mohalim* provides qualified practitioners for circumcisions. In 1988 the educational departments of both Movements united under the aegis of the Centre for Jewish Education which now serves all Reform and Liberal religion schools and assists wider educational activities. It is clear, therefore, that the RSGB and ULPS synagogues work together in many areas and have much in common. As it has been put colloquially, "they speak the same religious language and have very similar goals".

There are still certain differences in nuance between the two Movements, and there are three major issues that divide them. The first concerns Jewish status. The Reform adhere to the matrilineal line of descent, and recognise a person as Jewish if their mother is Jewish. The Liberals accept individuals as Jewish if they have any one parent who is Jewish, and providing that they have been brought up as Jewish. The ULPS argues that in a society where men and women often both share the religious upbringing of children, it is both illogical and sexist that the gender of the parent who is Jewish should determine whether the child is Jewish. It is the Jewish home life and education of the child that should be the deciding factor. The Reform believe it would be detrimental to overall Jewish unity to change the traditional definition of Jewish status. Nevertheless it is recognised that 'patrilineal Jews' (those with a Jewish father but non-Jewish mother) can have a strong

Jewish identity. Those that wish to regularise their status via the Reform Beth Din are given every encouragement, and are often granted exemptions from the full conversion course if they have already led a Jewish life.

A second difference concerns the requirements for conversion. The courses run by the ULPS and RSGB are virtually identical in terms of length of time, study topics, home practices, synagogue attendance and circumcision for male proselytes. However, in the Reform all candidates undergo the traditional rite of *tevilah* (ritual immersion), whereas this is not demanded by the Liberals. For many years *tevilah* was not a Reform requirement either, but it was re-introduced in 1977 to harmonise RSGB practices with those worldwide. It was also felt to be a meaningful rite that symbolised the new religious identity of the proselyte. Despite this discrepancy, Liberal proselytes are considered fully Jewish as it is the policy of the RSGB to recognise proselytes accepted into Judaism by any other *Beth Din*[1].

The third difference occurs in divorce procedure. The Reform urge couples undergoing a divorce to obtain a *get* and thereby terminate the relationship both civilly and religiously. A *get* is essential before either partner can remarry in synagogue. The Liberals regard a civil divorce as sufficient and do not insist on any other Jewish ceremony. Liberals who had remarried without a *get* would be accepted as husband and wife if they transferred their membership to a Reform synagogue; however, if the second marriage had not yet occurred, the partners would be asked to obtain a *get* before the wedding could take place in a Reform synagogue. It should be noted that whilst policies over *tevilah* and a *get* are significant differences between RSGB and ULPS, in Orthodox eyes there is no distinction between the two Movements, as they do not recognise the converts of either of them and do not accept a Reform divorce as valid.

A variety of other, lesser differences also occur although they may not apply to every synagogue. Thus all Reform communities insist that a certain degree of *kashrut* is observed at synagogue functions, whether by serving *kosher* meat only, or by separating milk and meat products. Some Liberal communities do likewise, but others have no objections to *non-kosher* meat. All Liberal synagogues observe *Rosh Hashanah* for one day only, as do some Reform congregations, although many others hold a second day service. Local custom and the personality of the Rabbi are often more of a determining factor in the religious character of a community than the label

---

1 Assembly of Rabbis, 10th July 1957

'Reform' or 'Liberal' that is attached to it.

The idea of a merger between the two Movements is suggested frequently, and serious attempts to explore the possibilities of a union were made in 1985. The eventual decision not to merge was based partly on the three major differences already mentioned, which were felt by some to be too large to be bridged. Others pointed out that all three were limited to status areas that might never affect most members of the RSGB and ULPS, whilst there were ways of harmonising the discrepancies given sufficient will on both sides. It is likely that in future decades, further efforts will be made to have a unified Progressive Movement, especially if changes occur in the procedures of either Movement that minimise those particular differences. In the meantime there is a close level of co-operation in areas of common interest. In addition many neighbouring local Reform and Liberal synagogues have, of their own accord, formed local links. They hold joint events, share resources, and their Rabbis exchange pulpits. Many of their members will state that they have a Reform or Liberal identity and feel more at home in one type of synagogue than the other, but the ideology of the two Movements is so similar that in practice they often do not mind joining whichever synagogue is the nearest.

5. WHAT IS THE ROLE AND AUTHORITY OF A REFORM RABBI?

The role of the Reform Rabbi is varied and demanding. Indeed the congregational Rabbi is often expected to be a 'jack of all trades' and master of every one. The most visible duty of the Rabbi is conducting Sabbath and Festival services. Reform Rabbis usually lead the whole of the service whereas their Orthodox counterparts often read only the *Torah* section with a *chazan* responsible for the rest of the service. A further difference is that a sermon is expected on every Sabbath. In some synagogues this occurs at both the evening and morning services; at others it is only during one of the services, with an explanation of the *Torah* portion occurring at the other one. Services for personal events such as a marriage, funeral and *shivah* are also taken by the Rabbi. Another major activity is educational work. This takes place at all levels of the community including the Religion School, Adult Education, Proselyte Classes, *Shabbat* Study Groups and special sessions connected with the festivals. Equally important is the pastoral role. This entails visiting those who are ill, whether at home or in hospital, those who have been bereaved, and those who are elderly or unable to attend synagogue. It also involves assisting with a whole range of personal issues, whether marital difficulties, loss of faith, depression or other crises. This is the invisible work of Rabbis, often the most time-consuming, but only known about by the one or two people involved in each case. In recognition of the widespread nature of such problems and the need to respond professionally, many Reform Rabbis are trained in marriage guidance, psychotherapy or other forms of counselling. This is a major development in the skills of a Rabbi and has proved of great benefit in communal life.

What lies behind all the sermons, classes and private conversations is the very essence of Rabbinic activity: providing religious guidance on moral, personal and ritual questions. Such questions might include the ethical demands of a business problem, whether one should say *Kaddish* for one's first spouse after re-marrying, what blessing should be said if one has to eat food on *Yom Kippur* for health reasons, how to give one's children a strong Jewish identity, why spiritualism is discouraged, and when to tell an adopted child about his origin. Some Rabbis publish examples of such questions along with the response given in their synagogue newsletter, both as an educational device and so as to build up a body of modern Reform responsa. It also helps members to understand what help they can look to their Rabbi to provide. Issues affecting the community as a whole are also dealt with by the Rabbi, such as the format of a *bar/batmitzvah* or synagogue activities permitted on the Sabbath. In some communities a Ritual Committee assists the Rabbi in decision-making, partly to involve a lay perspective and partly to help with administrative details.

Rabbis are expected also to be involved in the wider aspects of the community, such as social and cultural events. Thus periodic appearances at the Mothers and Toddlers, Youth Groups and Friendship Club are important. Indeed most Rabbis welcome this as an opportunity to meet those who are part of the community but who do not necessarily attend services, or to see those who are synagogue-goers in a different milieu. The Rabbi is also part of the general policy-making body of the synagogue, and has an automatic place on Council. This too differs from Orthodox Rabbis, many of whom are seen as occupying a religious role only and are divorced from the organisational aspects of the community.

Much work is done by the Rabbi in the general community as well. This might include speaking to groups such as Rotary, Scouts, schools, churches and Women's Institutes on Jewish life, establishing relations with clergy of other faiths, representing the synagogue on local bodies, or leading courses for religious education teachers on Jewish beliefs and practices. It is also usual for the Rabbi to play a role within the Reform Movement as a whole. This could entail serving on committees, assisting with youth holiday camps, visiting synagogues without a Rabbi, or other involvements. In addition, all Rabbis who serve an RSGB community are called upon in rotation to sit as a member of the Reform *Beth Din*.

The authority of Reform Rabbis derives from their *semichah* (ordination). In Britain this is awarded by the Rabbinical College, the Leo Baeck College, following a five year course of study. During that time one learns both traditional Jewish sources and modern pastoral skills as well as gaining some practical experience in congregational and educational work. The *semichah* is not accepted by Orthodox authorities but is recognised worldwide by Conservative, Liberal and other Reform communities.

The authority of Rabbis in their own congregation is tempered by two considerations. First, as a member of the Assembly of Rabbis, the professional body to which all Reform Rabbis serving British communities belong, there are certain strictures which must be observed, such as not officiating at mixed-faith marriages[1]. Such decisions are taken collectively and voted upon, for there is no Reform Chief Rabbi who asserts central control. Secondly, all status questions must be resolved by the Reform *Beth Din*, such as cases of conversion, divorce and adoption. Most other religious aspects of congregational life are the responsibility of the Rabbi concerned; for example, which prayers to read in English, whether non-Jewish caterers can be used for synagogue functions, and what type of activities are suitable for fund-raising. Thus in matters of communal observance the Rabbi has considerable influence, even though in personal observance Reform is strongly attached to the principle of individual religious freedom. The style of most Rabbis is not to issue proclamations to the laity but to discuss questions with them, thus involving and educating the community in the process and using decision-making as a teaching method. It might be added that there are occasional disagreements between the Rabbi and congregation over certain issues, but Rabbis who enjoy the confidence of their community usually find that their advice is followed. No Rabbi, Orthodox or Reform, can impose their authority on the congregation unless they first earn its respect.

---

1 Assembly of Rabbis Revised Constitution, 12th January 1981

As each Rabbi is independent of central control save in the two aspects already mentioned, and as each congregation within the RSGB is autonomous, considerable variations can occur between Reform communities. Thus one synagogue may have an organ and a choir and read substantial parts of the service in English, whilst another may have neither organ nor choir and read most of the service in Hebrew. Each has its own *minhag* (custom) that has evolved over the years as a result of the character of its membership and the personality of its Rabbi. As a result, there is often greater variation between the services in one Reform synagogue and another than between those of one United Synagogue and another. However, there is still a broad conformity between all Reform communities, each using the same prayer book and subscribing to the same principles of a modern approach to Jewish life.

6. HOW HAS REFORM JUDAISM CHANGED?

Being open to both re-evaluation of tradition and to contemporary influences, Reform has undergone certain changes in the last few decades. Their accumulative effect has been to make Reform appear more traditional than it was previously although its essence remains the same. The changes are primarily due to the blow dealt by the Holocaust to the spirit of optimism and universalism that had dominated Reform thinking beforehand, and indeed that of many Jews generally. Prior to the rise of the Nazis there was enormous confidence among the majority of Jews that they were in harmony with European society. Cultural and scientific achievements were ever-increasing, the age of reason heralded the demise of prejudice, the world was progressing towards a glorious future, and the 'Jewish problem' seemed to have been resolved. Jews identified with their fellow citizens, loved their neighbours as themselves, and imagined that together they would advance steadily towards the Messianic era. All this was shattered by the return of anti-semitism in the most devastating form ever known. Jews were reminded once again of the destructive elements within humanity and of their own separateness from all other people. Optimism was replaced by scepticism, universalism by particularism. There was a closer identification with fellow Jews because they were Jews. There was a search for specifically Jewish roots and a return to folk traditions. The Jewish nationalism that most Jews had formerly dismissed as an alien distraction was now welcomed by many as the new path to redemption. More recently Yiddish, once despised as the language of the ghetto, has experienced a minor revival in a wave of nostalgia for the private language of former times, and in recognition of the rich cultural heritage to which it had given rise.

The impact of these powerful changes can be seen throughout post-war Jewry. They are evident, too, in Reform Judaism and can be identified in four main areas: self-identity, status issues, ritual observances and source-texts.

The more intense identification with Jewish causes has led to a rejection of the generally anti-Zionist stance of early Reform thinking. It was realised, firstly, that a Jewish state could prevent the recurrence of Jews being prey to the whims of the host community; and secondly that it could fulfil the many prayers yearning for a return to the land of their biblical ancestors. It was both opportune politically and valid religiously. Today the Reform Movement is linked to the World Zionist Organisation, has numerous educational and fund-raising activities in support of Israel, and has encouraged programmes promoting *aliyah*, particularly amongst its youth. Another manifestation of the concern to reinforce Jewish identity is the establishment of the first Reform Jewish day school, Akiva, as well as the rise of nursery schools in many Reform congregations. Again this departs from the former days when all hints of separatism were abhorred. Now it is felt to be a legitimate way of inculcating Jewish knowledge and values in partnership with English lifestyle and culture.

The concern for the totality of Jewish life and the awareness of *k'lal Yisrael* has led to an increasing desire to be in harmony with the general Jewish practices in status issues. It is felt important that Reform status procedures should correspond as closely as possible with those of other Jewish groups without compromising a Reform perspective. Thus the writing of a *get* in cases of divorce was reinstated in the 1940s and made obligatory for those wishing to remarry in a synagogue. Similarly, *tevilah* was reintroduced in 1977 for all male and female proselytes. The fact that Orthodoxy has not accepted Reform conversions or divorces, even though they now fulfil the traditional requirements, is a matter for great regret.

Greater traditionalism has affected ritual observances too. The synagogue liturgy now includes many traditional prayers omitted from previous editions. Thus the Daily and Sabbath Prayer Book issued in 1977 re-introduced the blessings before and after the reading of the *haftarah*, the blessing for putting on *tefillin*, and the second paragraph of the *Aleinu*. Similarly the High Holy Day Prayer Book issued in 1985 re-introduced the *Selichot* Service, the

Unetaneh tokef prayer, and the full traditional version of the *Kol Nidrei* prayer. In many synagogues the practice of sitting after the first three paragraphs of the *Amidah* has been replaced by standing throughout the remaining paragraphs. Some synagogues that once used an organ at Sabbath services have dispensed with it. The canonicals (gowns and bands) previously worn by most Rabbis have been abandoned by many today, while the small silk *tallit* has often grown into a large woollen one. Some congregations have re-introduced a second day *Rosh Hashanah* service, provision for which has been made in the new High Holy Day Prayer Book[1]. Most congregations have adopted definite policies regarding the *kashrut* of food served on synagogue premises. They insist either that all meat should be *kosher* and milk products be separated, or that only milk and vegetarian products should be used. Previously rules on *kashrut* were much laxer in many congregations.

The concern for Jewish roots is apparent too in the source texts used for sermons and study groups. In the past most addresses focused primarily on ethical and moral principles, exhorting congregants to purer and more spiritual lives. Nowadays they are equally concerned with Jewish tradition and customs, educating the community as to how best to put a Jewish lifestyle into practice. Quotations that once came exclusively from the Prophets are today outnumbered by references from the *Talmud*. Study groups which once pored over theological and philosophical works have given way to those concentrating on Rabbinic commentaries or *Chasidic* texts. Interest in *halachah* and the 'Jewish way of doing things' has replaced the pursuit of pure spirituality and the path of ennobling rectitude. Indeed, the pendulum has swung so far that there have been calls for a return to the moral outrage of the Prophets. In addition the search for spirituality has led to interest in psychoanalysis and inner redemption[2].

It should be noted that these changes in Reform are differences of nuance rather than character. Reform still retains its modern approach to Jewish life. Indeed in other areas it has led British Jewry in its radicalism, such as ordaining women Rabbis and catering for female congregants through the introduction of inclusive language in the prayer book. Major initiatives have taken place in matters that once were considered 'political' and beyond the

---

1 *Forms of Prayer*, Vol III, pp.881-908
2 *Soul Searching: Studies in Judaism and Psychotherapy* (ed Howard Cooper)

concern of religion, but which are now seen as the testing-ground of Judaism's concern for everyday life: nuclear arms, human rights, poverty and homelessness. Reform has also tackled issues that were previously taboo subjects, such as homosexuality and mixed-faith marriages. Neither are promoted but the genuine needs of individuals in both situations are recognised and practical steps have been taken to be more accommodating to them. In both instances, Reform has been unafraid to step into controversial areas when it felt that a new approach was necessary in the light of modern conditions. It would be wrong to measure whether British Reform has become more 'right-wing' or more 'left-wing'. Instead the best summary is that it has grown much more confident. Thus it feels able to re-adopt customs that were rejected by earlier generations, yet is willing equally to venture into areas from which they would have shied away. It retains both its respect for the traditions of the past, and its determination to respond to the needs of the present.

7. IS REFORM JUDAISM 'TRUE JUDAISM' OR A BRANCH OF JUDAISM OR A SEPARATE RELIGION?

It is hard for some Jews to view the nature of Reform dispassionately, being swayed either by their own personal sympathy or hostility to it. It is noteworthy, however, that the most adamant rejection of Reform comes from those who are generally unaware of what Reform Judaism stands for, who have never attended a Reform service, and who are therefore unqualified to judge it. If one was to imagine an objective analysis of Reform and Orthodoxy by a non-Jew, it would probably note that the services of both contain Hebrew, the major prayers are the same, the worshippers wear head coverings and prayer shawls, they celebrate the same festivals and observe the same calendar, they circumcise their boys, hold *barmitzvah* at thirteen, marry under a *chuppah*, recite *Kaddish* and sit *shivah* at times of death, eat and abstain from the same foods, share the same history, have the same regard for Israel, derive their tradition from the same source texts, and believe in the same incorporeal but revealing God. These vast similarities outweigh the variations in detail, and stamp the two as common heirs to the same tradition differently interpreted. Indeed, in matters of practice it is the details that separate Reform and Orthodoxy. Thus there is a different approach to which type of work is permitted on the Sabbath and how many people are required in order to recite *kaddish*, but a common agreement that the Sabbath should be a time of rest and that the *kaddish* be said for the departed. If there was less in common on the generalities of Judaism, then arguments about the particulars would not be so heated or even necessary at all.

It is clear, therefore, that the Jewishness of Reform is hardly an issue for debate, and the real question is who has the better claim to be 'true Judaism'. In this respect there is a certain imbalance of opinion between the two groups: Orthodoxy regards itself as the only correct teaching of Judaism and dismisses Reform as a fallacy, whereas Reform sees both Reform and Orthodoxy as valid branches of Judaism for those who subscribe to them. Part of the problem lies in the fact that in Britain it is only in the last fifty years that Reform has grown rapidly and has been opposed vigorously. It is noticeable that in the United States, where Reform has long dominated American Jewry, Orthodoxy has been forced to come to a public acceptance of Reform synagogues and Rabbis, if only as a sociological reality. For the past 400 years there had been a standard form of Judaism which was virtually uncontested. Rabbinic Judaism had reigned supreme, only temporarily worried by Shabbateanism in the seventeenth century and quickly absorbing *Chasidism* in the late eighteenth century. The change from a monolithic Judaism to a pluralistic one is a modern phenomenon to which Jewry has not yet fully adjusted. However, it is not without precedent, for Jewish life before the first century also witnessed several competing strands of Judaism with Pharisees, Sadducees, Essenes, Theraputae, Dead Sea sects and Hemerobaptists. There were considerable theological and ritual differences between them, although all existed within a recognised Jewish framework. Yet it was not necessarily the outstanding merit of the Pharisees that led to their domination and the eventual merge of all Jews into Rabbinic Judaism. It was the war with Rome in 67 CE which ravaged Israel, destroying both the Temple and the wilderness communes, and which left the Pharisees as the only group capable of responding to the chaos that ensued. The fact that they revolutionised Judaism and revitalised Jewish life is to their immeasurable credit; but it should not obscure the external circumstances that led to the supremacy of their interpretation of Judaism over that of their contemporaries. Thus the pluralism in Judaism today is merely a return to the pluralism that existed in earlier times and there is nothing un-Jewish about it. One can be religious without being Orthodox; one can be deeply committed to Judaism without maintaining every single observance of past generations.

The establishment of the Reform Movement, either originally in Germany or its British counterpart later on, was not motivated by a desire to create a new Judaism for its own sake, but to cater for the new lifestyle of Jews already in existence. Thus Jews had lost familiarity with Hebrew, no longer believed in the physical resurrection of the dead, did not desire the restoration of sacrifices, wanted greater decorum in services, lived too far from synagogues to walk there on the Sabbath, preferred to be cremated rather than buried, and favoured the re-introduction of instrumental music into Sabbath and festival services. As with the other great changes in the past (negating the death penalty, preventing polygamy, allowing interest-bearing loans to fellow Jews), it was sociological factors that prompted *halachic* changes. *Halachah* rarely initiated new trends in society but followed popular developments and legitimised them. In the same way Reform merely responded positively to the sociological changes amongst the Jews of the nineteenth and twentieth centuries, whereas by this time Orthodoxy was unwilling or unable to operate the flexibility that had once characterised the *halachah*.

It is significant that until 1958 the Reform Movement in England was known as the Association of Synagogues in Great Britain. It lacked the word Reform in its title, as did the first Reform synagogue and many subsequent ones. They deliberately avoided any nomenclature that would imply separatism from the mainstream of Judaism. From the beginning the Reformers saw themselves as a trend not a sect, and they did not require any adjectives to qualify themselves. It was only later that the term Reform was used when it was felt to be a positive attraction to those who might otherwise drop out of synagogue life altogether[1]. The term 'Reform Judaism' is a convenient shorthand for the Reform interpretation of Judaism. Thus while the label 'Reform Judaism' distinguishes Reform from other brands of Judaism, it also makes clear that it is closely linked to them and is engaged in the same task of continuing the traditions of Judaism, albeit from a particular perspective. Perhaps the situation might be compared to that in Christianity where several different denominations exist but are all recognisably Christian. After centuries of mutual persecution, including burning each other as heretics, they have come to a *modus vivendi* and realised that God is manifest in several different ways and that no one has a monopoly on the truth. Judaism has avoided the worst excesses of Christianity but has not yet learnt the lessons of tolerance. It would be highly regrettable if Orthodox-Reform

---

1 See Jonathan Romain, 'RSGB – Does It Need A New Label?', *Manna* (Winter 1987), p.2

differences were to continue to be another example of religion leading to antagonism rather than to harmony. Reform sees itself as neither superior nor inferior to Orthodoxy, but as an equally authentic expression of Judaism today. Authenticity does not mean that everyone else agrees with you, but that you have firm reasons for your faith and practice. The validity of Reform does not depend on Orthodox recognition, but on its confidence in its own history and mission. There is no attempt to detract from those who accept the tenets of Orthodoxy; instead there is a desire to offer a different approach for those unable to feel at home with Orthodoxy yet who are equally committed to the same dynamic Jewish heritage. Judaism is a 'tree of life' which has one trunk but several branches.

CHAPTER TWO

BELIEFS

I am the Lord your God who brought you out of the Land of Egypt, out of the camp of slavery.

Exodus 20.2

1. WHAT ARE REFORM BELIEFS CONCERNING GOD?

There is no separate Reform theology of God and its position is generally at one with the traditional view[1]. Indeed it is noticeable that although Reform would not subscribe to some of the thirteen principles of faith drawn up by Maimonides concerning the nature of the *Torah*, there is no disagreement with the first five on the essence of God. According to Maimonides' summary of Jewish belief, God is the sole creator, indivisible, incorporeal, eternal and unique. It is also accepted that there have been Divine revelations to humanity, whether in the mass experience of a whole people at Mount Sinai (Exodus 19.16ff), or in the small, still voice to a lonely and dispirited Elijah (I Kings 19.9ff), or out of a whirlwind to a Job who is desperately trying to make sense of the pain and confusion he feels (Job 38.1). Thus God is not only the God of grand designs, creating and legislating, but is also the God of each individual, with whom one can have a personal relationship.

The liturgy in the Reform prayer book largely follows the traditional prayers in its presentation, although it also contains some important departures. One difference is the avoidance of specifically male terminology when referring to God. Such imagery not only limits God but also alienates those worshippers who find it difficult to relate to a male stereotype (see IV.3). In addition, some of the new prayers that have been added try to overcome the modern hesitation in addressing God. In an age that values logic over faith, many Jews find it easier to concentrate on doing rather than believing. Even when beliefs are tackled, it is more often talking about God rather than talking to God. It is a problem common to Jews of all strands, with some avoiding the question of God by retreating behind the rules of the *halachah*, and others doing so by burying themselves in social action. In both cases it is much easier to deal with set tasks; confronting God would be unsettling and dealing with the unknown. Yet Judaism expects its adherents not only to follow the commands of God but also to attempt to hear the voice of God. Hence the addition of prayers that admit the difficulty and try to face the need to accept the reality of God in one's life[2]:

> Lord, a mystery surrounds my life. What comes before it and what lies after it are hidden from me. My life is very short, and Your universe is vast. But in the darkness is Your presence, and in the mystery, Your love.

---

1 Michael J Goulston, 'The Theology of Reform Judaism in Great Britain', *Reform Judaism* (ed Dow Marmur) p.53

2 *Forms of Prayer*, Vol I, p.65

My fathers put their trust in You, and You put goodness in their hearts and peace within their minds. May I be like them and may my reward be like theirs.

In every place, at every time, Your voice speaks with me. It leads me in the way of honesty and charity. It shows me truth and goodness. There are times when it is hard to hear You, and times when it is hard to follow You; and I know this is my loss.

In the quietness of this Sabbath I turn my thoughts to You. Help me to hear Your voice, find Your image in my soul, and to be at peace.

It must be stated that Judaism itself does not claim to have full knowledge of God – by definition the finite mind cannot fully comprehend an infinite God. We know only that which has been revealed, and what humanity is capable of grasping. In the Bible, the place one might expect a detailed exposition, the position is left vague. The very first verse of Genesis – "In the beginning God created the heavens and the earth, and the earth was void without form" – starts off by taking God's existence for granted and concentrates instead on the nature of the world. Even with the first Jew, Abraham, no details are given as to his religious search. "And the Lord said to Abraham, 'Get you out of your country, leave your family and your father's house, and go to a land that I will show you' ". (Genesis 12.1). Thus the presence of God is assumed, and it is humanity and its development that is the focus of interest. In the clearest moment of personal revelation to Moses, the most that he was permitted to see was the back of God (Exodus 33.23). It means that whilst there is a firm concept of God, there are also many gaps. Judaism has been content to base itself on belief in the general existence of God rather than on dogma concerning the exact nature of God. In Judaism a heretic is regarded not as one who believes the wrong thing about God, but whose immoral actions imply a denial of God.

It should be recognised, of course, that what Judaism says about God and what individual Jews believe is not necessarily the same. Many Jews subscribe to the views contained in traditional teaching as mentioned above, and yet still have their own particular image of God which for them fills some of the gaps. For some, God is the puppet master who pulls the strings and controls the world, setting humanity's future and working miracles. We are the 'Pinnochios' who act out God's pre-ordained moves. For others, God is the watchmaker who creates the mechanism, winds it up and then leaves it running on its own momentum. The world having been started and the basic pattern, God no longer intervenes in its workings and we are in control of our own destiny. For yet others, God is the supermarket manager who allows us in, lets us make our choices, but waits at the end with a checklist. Our freedom is limited by a final reckoning and we are recorded or punished accordingly. For others, God is our helpmate, the source of comfort to whom we can turn in time of loneliness or distress. The relationship may be based on our needs but God knows our nature and is always available to us. For others, God is our conscience, deep within and constantly tugging in a certain direction; always with us, but not always listened to. Alternatively, God works through our conscience. It matters not that there are different images for different Jews. What is important is that they help each individual come closer to a relationship with God. As the opening paragraph of the *Amidah* suggests, God should be both "God of our ancestors" whom we know through traditional teachings, and "our God" whom we have come to terms with personally through our own religious search.

A particularly powerful influence in the perception of God for some Jews today has been the Holocaust. For them the idea of a just and all-powerful God who could allow such atrocities to occur seems impossible. God cannot be both, otherwise God would have intervened in some way. Others have reached the same conclusion over individual tragedies, such as the unnatural death of a child. Answers that satisfied previous generations – that we cannot fathom the will of God, or that the sins of the generation were responsible, or that the injustices of this life will be compensated in the life to come – are no longer accepted by all today. Instead, some Jews feel that they can only believe in a benign God who created the world but chooses not to intervene in its affairs. The revelation at Mount Sinai was a 'one-off' event and God will step into human history no more. The prayers one utters for God's help can only be answered in terms of strengthening the ability and resolve of that person to tackle life's problems. According to this view, it is sufficient that the presence of God is known and can inspire human beings to follow in certain directions; the course of human destiny is entirely in the hands of humanity and dependent on how it responds to God's revelation. Other Jews find it difficult to develop a view of God that encompasses both their faith and their doubts, and are content to let the matter float unresolved.

The tendency amongst many Jews to describe Judaism as a way of life rather than a faith may seem to give a low priority to the importance of faith. However, it reflects the fact that it is the consequences of faith, rather than the faith itself, that are significant. Arising from belief in God, however expressed, are several statements that are also indispensable to Judaism: that the world has a purpose, that life has meaning, that all people are equal, that each individual is unique, needs to be treated with dignity, and has a role to play. In similar vein, it is the practical consequences of prayer that are as important as the act of communion itself. Thus Jews pray to God not only to praise God, but also to remind themselves how they should behave. By declaring how God cares for the living, supports the falling, heals the sick and frees prisoners[1] one expresses appreciation of the attributes of God and also sets out a programme for one's duties as a Jew. Belief and action are inseparable in Judaism. The Reform prayer book both affirms the presence of God in daily life and proclaims the path of righteousness which the Jew is obliged to follow.

2. WHAT IS THE REFORM UNDERSTANDING OF THE CONCEPT OF THE MESSIAH?

The term 'Messiah' literally means 'The Annointed One' and occurs with a variety of applications in the Bible ranging from the Patriarchs to King David to the non-Jewish emperor, Cyrus. However, it later became associated with the concept of a future redeemer. Even in this sense there is no consistent doctrine, save that at some future time a new age will come, headed by the Messiah, in which many of the problems of conflict in the world will disappear. Over the centuries different interpretations and details have been added by Jewish tradition. Reform subscribes to the idealised picture painted in the later books of the Bible of life in Messianic times. It is an era of peace in which justice and righteousness reign supreme and all live in harmony. In such a time swords will be beaten into ploughshares (Micah 4.3), while even in the animal world the wolf shall lie down with the lamb (Isaiah 11.6). The benefits will apply not only to Jews but to all people, and there will be universal tranquillity and co-operation. (It is, of course, the absence of such world-wide peace that is one of the reasons why Christianity's claim that Jesus was the Messiah has never been accepted by Jews. Another factor is that in the Jewish understanding there is no hint that the Messiah will be an object of worship or divine, nor that the Torah will be abrogated by the Messiah's coming.)

---

1 *Forms of Prayer*, Vol I, p.37

Reform thinking differs from Orthodoxy in two respects. First it rejects some of the roles allocated to the Messiah – that he will rebuild the Temple, restore the sacrifices and regather all the exiles to the Land of Israel. There is no desire to see a re-emergence of the sacrificial cult which is regarded as a stage in the religious history of Judaism that has long been surpassed. A return to it would be a regression, and references to such hopes, still prominent in Orthodox liturgy, have been deleted from the Reform prayer book. Second, Reform has extended the notion that the most important feature is not so much the actual person of the Messiah but the era of peace that the Messiah will usher in. As a result, references to 'the Messiah' have largely been changed to 'the Messianic Age'. Emphasis has thus been shifted from the coming of a single individual to the quality of life that will arise for all.

Despite Judaism's firm belief that there will be a Messianic Age, there is no definitive opinion as to when it will occur. Indeed, two opposing traditions have developed: according to one, it will be when the world has sunk into total depravity and only the Messiah's coming will save it from destruction; according to the other, it will be when the world is on the brink of perfection and the Messiah's arrival will be the final seal. Reform thinking prefers the latter interpretation because it avoids the dangers of a personality cult and instead emphasises the duty of all people to work towards the coming of the Messianic era. Rather than denying responsibility for the state of the world or claiming that individuals lack the ability to have any effect, it is the task of every person to contribute to its betterment. The saying of Rabbi Tarphon has taken on the status of a motto in Reform circles – "It is not your duty to complete the work, but neither are you free to desist from it" (*Avot* 2.16; some editions 2.21). *Tikkun olam* ('repairing the world') has become a key phrase that reinforces the importance of collective effort to achieve a better society. The small successes of each individual can gradually build up and bring ever closer the Messianic Age. It is accepted that the coming may not be imminent, and Reform does not have a Messianic timetable. Indeed, after the Holocaust some consider the notion of a world free of fear and hurt to be an impossible dream. The transformation required in human nature defies imagination. Nevertheless, resignation and despair are not the answer; maintaining the vision of perfection is essential and striving towards it is fundamental to Jewish existence.

In Reform thinking, therefore, the Messianic Age is not dependent purely on God's intervention but is an aim towards whose attainment humanity can play an active role. Consequently it does not accept the view of those Orthodox groups which claim that the establishment of the State of Israel by humans was sacrilegious because it usurped the role of God. Reform also does not support the view expressed in some nationalist circles that the State of Israel is the panacea for all Jewish problems and that its creation has heralded a new age. Instead Reform abides by its belief that universal peace is the only criterion by which the Messianic Age can be judged, and that each moment spent waiting for its coming can also be used to hasten it.

3. IS THERE A SPECIFIC APPROACH TO SUFFERING IN REFORM THINKING?

One of the most commonly asked religious questions is "Why is there so much suffering in the world?" It is posed so often partly because most people experience a degree of suffering at some point in their life, and partly because there is no obvious answer. The issue is made even more puzzling by the fact that suffering befalls people who are thoroughly good and who do not 'deserve' to suffer, while those who act immorally sometimes appear to escape any suffering. For many people it seems not only incomprehensible but grossly unfair; it runs counter to their understanding of Judaism, which they associate with providing explanations and promoting justice.

There have been numerous attempts to resolve the problem by Jewish thinkers, ancient and modern. None have received universal acceptance, although they have each appealed to different people and given a degree of comfort to many of those concerned. Reform does not claim to have discovered a solution although it does reject certain stances which cause as many problems as they solve and it veers towards others. It recognises that the point of searching is not just to satisfy intellectual curiosity but is to help people perplexed by the suffering they experience or see around them. In the absence of a definitive answer, the value of any response must be judged by its ability to give such help, in keeping with the general tenets of Judaism.

The most traditional response is that suffering is not accidental but is part of a system of reward and punishment. It is retribution from God for faults we have committed either recently or in earlier years. Put colloquially, 'we get what we deserve'. This can be detected in various passages from *Torah* – Exodus 20.5 where punishment or reward is promised for those who disregard or obey God's commands, Leviticus 14.1-19 where a person cleansed of leprosy offers a guilt offering and a sin offering before being fully re-admitted into the community – but it has several limitations. It does not help when dealing with the death of a righteous person, or of a young child who did not even have the opportunity to act badly. There are too many exceptions to take it seriously.

A varying argument put forward, particularly in some Orthodox circles, is that suffering is the result of collective guilt. Individuals may not have erred but their generation has sinned, and so they are swept away along with the moral decay around them. The proposition is horrendous, for it suggests it is theologically acceptable for an innocent person to suffer because of the sins of others. Clearly, there is a relationship between the individual and the surrounding society, and a responsibility to contribute to its general welfare, but that cannot justify including the righteous in the punishment of the wicked. It would not reflect well on a God who operated in this way, as Abraham pointed out with regard to Sodom and Gomorrah: "Shall not the Judge of all the earth do justly?" (Genesis 18.25).

A different reason given is that suffering may seem unfair but has the purpose of teaching the lessons of humility and sensitivity, harnessing our pride and making us aware of the frailties of life. This, too, is flawed for it would be a cruel God indeed who used human beings as a blackboard, who crippled or terminated one person's life in order to educate others.

Another response is to assert that although we cannot see a purpose behind the tragedies that occur, there is a pattern and plan on the larger and long-term canvas of God's view of life. We have to trust that all will be revealed at some time. A similar 'not in our time' approach is to declare that all the ills of the world will be compensated for in the life to come. Both positions have the merit of being honest enough to postpone an answer to an unspecified and distant date. They also reflect the reality that there is much that is beyond our control. Like Job we have to acknowledge our limitations, and this admission can provide a release from being weighed down by an unfathomable mystery. Nevertheless, some people will find it unsatisfactory to think of themselves as part of a Divine jigsaw that they may never see completed. It also denies the importance that they attach to the events of this world and is no remedy for what goes wrong.

All these answers are based on the premise that God is totally responsible for the course of the world and so all suffering must come from God. They therefore seek to explain why God instigated treatment that so often seems unfair. As a result the reasons given are largely intended to exonerate God from blame and to show why the individual concerned deserved to suffer.

An altogether different approach that is increasingly advanced, especially in Reform thinking, is that God is not the source of suffering. It follows the view of God already suggested (see II.1) that God does not intervene in the world and is not responsible for everyday affairs. God is not all-powerful or, rather, chooses not to exercise full power. The world is in the hands of humanity. Misfortunes happen not because of a person's guilt or because of God's will, but simply because such things happen. Sometimes specific causes can be traced. They include human error, such as careless drivers on slippery roads; or human evil, such as an armed gunman killing a bystander during a bank raid; or human frailty, such as the cancer or other fatal diseases that strike at so many people that no-one can say "why me and not anyone else?"; or natural disaster, such as a freak wave that drowns children playing on a beach. In all cases, the effect is terrible, but the cause lies not in God but in the way of the world, which is a much more dangerous and unpredictable place than we imagine. The idea of reward and punishment can still apply, although it has to be transferred from material terms to inner feelings. Good people may well experience suffering but they will also have a sense of integrity and be at peace with themselves. Wrong-doers may escape misfortune but they will never be free of the guilt or foreboding that their lifestyles generate.

Where was God in Auschwitz? Why did God let the Nazis kill so many innocents? According to the above view, the question has to be rephrased. It should be "Why did some people decide to use their God-given freedom for such destructive ends?" More positively, it also needs to be remembered that other people used that same freedom of choice to resist the evil. By the same token, suffering is not the only experience of life. There is much joy and beauty to be appreciated. Accidents, disasters and tragedies are only called by such names because they go against the normal expectation of daily life as routine and safe.

Some extend the theme of the limited God by emphasising that it still includes a caring God[1]. God may not intervene, but God is available. Humanity may suffer because of the way of the world, but it is not alone. One can always turn to God who not only cares about individuals but suffers with them. It is a theme to be found in both biblical and *talmudic* sources (Isaiah 63.9; *Berachot* 29a) which contain the image of a weeping, suffering

---

1 Albert H Friedlander, 'A Suffering God in the Jewish Tradition', *Manna* (Spring 1989)

God. This does not answer the question of human suffering, but it can provide support for those in distress who lift up their eyes to the hills looking for help.

Of course, this view of suffering – not as punishment that is deserved but as a natural part of life – will not find favour with all. It is presented as a possible explanation for those who find the other ways inadequate. Ultimately, the only statement that can be made without fear of contradiction is that we do not know why suffering exists and what determines who experiences it. Sometimes it is better to acknowledge the lack of certainty and the frustration that comes with it. Answers are not right or wrong, but helpful or unhelpful. It means that many responses are possible and it is up to each individual to find what is meaningful for them and to assist others facing a trauma to come to terms with it in their own way.

4. WHAT IS THE REFORM ATTITUDE TO THE AFTER-LIFE, SPIRITUALISM AND ASTROLOGY?

Unlike Christianity, Judaism has never had a clear map of the hereafter. From a variety of inconclusive references in the Bible, two different doctrines arose: first, the notion of the immortality of the soul held that from the time of death, the soul lives on separately from the body and has continued existence (Proverbs 12.28, *Shabbat* 152b). Secondly, the notion of the resurrection of the dead asserted that a person died at the time of death (both body and soul) but would revive and be resurrected bodily in the Messianic era (Daniel 12.2, *Sanhedrin* 10.1). The latter belief came to be particularly important for Rabbinic Judaism and was one of the main distinctions between the Pharisees and the Sadducees. In time the two doctrines merged to form the belief that a person's soul survived the death of the body and lived on until the Messianic age when it was reunited with the body and the person resurrected. This is expresssed in the second paragraph of the *Amidah*, said at every daily, Sabbath and festival service, which concludes "Blessed are You Lord, who revives the dead"[1].

Amongst Reform Jews the belief in the literal resurrection of the body is no longer maintained and only the belief in the immortality of the soul is accepted. The difference between the Reform position and that of the

---

1 *The Authorised Daily Prayer Book* (ed S Singer), p.47

Orthodox is reflected in the different Reform translation of the above blessing which is rendered instead as "Blessed are You, Lord, who renews life beyond death"[1] – thus referring to the immortality of the soul, but not the resurrection of the body. The exact nature of the state of the soul after bodily death has never been defined in Jewish tradition, and this attitude is shared by Reform on the grounds that such existence is beyond our comprehension, and any comment can only be in the nature of speculation. All that can be stated is that, whilst life as we know it is limited to our current stay on earth, there is life after death. It is not necessarily more desirable and to be valued above this life, but rather a different stage. In the absence of any further details, the best policy is to concentrate on the merits of the world we know and to use life here to the full. For many, therefore, the good deeds that we perform are because it is right to act in such a way rather than to earn reward in the next life. The doctrine of reward and punishment, whereby one's merits or faults are recompensed accordingly in the world to come, is essential to Orthodoxy. In the Reform it is neither denied nor enlarged upon, and is left a matter of individual belief. Some find it a helpful notion, through which many of the apparent injustices of this world are redressed in the next world. Others see it as operating in this world, albeit not necessarily in material terms, but in the sense of integrity that a righteous person has, and the guilt and foreboding felt by those who have committed wrongs.

It follows from the above that humans do have some sort of existence even after they have experienced bodily death. It has long been the desire of many to try to pierce the mystery and to communicate with the spirits of the dead. Spiritualism and seance sessions are but modern examples of such attempts which go back to the earliest time. In the Bible they are forthrightly condemned and one who is "a charmer ... or consults ghosts or a familiar spirit" is considered an abomination to God (Deuteronomy 18.10-11). The instance of the Witch of Endor supposedly summoning up the spirit of the dead prophet Samuel to speak to King Saul is puzzling, and many suggest that it was Saul's imagination that conjured up Samuel's presence (I Samuel 28.13-14). Even if the episode is taken to have been a real occurrence, or if modern seances appear to have astoundingly accurate results, the Jewish position remains. It is not doubted that there is a spirit-world; it is merely stated that it is a realm best left alone. This world is the area of our concern and it is wrong to dabble in matters whose true dimension is beyond our ken.

---

1 *Forms of Prayer*, Vol I, p.37

Two pragmatic objections must also be mentioned. First, it can be very dangerous allowing oneself to be controlled by mediums or spiritualists upon whose guidance one may become totally dependent. It can be particularly harmful for those whose emotions are vulnerable and who are open to manipulation. Secondly, the attempt of those who have been bereaved to contact dead relatives is a refusal to accept that they have died and an attempt to 'keep them alive'. Whilst such acceptance can be a difficult and long process, it is an essential stage in one's gradual recovery from mourning and in one's ability to re-enter the flow of life and establish new relationships. Psychologically, it is far more healthy slowly to come to terms with one's loss, including the things that were unsaid and the quarrels that were unresolved, than to try to pursue them beyond the grave.

Astrology, along with reliance on horoscopes, are other practices that are viewed with disapproval. Condemned in the Bible (Isaiah 47.13; Jeremiah 10.2), astrology was treated as a respectable science in *talmudic* times. It was accepted by many Rabbis that every person had their own star which was their patron from conception, guided their fate and linked them with others born at the same time (*Shabbat* 53b, *Megillah* 32a, *Nedarim* 39b). In modern times, however, it is recognised that an individual's life is affected by many different influences, including genetic factors, early upbringing and social environment. Moreover, astrology is a form of fatalism in which one's personal direction is pre-determined; it contradicts Judaism's insistence on free-will and the choices that everyone is able to make as to the course of their life. Those who rely upon astrology to make decisions or who use it to attempt to discover what the future holds are in danger of being disappointed, if not led astray, to their detriment. This is not to deny that the time of one's birth may have a certain significance; rather it is to warn against putting one's trust in speculation and to assert the importance of individual responsibility.

CHAPTER THREE

CYCLE OF LIFE

To everything there is a season and a time for every purpose under heaven ... a time to be born, and a time to die ... a time to mourn, and a time to dance.

Ecclesiastes 3.1-4

1. WHAT SPECIAL CEREMONIES TAKE PLACE ON THE BIRTH OF A CHILD IN REFORM SYNAGOGUES?

Birth

The birth of a child is a momentous occasion for parents. It is recognised as such by Judaism and various rituals take place which are designed to achieve three objects – to give expression to the emotions of the family, to emphasise from the start the Jewish identity of the child, and to provide a communal welcome to what is an addition also to the family of Israel.

Circumcision

Brit milah (the covenant of circumcision) is the oldest Jewish ritual. It is also referred to as a *bris* by those who use the *Ashkenazi* pronunciation of Hebrew. It is first mentioned in Genesis 17.10-14 and marks the special relationship between God and the Jewish people. For parents it is a physical expression of the faith and traditions into which the child has been born and which they will pass on to him. It is performed on the eighth day after birth (the day of birth counting as the first day) even if it falls on a Sabbath or festival. The only delay is if there should be a problem with the health or weight of the child, in which case the circumcision is postponed until the child is well. The person who performs the circumcision – a *mohel* – should be a trained expert and belong either to the Initiation Society or to the Association of Reform and Liberal *Mohalim*. The Association was formed in 1988 because members of the Initiation Society would not circumcise sons of women who had converted under the auspices of Reform and Liberal synagogues. Members of the Association are both fully qualified doctors and trained *mohalim*. A medical circumcision performed by a hospital doctor is deemed valid, but it is not recommended as it is devoid of any Jewish ceremony. It can also be a more complicated procedure and is performed by doctors who are not usually as proficient in circumcision as are *mohalim*. If possible *brit milah* takes place in the parents' home, where they will be most at ease, but it can occur elsewhere equally well, including the *mohel's* surgery or the hospital if the mother is still there. There is no objection to women being present at the *brit milah*, although it is usually the custom for the mother not to attend because of the distress she may feel. Members of the family or close friends can be given a role in the ceremony: the *kvatterin* (godmother) takes the baby from the mother and brings him into the room, handing him over to the *kvatter* (godfather) who gives him to the *mohel*. During the circumcision the child is held by the *sandek* (the holder). The father makes a declaration and recites a blessing. The response of those present indicates the multi-faceted significance of the ceremony[1]:

> May his father and mother rejoice in him. With love and wisdom may they teach him the meaning of the covenant which he has entered today so that he may practise righteousness, seeking truth and walking in the ways of peace. May this young child grow into manhood as a blessing to his family, the family of Israel and the family of mankind.

It should be noted that circumcision does not make the boy Jewish. Jewish status is derived automatically from being the child of a Jewish mother.

Baby blessing for girls and boys
A few weeks after the birth of a girl, a special ceremony occurs in synagogue when the parents come up to the Ark and each reads a prayer of thanksgiving. The mother's prayer includes the words[2]:

> As she grows in body and in mind, may the law of truth be found on her lips and the love of justice in her heart. May she be a blessing to those around her and bring honour to Israel in the sight of all mankind. Lord, be with me and my husband; may our love for our child draw us even more closely together in helpfulness and in trust.

The Rabbi then invokes a blessing upon the child. The ceremony can be conducted privately at any time, but is usually held in front of the community during a Sabbath service. It differs from the procedure in Orthodox synagogues where the father is given a *mitzvah* at the Sabbath service following the birth of his daughter; thus it does not involve the mother, who may not even be present if she is still recovering from the birth, while the child is also not present. Another difference is that in Reform synagogues the ceremony is often performed for boys in addition to their circumcision. The reason is partly to celebrate the birth with the wider community, and also because the parents are now more relaxed than at the circumcision and so can enjoy the occasion more. As a way of sharing their happiness, some families like to provide a special *kiddush* after the service. Others make a donation to the

---

1 *Forms of Prayer*, Vol I, p.313
2 Ibid, p.285

synagogue or to a charity specifically concerned with children's welfare, whilst another option is to plant a tree in Israel in the child's name.

Naming

Jews may have adopted secular forenames and surnames in the last two centuries, but they still maintain separate Jewish names. These are used in various religious contexts such as when one is called up to the reading of the *Torah* in the synagogue service, or on Hebrew documents such as a *ketubah* (marriage certificate). The Jewish name of a boy is given at his circumcision and that of a girl at her blessing in a synagogue. A variety of traditions exists for choosing a forename: after deceased relatives to perpetuate their memory (the *Ashkenazi* custom); after living relatives as a way of honouring them (the *Sephardi* custom); the Hebrew translation of, or nearest sound-equivalent to, one's English forename. A new tradition introduced by Reform synagogues is that the second part of one's name, which was previously just the first name of one's father, should now also include one's mother. Thus if a son, Daniel, was born to parents by the name of Michael and Sarah, his Hebrew name would be *Daniel ben Michael v'Sarah*. It has been the official Reform policy since 1988 to recommend the use of both parents' names for naming children, although it was practised widely before this date[1]. Adults given originally just their father's name can add their mother's name of their own accord if they so desire. Should a child have a non-Jewish father, options for the child's second name include using the mother's name plus either the Hebrew equivalent of the father's name, or the name of the maternal grandfather, or the substitute 'Israel'; alternatively one can just use the mother's name. Bearing in mind that one's Jewish name should not be a source of embarrassment, the author suggests that the above options are used in this order of preference.

Redemption of the first-born

The ceremony of *pidyon ha'ben* (redemption of the first-born) involves the father of a first-born son who is 31 days old presenting the child to a *cohen* and then redeeming him by buying him back with five shekels. This act recalls the special religious status of first-born sons in biblical times before they were replaced by the Levites as the religious officials (Numbers 3.40-

---

1 Assembly of Rabbis, 20th January 1988

51). However it is rarely performed in Reform synagogues primarily because the role of a *cohen* has been abolished owing to its problematic nature (see IX.7). Moreover, the ceremony discriminates against other children – subsequent boys or a first-born girl, and even a first-born boy born after a miscarriage; none of these are deemed eligible for the ceremony whereas they are equally important and should be treated as such. In addition the ceremony can be regarded as being superficial in purpose, for it is not intended that the father really give away his son and not redeem him, an act which would be invalid legally.

Non-Jewish children
A child with a Jewish father and a non-Jewish mother is considered non-Jewish, as Jewish status is conveyed through the mother's line. However, it is recognised that many Jewish fathers wish to maintain certain Jewish traditions, particularly that of having a newly born son circumcised. Most Reform Rabbis would encourage this, as it would facilitate any future conversion of the child, either when still a minor or in adulthood. In such cases a *mohel* would perform the circumcision in the usual way save that the blessing would be omitted. The consent of the mother would be a necessary pre-requisite, whilst the *mohel* would remind both parents that circumcision itself does not confer Jewish status on the child. A baby blessing in synagogue would not occur unless the mother was in the middle of a conversion course, in which case the blessing would take place after she and the child had been admitted to Judaism[1].

2. WHAT DOES A *BARMITZVAH* INVOLVE IN REFORM SYNAGOGUES AND WHAT IS A *BATMITZVAH*?

A *barmitzvah* (son of the commandment) refers to the ceremony marking the religious 'coming of age' of a boy who reaches thirteen years (*Avot* 5.1; *Yoma* 82a). It is based on a legal concept marking the time from which the child becomes responsible for the obligations of Jewish Law. It reflected an era when a thirteen year old may already have been at work and was treated as an adult. This is not the case nowadays, and so the *barmitzvah* ceremony

---
1 eg Assembly of Rabbis, 1st March 1965

has come to have other ramifications. It is a valuable way of reinforcing the boy's identification with Judaism and encouraging continued practice and study of the faith. It also acknowledges the physical and emotional changes he is undergoing by giving him prominence and a new position within the community. At the same time it symbolises for his parents the new relationship that they should have with him. As there is no religious distinction between the sexes, and as girls undergo major bodily and attitudinal changes too, Reform regard a ceremony for them as equally important. Moreover, as girls in Reform religion schools (and day schools) receive the same Jewish education as do boys, it is considered only natural and just that they should have a similar public ceremony. This takes exactly the same form as the *barmitzvah*, occurs when the girl has reached 13 years and is called a *batmitzvah* (daughter of the commandment). Virtually all Reform synagogues conduct *bar/batmitzvah* ceremonies when boys and girls attain the age of 13. However, one or two synagogues postpone the ceremony to the sixteenth year when, it is felt, the individuals have a greater understanding of their religious obligations, and by which time their maturity is more akin to that of a thirteen year old in ancient times. This policy also has the benefit of helping to maintain formal Jewish education until 16 years and providing the students with a much greater appreciation and knowledge of Judaism as a result[1].

The *bar/batmitzvah* ceremony varies slightly in different Reform synagogues, but generally involves the person reading the weekly portion from the scroll of the *Torah* on a Sabbath morning (some read, some chant, some read and translate) as well as saying the blessings before and afterwards. The child is usually responsible for the whole *Torah* reading rather than just the last few verses (*maftir*) as is common in many Orthodox synagogues. In many synagogues they then read the *Haftarah*, the weekly reading from the Prophets, along with its blessings. In some synagogues they also give a short explanation of the *Torah* portion, and even deliver a sermon based on it resulting from their Jewish studies. In addition many lead some of the prayers in the service or read certain sections such as the Ten Commandments. It is also usual for them to read a special prayer regarding the occasion, the male form of which includes the declaration[2]:

---

1 See A M Bayfield, '*Barmitzvah* – Is Nothing Else Sacred?', *New Ideas in Progressive Jewish Education*, No 13 (December 1977)
2 *Forms of Prayer*, Vol I, p.291

In the presence of my teachers, the leaders and the members of this holy congregation, I am now prepared to take upon myself the duties which are binding on all the family of Israel. I ask their help in the years that lie ahead to strengthen my loyalty and devotion so that I may grow in charity and good deeds. I think also of those who have gone before me, who through all the troubles of the world preserved this heritage of holiness and goodness, so that I should enter into it now.

May I be a true *Barmitzvah*, a son of the commandment, taking my place in the community of Israel, accepting its responsibilities, rejoicing in its blessings. May I be a witness to the living God and His goodness, and the tradition that lives within me.

I remember all those who have helped me to reach this time. I give thanks for the love and care of my family, the patience and instruction of my teachers, and the support and companionship of my friends.

In the *Torah* I have read the word of God. With your help may I go on to fulfil it in my life.

Very often this prayer is read in front of the open Ark, with their parents standing beside them; in some synagogues there is a ceremony of the father handing to his child a scroll of the *Torah* to symbolise the chain of tradition being passed from one generation to the next. Part of the Rabbi's sermon is usually devoted to the significance of the occasion and the challenges facing the particular individual. It is often followed by a special blessing by the Rabbi. The blessing recited in Orthodox synagogues by the father – "Blessed is He who has freed me from the responsibility of this child" – is not said, as it is recognised that nowadays a thirteen year old is still very dependent on its parents and is only beginning the process of maturation. After the service the family usually provides a *kiddush* for the whole congregation, although lavish celebrations are discouraged, so as not to discriminate between rich and poor families.

Relatives and friends giving gifts to the boy or girl are encouraged to choose gifts of Jewish significance appropriate to the occasion, such as a Jewish ritual article, a Jewish book or a certificate of trees planted in Israel in their name. Many families will have a private celebration afterwards and, whilst it is appropriate to acknowledge and enjoy such a special occasion, the party should not be on such a scale that it overshadows the *bar/batmitzvah* ceremony. Similarly, parents should not fall into the trap of spending more time discussing the catering arrangements than they do helping their child with the *bar/batmitzvah* studies. Many Rabbis encourage the families concerned to share their happiness with those less fortunate than themselves by donating to charity a percentage of the cost of their celebrations (and perhaps also of the financial gifts received). If the child is involved in deciding the amount given and the cause chosen, the act can also carry great educational value, signifying both the importance of charity and the new responsibility accorded to the child.

Prerequisites for the *bar/batmitzvah* are that the children have attended religion school for a minimum number of years, and have acquired a basic grasp of their Jewish heritage. Familiarity with synagogue services is also mandatory. In the absence of such knowledge the ceremony may be postponed until greater appreciation of Judaism has been gained. This applies particularly if children have not attended religion school until shortly before their thirteenth birthday in which case some Reform synagogues demand a minimum study of two years before a *bar/batmiztvah* can take place. Special arrangements are often made for the handicapped so as to enable them to have a *bar/batmitzvah* ceremony even if they cannot manage all the usual requirements. What occurs after *bar/batmitzvah* is equally important. Most Reform synagogues have post-*bar/batmitzvah* classes which the young people are encouraged to attend so as to continue their Jewish education formally for at least another two years. In some cases this concludes with a *ben/bat Torah* ceremony whereby the individual takes the whole of the Sabbath morning service or the service at *Shavuot*. As the festival which commemorates the revelation at Mount Sinai and the bond which was cemented between God and Israel, it is an appropriate occasion to celebrate the commitment of the teenagers to the community. Other synagogues provide special tuition to enable teenagers to study for the GCSE religious studies examination (Jewish options) which is then taken at sixteen years simultaneously with the other subjects being studied at school. Additional ways of involving them in synagogue life include giving a *mitzvah* during the High Holy Day Services to those who have had their *bar/batmitzvah* during the previous year, or of asking them to re-read their *Torah* portion when it occurs again in future years. Common to all Reform synagogues is the conviction that Jewish learning and involvement is a lifelong activity. The ceremony of *bar/batmitzvah*, which is sometimes regarded erroneously as the end of one's Jewish education, is seen merely as the beginning of a different stage in one's Jewish development.

It is noticeable that the growing popularity of a *batmitzva*h for girls in the post-war period has encouraged Orthodox synagogues to have an equivalent ceremony, the *bat chayil* (daughter of worth). However, this takes place a year earlier at twelve, usually involves a group of girls rather than an individual, occurs on a Sunday afternoon, and entails reciting psalms or special readings rather than the main prayers or the *Torah* portion. A recent development in Reform synagogues is that a number of people who never had a *bar/batmitzvah* in their youth choose to have the ceremony in later life. These include women who were brought up in Orthodox synagogues, men who never had the opportunity because of war-time conditions, and proselytes. They find the study preparations very challenging, while the occasions themselves are a very moving re-affirmation of their Jewish commitment and their involvement in the local community.

3. WHAT ARE THE DISTINCTIVE PROCEDURES OF A REFORM WEDDING?

Reform Rabbis meet with a couple well before their wedding so as to make all the arrangements. The Rabbi will ask the couple for proof of their Jewish identity in order to fulfil the requirements of both Jewish Law and civil law. Producing the *ketubah* of their respective parents is the easiest way of ascertaining Jewish status (or a certificate from a *Beth Din* for those converted or adopted). However, if these are not available, synagogue membership or verbal affidavits by others is often deemed sufficient. If either party is divorced and the previous partner was Jewish, they need to obtain a *get* (Jewish certificate of divorce) if they have not already done so (see IX.4)[1]. *Chalitzah* – the obligation of a man to grant a release to his deceased brother's childless widow before she can remarry – is not required. This custom arose from Deuteronomy 25.5-9 and the need to protect a woman without husband and children in a society where women were at risk and generally dependent on men for support. However, it has long lost its relevance, while its purpose was often frustrated because widows were prevented from remarrying by brothers-in-law who, for malicious or mercenary reasons, refused to release them[2].

---

1 Michael Curtis, 'The *Beth Din* of the Reform Synagogues of Great Britain', *Reform Judaism* (ed Dow Marmur) p.135
2 Idem

Several of the prohibitions banning certain unions or limiting times of marriage, which are still observed in Orthodox synagogues, are no longer maintained. Thus a *cohen* is permitted to marry a divorcee or proselyte in Reform synagogues[1] while a *mamzer* can marry any Jew[2]. The ban on a person marrying the paramour has been changed to allow the marriage of those who have committed adultery with each other in cases where the marital relationship had already broken down before the adultery occurred[3]. The delicate issues involved in this policy have often been debated by the Assembly of Rabbis but it has been felt that in cases where the adultery is 'technical' – eg when still legally married to, but already separated from, their spouse – the person should not be prevented from marrying their paramour once their divorce has been arranged. Because of the complexities involved, each application has to come before the Standing Committee – a sub-committee of the Assembly of Rabbis – which examines cases of special difficulty before they go to the Reform Beth Din. Special permission has also been given in cases where the adultery occurred a considerable time beforehand and since which the couple have established a stable home[4].

The waiting period of 91 days for a woman who divorces and then remarries, insisted upon in Orthodox synagogues, is not required in Reform synagogues as it is felt that the original reason for this custom – the difficulty of ascertaining the paternity of a child born six months after the remarriage – is unlikely to be applicable today[5]. Weddings are not held on Sabbaths, festivals (with the exception of *Chanukah* and *Purim*) or on *Tishah B'Av*[6]. However, they are permitted in many Reform synagogues at all other times, including on now obsolete fast days and during the *Omer* period, because the importance of marriage is held to outweigh the unpleasant historical associations with those days in the first and second centuries. Women are not obliged to go to the *mikveh* before the wedding, although it is an option for those who wish to do so (see V.3). Unlike many Orthodox synagogues, the menstrual cycle of the bride-to-be is not regarded as a criterion for fixing the date of the wedding.

---

1 Idem
2 Idem
3 eg Assembly of Rabbis, 28th May 1969, 5th May 1975, 5th March 1981
4 eg *Current Procedures,* p.7
5 Michael Curtis, ibid, p.136
6 eg *Current Procedures,* p.5

Many Rabbis will raise the wider issues of the couple's relationship with each other and with their respective families. They seek to ascertain whether any problems exist that should be tackled before the wedding takes place, either through the Rabbi or through marriage guidance[1]. They also discuss the commitment and responsibility that marriage entails, and emphasise what a significant step it is even for those couples who are living together already. For most couples, an enormous amount of effort and planning goes into the wedding, a day that lasts a few hours at most. It is even more important to devote the same energy and preparation to the marriage itself to ensure that it is long-lasting and successful. There are no guarantees of success, but certain elements are extremely important: that the couple know each other well and are aware of each other's expectations; that they have the ability to communicate properly and resolve problems that arise between them; that they have discussed and agreed upon major issues that will face them (such as financial arrangements or children and their upbringing); that they are committed to upholding their marriage vows, with fidelity in marriage being sacrosanct; and that their two families are brought together harmoniously and, where possible, welded into an amicable relationship. In addition the Rabbi will be concerned as to whether the couple are able to run their home and bring up any family in a Jewish way, and will discuss the best method of achieving this. In cases where either or both partners lack any Jewish knowledge they may be asked to attend adult education classes before their marriage takes place[2]. In a few exceptional cases Rabbis have refused to officiate at certain marriages in their communities when they considered that one partner had behaved despicably to their former spouse and the Rabbi, knowing the family circumstances, could not in good conscience assist with the new marriage[3]. However, so as not to deprive the couple of their right to marry, they are referred to a Rabbi from another community who will officiate at the ceremony.

The venue of a wedding is up to the discretion of the Rabbi in consultation with the couple, but the general policy is for the ceremony to take place in a synagogue so as to emphasise the religious aspects of the occasion. In 1977 the Assembly of Rabbis declared that it "regrets the commercialisation of marriage ceremonies that may occur when hotels or catering halls are the venue for marriage services and re-affirms the centrality

---

1 See the recommended course in Dow Marmur *The Jewish Family Today and Tomorrow* p.5
2 eg Assembly of Rabbis, 9th November 1960
3 eg Assembly of Rabbis, 18th April 1961

of the synagogue in Jewish life"[1]. The author suggests that another alternative is to return to the custom of having marriages in the open air. Marriages occasionally take place in the couple's home or garden, particularly if it is a second marriage or a Jewish ceremony for a couple already civilly married.

The ceremony itself is based upon the format developed over the centuries: the couple stand under a *chuppah*; there are some opening psalms, usually sung by a *chazan* or choir; blessings are made over wine and over the *chuppah*; the traditional formula of the marriage oath is uttered; there is the recital of the *Sheva brachot* (the seven blessings at the end of the ceremony); and a glass is broken underfoot to a chorus of "*mazeltov*".

Reform weddings also have some extra features. In keeping with the equality of women in Reform synagogues, the bride has an active role in the actual moment of marriage: after the groom has given her a ring and recited the traditional marriage formula, she has the option of presenting him with a ring; the bride also makes a reciprocal vow, declaring in Hebrew "And you are married to me in holiness according to the law of Moses and Israel"[2]. As it is now the general custom for women to wear their marriage ring on the third finger from the thumb on their left hand, the ring is often placed there during the ceremony. This is felt to be more appropriate today than the custom of putting the ring on the index finger of the right hand and then transferring it after the wedding, as is done in other synagogues in deference to a previous tradition.

Another difference is the text of the *ketubah* that is used. It is written in Hebrew rather than in Aramaic, and omits the traditional references to the financial agreements concerning the dowry and a settlement in case of divorce. This was once very important to record but now has no legal relevance. Instead the *ketubah* stresses the nature of the relationship being entered – "a covenant of love and companionship, of peace and friendship". It also emphasises the reciprocal obligations of the couple to cherish, respect and support each other. Instead of being male-oriented, it treats both as equal partners with shared responsibilities. In many synagogues it is customary to sign the *ketubah* during the ceremony in contrast to the Orthodox custom of signing it just before the ceremony. Moreover, both the groom and bride sign the document, whereas the Orthodox require only the groom to do so, with the bride's signature being optional. Similarly in the Orthodox synagogues,

---

[1] Assembly of Rabbis, 28th November 1977
[2] *Forms of Prayer*, Vol I, p.281

the witnesses to the *ketubah* have to be males only. In Reform synagogues, of course, women are regarded as equally competent and can act as witnesses for the *ketubah*. After the signing, the couple are not obliged to perform *yihud* (time spent alone together), originally the moment when one consummated the marriage, but can join their families and guests immediately.

A substantial part of the marriage ceremony is custom rather than law. Many Reform Rabbis will point this out and explain that certain traditions can be varied to suit the wishes of the couple and to make the wedding as personal as possible. Thus whilst the bride usually enters the *chuppah* after everyone else is present, the bride and groom can both be under the *chuppah* together at the start of the service or enter together. If the bride does make a separate entry, there are many options as to who can accompany her: the two mothers (an old Jewish tradition), or her father, or someone else special to her. Rarely performed is the custom of *bedeken*, whereby the groom checks the identity of the bride before the ceremony starts so as to avoid Jacob's mistake in marrying the wrong bride (Genesis 29.20-26). Except for arranged marriages in which the couple hardly know each other, such a precaution is unnecessary and most couples prefer to meet under the *chuppah* on their wedding day. When a *bedeken* does occur, it is often a mutual identification and the Rabbi asks both bride and groom to confirm that the other is the person they wish to marry.

The roles of best man and bridesmaids do not derive from Jewish tradition but have been borrowed from English culture. Thus they have no religious function in the marriage service, unlike the two *edim* (witnesses) who sign the *ketubah*. Nevertheless, the best man and bridesmaids can be very useful ways of involving family or friends in the ceremony, while they also echo the earlier Jewish custom of both bride and groom each being attended by friends as they approach the *chuppah*. It is also possible that instead of the usual type of *chuppah*, an embroidered canopy resting on four self-supporting poles, the *chuppah* could be a large *tallit* (perhaps that of the groom) tied to four poles and held up by four friends or members of the family. Another variation is that instead of the *chazan* or choir singing the *Sheva brachot*, they can be sung or said by seven relatives or friends of the couple. Instrumental music can be an important part of the ceremony, with some synagogues offering a variety of melodies traditional for the entry and exit of the couple, while other synagogues allow the couple concerned to choose music that is special to them.

Other ways of making the ceremony as personal as possible are to use the *kiddush* goblet belonging to the couple (or to their family) for the wine that is drunk under the *chuppah* rather than using the synagogue one. There is also a return to the tradition of using an illustrated *ketubah*, while couples with artistic ability (or with artistic friends) can design their own version. There are no specific requirements as to wedding wear, save that bride and groom should be dressed decorously. The Rabbi may mention certain traditions, eg a veil for the bride or a *kittel* (white robe) for the groom, but the choice is left entirely to the couple. It is not necessary for a groom to wear a *tallit* under the *chuppah*, although there is no objection to his doing so.

4. ARE REFORM MARRIAGES RECOGNISED BY OTHER JEWISH AUTHORITIES?

Reform weddings fulfil the traditional requirements for a Jewish marriage: the exchange of a ring, the oath of marriage, and the signing of the *ketubah* in front of two Jewish witnesses (*Kiddushin* 5b, 9a). As a result they are recognised by all Reform, Conservative and Liberal synagogues in Britain and abroad.

In Orthodox circles the validity of marriages in Reform synagogues is sometimes called into question. However, this is largely the result of ignorance or a deliberate attempt to mislead others. The definitive answer is that, except in cases where a Reform conversion or divorce was involved, all Reform marriages are valid according to the most Orthodox interpretation of Jewish Law. Moreover, the children of such a Reform marriage are considered fully Jewish in Orthodox eyes and would be eligible to marry in an Orthodox synagogue if they so wished. This has been acknowledged formally by the Office of the Chief Rabbi of the United Synagogue in a letter stating: "No responsible Orthodox authority would ever deny that where a marriage took place ... which could have just as well taken place in an Orthodox synagogue, the children of such a marriage could become members and indeed be married in an Orthodox synagogue"[1]. It should also be noted that a divorced person who was married originally in a Reform synagogue and wishes to remarry in an Orthodox synagogue is generally required by the Orthodox authorities to obtain a *get* before the second marriage can take place. This is a further indication of the recognition given to Reform marriages.

---

1 Rabbi A M Rose (Secretary to the Chief Rabbi) to Rabbi S Brichto, 28th November 1967

The basis for this recognition is that the venue of one's marriage (an Orthodox or Reform synagogue) and the status of the officiant (Orthodox Rabbi, Reform Rabbi or even a lay person) are irrelevant. The important elements are that a Jewish man and a Jewish woman, both free of any other marital obligations, make the formal declaration of Jewish marriage, and exchange an item of worth (nowadays a ring) in the presence of two Jewish witnesses. Providing these conditions are fulfilled, under whatever auspices, then the marriage is deemed valid according to all Jewish authorities. The children of the marriage are regarded as fully Jewish and perfectly legitimate.

The Reform marriages that are not recognised by the Orthodox are those where the status of one partner derives from the decision of a non-Orthodox *Beth Din*. This is because the Orthodox do not accept the authority of Reform Rabbis and so do not regard as valid the Reform *Beth Din* or its decisions. These cases would include those who were converted, adopted or obtained a *get* through the Reform *Beth Din*. Such individuals are deemed ineligible to have a Jewish marriage, and any ceremony that takes place is considered null and void. In the eyes of the Reform, however, there are no impediments to these marriages and they are considered valid and binding. Moreover, Reform synagogues are empowered by the civil authorities to register marriages under the 1949 Marriage Act. This confirmed rights granted originally to the West London Synagogue and subsequent Reform congregations in the 1857 Dissenters Chapel Act. Reform marriages are therefore recognised by the State and carry full legal force. It should be noted that in order to minimise any mistaken impression, those whose marriages might not be accepted by the Orthodox authorities – or their children in Orthodox Jewish day schools – are informed of this fact before marrying in a Reform synagogue. Whilst this might disappoint some of the individuals involved, there are so many Reform and other non-Orthodox communities in Britain and throughout the world that they will generally find a synagogue that welcomes them.

In the vast majority of cases, therefore, no problems arise for a couple or their children if they marry in a Reform synagogue. Moreover, it is felt by many people that if they are to be married in synagogue, it should be in one whose policies and practices correspond to their own religious feelings and are in accordance with the Judaism in which they wish to raise their family.

5. WHAT IS THE REFORM ATTITUDE TO HOSPICES?

Hospices are a relatively new phenomenon. The first one in Britain was founded in 1905, but most others date from the last two decades. In many ways they provide a service that once took place at home when extended families lived together and died in each other's presence. If someone was dying the rest of the family would gather round the bed, children included, and would stay with the person to their end. There was always someone at home to look after an infirm relative whereas today, owing to the trend to live in small family units, elderly relatives often reside alone and die alone. Alternatively, when they cannot look after themselves, they are transferred to old age homes or geriatric wards where professional carers tend to their needs and oversee their last moments. Another prevailing trend in modern society is to regard death as unnatural and to be delayed in every way possible. As a result, nursing staff and doctors at hospitals constantly seek medical cures and view the death of a patient as a failure. Whilst this is highly desirable in most cases and leads to people enjoying a longer life, it is a problem for the terminally ill, as many medical institutions are not orientated towards caring for those whom they cannot cure. In a situation where neither relatives nor professionals cater for the dying, hospices offer specialist care for the dying with constant attention in peaceful surroundings. No treatment is given to the ailment affecting the person, although drugs are administered to control any pain the person is suffering and to make the final days as stress-free as possible.

Despite their noble intentions certain objections can be raised against hospices. One is that by sending a relative to a hospice one is accepting that the person has no possibility of a cure and that death will follow shortly. It can be seen as 'giving up', whereas the Jewish attitude has been always to maintain hope and believe that conditions might improve. Thus Isaiah is rebuked for telling King Hezekiah that he was about to die when he was seriously ill, whereas in fact he was healed through a combination of prayer and medicine (II Kings 20, *Berachot* 10a). The preservation of hope is given practical expression in the confession to be said by the dying, which is given the more encouraging title of "prayer during dangerous illness" and which does not exclude recovery[1]:

---

1 *Forms of Prayer*, Vol I, p.294

You are the Master of my life and death, may it be Your will to heal me and keep me in life. But if it is time for me to go forward, through death to life everlasting, give me courage and trust to ease my journey.

The tacit acceptance of the inevitability of death by entering a hospice may come as a great shock to the patients themselves who may not have realised beforehand how seriously ill they were and who may become despondent and lose all will to live. This argument can be countered by the point that if there was the slightest possibility of any remedy the person would still be in hospital and it was only because all known medical treatment had failed to contain the illness that they had gone to a hospice. In addition the staff at hospices are well aware of the emotional trauma faced by patients and relatives alike, and are trained to deal with them as much as with the physical problems.

Another objection is that pain-killing drugs often have a side effect of speeding up the onset of death because of their effect on weakened organs. This might be said to fall into the category of euthanasia, which is regarded as unacceptable in Jewish eyes and akin to murder (see XI.5). However, in this case it can be argued that the pain arising from not having alleviating drugs could do as much damage to the patient as the side effects of the drugs. Moreover, the drugs are not intended to kill the patient but to enhance the quality of what little remains of their life. Given that the purpose of such drugs is benign, their use would be justified.

There are also positive advantages to hospices which must be mentioned. In many cases the family of the person concerned cannot look after the patient at home – either because of the physical difficulties involved or because of the emotional strain. Nor might they be able to provide the specialised administration of drugs that is necessary. Those who might otherwise be in hospital and subject to a strict regime concerning mealtimes and visiting times, geared more towards those whom the hospital will cure and discharge, find that the regulations in a hospice are much more appropriate for their particular needs, with greater care for individual diet and virtually unlimited visiting hours. Another benefit is that the approach of death is dealt with as a natural part of life which can be talked about openly and faced with equanimity. The fact that both the patient and their family acknowledge the terminal situation can lead to their being able to talk about it without pretence, have important conversations concerning last wishes, provide an opportunity to heal family quarrels and give the patients the right atmosphere in which to set their affairs straight. Thus for those whose demise is imminent and whose family are unable to provide the necessary care at home, hospices can provide a gentle way of passing one's last days.

6. WHAT HAPPENS AT THE TIME OF DEATH, AND WHAT IS THE REFORM ATTITUDE TO AUTOPSIES AND ORGAN TRANSPLANTS?

Non-Jews touching the body
For Orthodox authorities it is strictly forbidden for non-Jews to touch the dead body of a Jew. This ban dates back to ancient times and relates to pagan practices of mutilating dead bodies, or of using the blood for ritual purposes. Reform recognises that such customs are not present today and considers that there is no justification for the prohibition being maintained[1]. It would also be highly insulting to the doctors and nurses who took such care of the person whilst alive to consider them untrustworthy after death. If non-Jewish hospital staff wish to remove the body of a Jew who has died to a different room, clean the body and straighten the limbs, this is permitted. The only caveat is to ensure that the person's hands are placed alongside the body and are not crossed.

Taharah
It is recommended that *taharah* (ritual washing of the corpse) should take place in addition to any normal washing that may have been done[2]. It is performed either by a *chevra kaddisha* (holy brotherhood), a trained group of members of the synagogue, or by the Jewish Burial Society. The body is washed and dried in a prescribed manner, dressed in a set of shrouds and placed in a plain coffin. *Taharah* is not considered necessary in cases where a person has died of an infectious disease and the bodily fluids could endanger those washing the body.

Post-mortem/autopsy
Requests for a post-mortem are resisted in certain Jewish circles because they delay burial and conflict with the ban against making cuts on a body. However, Reform synagogues consider them permissible because the

---

1 Assembly of Rabbis, 24th August 1955
2 Idem

medical knowledge that is gained from them can be used to save the lives of others. In cases where they are required legally, the principle applies that "the law of the land is the law" and has to be obeyed (*Nedarim* 28a).

Watching the body
The tradition of having *vachers* (watchers) who stayed with a corpse until the time of burial had the practical purpose of guarding against rodents or body snatchers (*Berachot* 18a). Now that Burial Societies have their own mortuaries which are safe from disturbance, it is not necessary to have watchers as well. Some, however, may consider it appropriate that the body should not be left alone out of respect for the deceased person. In this case the author suggests that the watching could be done by the relatives or friends of the person concerned, and not by paid strangers as has become the general custom.

Organ Transplants
The issue of using the organs of a dead person to benefit a living person has aroused controversy because it transgresses the laws which ban mutilation of a corpse and benefiting from a corpse (*Hullin* 11b; *Avodah Zarah* 29b). However, these objections are overridden by the principle that saving a person's life takes precedence over all other commands except the prohibition against murder, incest or idolatry (*Pesachim* 25a). An important caveat is that it is not permissible to save one person's life at the expense of another person's life. Thus it is essential to establish that the person donating the organ is dead before it is removed. As a result of medical advances, this means that not only has the heart stopped beating but also that brain death has occurred. It would be tantamount to murder to hasten the death of the donor or to ignore any possibility of a resuscitation. In view of these complexities, as well as the original objections, Orthodox authorities only permit organ transplants when there is a specific recipient who needs the organs immediately and who would otherwise die. However, because of modern methods of preserving organs and the ability to communicate world-wide, Reform synagogues permit taking organs for cases not known about at that moment but which are likely to arise[1]. The use of organs that are not necessary to save life but which can greatly improve the quality of life – such as the eyes for corneal transplanting – is also permitted. It is considered meritorious for those willing to donate organs after

---
1 Assembly of Rabbis, 11th July 1962

their death to carry donor cards so as to assist the procedure of saving the lives of others[1]. Where no record of a person's wishes exists and their organs are required by the medical authorities, the next of kin have the right to permit it[2].

A closely related subject is that of donating organs from a living person, such as a lung or bone marrow. This is permitted provided that it does not endanger the life of the donor. It should not be done for commercial reasons but sparingly, in limited circumstances, such as when a close relative is the recipient. Conversely it is permitted for a Jew to receive organs, whether from a Jew or non-Jew, that will enhance or save his/her life. The same permission applies to use of animal organs including *non-kosher* animals, such as transplanting a pig's heart-valve into a human body. Whilst there might be an element of revulsion at the thought of having an animal organ inside a human being, the general principle of the overriding priority to save life applies. The use of animals also avoids all problems associated with human organs – mutilation, benefit and particularly that of ascertaining time of death.

Donating one's body to science

An unusual but occasional occurrence is that some people wish to leave their body to science after their death so that it can be used for research purposes. This goes against the tradition of respectfully disposing of a corpse via burial or cremation and also denies mourners an opportunity to bid farewell to a person at a funeral service. Nevertheless, the motives of such a request are laudable, and medical knowledge will be furthered by it to the benefit of others. In such cases a *shivah* or other mourning rites may take place starting from the time of death, even though the body may not be disposed of for some considerable time.

7. HOW ARE REFORM FUNERALS CONDUCTED?

Timing

It is customary to hold the funeral as soon as possible after the time of death. However, it is not generally the practice to have the funeral the same day as the person dies, as some Orthodox synagogues do, for it can be too quick for

---

1 Assembly of Rabbis, 16th November 1981
2 Assembly of Rabbis, 27th May 1968

the family to prepare themselves emotionally, or for others to be informed. Most funerals take place within one to three days, although delays occur in certain circumstances, such as to allow time for a close relative who is abroad to be contacted and make arrangements to attend. This follows the tradition in *Mo'ed Katan* 22a which gives exceptions to the general rule of burying someone as soon as possible (*Sanhedrin* 46b). Funerals do not take place on Sabbaths and festivals.

Clothing
It is usual for mourners and all attending a funeral to wear black clothing or at least dark colours. Although some assume that this is an imitation of Christian customs, it is in fact an old Jewish tradition dating back to *talmudic* times (*Shabbat* 114a, *Yoma* 39b). In the Bible mourners often rent their garments (Genesis 37.34, Leviticus 10.6) as a dramatic and highly physical sign of their grief (a mourner is defined as one who has lost a parent, spouse, sibling or child). This led to the tradition of *keriah* (cutting) whereby a symbolic cut of a few inches is made into the clothing of a mourner shortly before the funeral commences. However, for many people, cutting one's clothes is no longer an appropriate expression of grief and can cause distress rather than be helpful. It is, therefore, no longer insisted upon in Reform ceremonies[1].

The Service
The service is short and decorous, consisting of a combination of Psalms and prayers appropriate to the occasion. It begins by accepting the reality of the human condition and our need for support:

> In the presence of death let us not fear. We share it with all who have ever lived and with all who will ever be. For it is only the dust which returns to the dust as it was, but the spirit returns to God who gave it, and in His hand is the care of every soul.
> The world we inhabit is a corridor to the world beyond. We prepare ourselves in the corridor to enter His presence. He is our employer who knows our sorrows and our labour. Faithful is He to give us the reward of our good deeds.
> He redeems us from destruction and leads us in the way of everlasting life.

---

1 Assembly of Rabbis, 14th June 1950

60 FAITH AND PRACTICE

The service also recognises the pain of the mourners: "Support us, Lord, when we are silent through grief! Comfort us when we are bent down with sorrow! Help us as we bear the weight of our loss! Lord, our Rock and our Redeemer, give us strength!" Alongside the other set prayers in the funeral liturgy, some Rabbis encourage the inclusion of a poem or prose reading that was particularly valued by the deceased, or applied to them, or was written by them. This not only makes the service more personal, but the task of finding appropriate material (and perhaps reading it out themselves) can be helpful for the mourners. In keeping with Reform practice, Hebrew and English are both used, whilst men and women are not separated. There is no attempt to discourage women from attending funerals, as happens in some Orthodox circles. They have as much right to come as do men, whilst if they themselves are the mourners it is more helpful for the grieving process if they are present at the ceremony.

There is also no distinction concerning someone who is a *cohen*, whereas in Orthodox circles they are not allowed in the same area as the coffin and do not come to the grave unless it is for their own immediate relatives. This originated in the biblical laws forbidding priests to have contact with a dead body – which is taken to include being in the same room as a corpse – as it renders them ritually impure and unable to conduct Temple sacrifices (Leviticus 21.2-4). Reform synagogues regard such regulations as redundant following the destruction of the Temple in the year 70 CE (see IX.7). The service usually takes place in a chapel at the cemetery, after which the mourners follow the coffin to the graveside for the concluding prayers. Some Rabbis prefer to conduct the whole service at the graveside. The service always includes a eulogy concerning the person who has died. Orthodox synagogues maintain the tradition that a eulogy should not be given on certain dates (eg on the New Moon, throughout the month of *Nisan*, the first seven days of *Sivan*, the days before *Rosh Hashanah* and *Yom Kippur*, and on *Chanukah* and *Purim*) as these are all special occasions and should not be saddened. However, as the funeral still takes place then, Reform considers it unrealistic to expect those attending to be unaffected by their grief. It would also be inappropriate not to praise the attributes of the deceased or to offer the mourners words of comfort.

The service concludes with the recitation of the *Kaddish* by the closest relative to the deceased. The Reform principle of equality of the sexes means that if this is a woman, perhaps the wife or daughter of the person who died, then she is the person who says the *Kaddish*. This differs from the Orthodox custom whereby women do not usually say the *Kaddish*, but a man is deputed to say it in her stead, even if he is not related to the family at all. The last act for all those attending a burial is to assist in the filling in of the grave, women included, if they so desire. It is both as a sign of respect for the deceased and an important stage in the mourning process, often being the ritual that most makes one come to terms with the fact that the person has died. All those who knew the deceased or the family are encouraged to attend the funeral, both to honour the dead person and comfort the mourners. However, Reform synagogues do not insist upon a *minyan* (a quorum of ten adult males) and the lack of it does not prevent the service proceeding in the normal way (see IV.8). Upon leaving a cemetery, taps and basins are available for washing hands. The custom has many possible origins: symbolically showing that one is not responsible for the death of the deceased (based on Deuteronomy 21.6-7); a superstitious practice to shake off the dead spirits and prevent them from following mourners; psychologically cleansing oneself of sadness and returning to everyday affairs. It is not regarded as obligatory, but optional for those who so wish.

Flowers

Flowers are not permitted at Orthodox funerals in Britain, as it is regarded as a Christian custom. However, this ignores the fact that Christian funerals originally lacked flowers too, and thus it is an innovation common to both faiths. Moreover, the *Talmud* hints that myrtle was placed on coffins on certain occasions (*Betza* 6a), while flowers are common at funerals in Israel today.

Some Reform synagogues discourage the presence of flowers at a funeral, either out of conformity with the traditional ban, or so as to avoid extravagant sums of money being spent. Other Reform synagogues permit them, providing this corresponds to the wishes of the mourners. Flowers can be helpful in a number of ways: allowing those attending to show the mourners a caring that they would find hard to express in words; adding a touch of colour to an otherwise bleak occasion; and being a source of comfort to the mourners. Some synagogues permit only the immediate family to bring flowers in order to limit the expense involved. Reform Rabbis often point out that sending a donation to charity in the name of the deceased (particularly one that meant a lot to the deceased or that was connected with his/her illness) is another, and more enduring, way of providing a memorial.

Donations

A custom that is strictly forbidden by Reform synagogues is that a mourner should give money as a gratuity to the Rabbi conducting the service or to those responsible for digging the grave. Funerals involve expenses, particularly to non-members, but these are arranged through official accounts and settled at another time. It is considered totally inappropriate for mourners to be distracted from their grief at the time of the funeral and for financial transactions to take place at the cemetery. The same applies to the *shivah*. Moreover, the Rabbi is a salaried professional and neither expects nor wishes to be tipped. If someone not acquainted with this policy attempts to make a contribution to the Rabbi, they are advised to send a donation instead to the synagogue at a later date. Money that is sent to the Rabbi is passed on to the synagogue or put into the discretionary fund that most Rabbis operate to help individuals within the community in need of financial assistance.

8. WHAT MOURNING CUSTOMS ARE PRACTISED BY REFORM?

At the time of death

There are many minor customs as to what should be done at the time of death, such as covering all mirrors in the house of mourning and pouring away any standing water. These are based on superstitions: in the former case lest the departing soul be trapped in the mirror or lest the corpse be reflected and herald a second death in the household; in the latter case lest the water be contaminated by the spirit passing through it. However, modern justifications have been added, such as a mirror being an object of vanity and therefore inappropriate to gaze into when a life has just been lost. These customs are not regarded as obligatory in Reform synagogues, although it is recognised that they can be helpful, as many people feel the need to 'do something' at the time of death to fill the vacuum and the sense of impotence that they experience[1].

Shivah

The purpose of the *shivah* – the seven days of mourning – is to be a comfort and help to the mourners. For centuries it has succeeded in doing so, and has provided a structure both for the mourners to express their grief and come to

---

1 Assembly of Rabbis, 14th June 1950

terms with their loss, and for the surrounding community to give practical and emotional support. Observing *shivah* is therefore encouraged by Reform synagogues today, although with sufficient flexibility so as to take account of modern conditions and preserve its purpose of assisting the mourner. Thus normally the mourner would remain at home for seven days after the funeral, receive visits from family, friends and members of the community throughout the day and have prayers there every evening except Friday night. Included in the service is a special memorial prayer[1]:

> Lord God, source of all being and foundation of life, what can we say to You, for You see and know all things. In Your wisdom You formed the Universe and in Your love You provide for all Your creatures. What can we do, but acknowledge Your power, accept Your gifts with gratitude, and according to Your will, give You back Your own.
> Lord God, may the light of Your presence shine on us as we gather here, our hearts bowed by the loss of .... whom You have gathered to Yourself. Accept in Your great mercy the earthly life which has now ended and shelter with Your tender care this soul that is so precious to our hearts.

Food is often provided by visitors so that there is no need for the mourners to shop or cook. However, in cases where a seven-day *shivah* is not feasible, such as if there is no local community and mourners would merely be at home alone and even more despondent, it is often better to shorten the period of *shivah*. This might entail sitting for only three days, based on the tradition that it is the first three days after the funeral that are the most important period (Palestinian Talmud *Mo'ed Katan* III, 82b), or for whatever length is appropriate to the situation. During the *shivah* it is customary to have a candle lit in memory of the deceased, and it is recommended that this should take place for the full seven days even if the public mourning is shortened[2]. The tradition of sitting on low stools is a substitute for sitting on the ground itself (II Samuel 13.31). Nowadays it serves to distinguish the mourners from others, and to symbolise their grief in that they are 'feeling low'. The custom is regarded as optional and Reform synagogues do not necessarily provide special stools[1]. Personal rituals during the *shivah* such as abstaining from

---

1 *Forms of Prayer*, Vol I, p.299
2 Assembly of Rabbis, 14th June 1950

shaving, washing and wearing leather footwear are left to the individual[2]. A traditional prohibition that is discouraged by Reform synagogues is the ban on mourners greeting acquaintances[3]. It was intended to emphasise the grief of the mourner and to avoid jocularity, but it is felt to be inappropriate today when many people feel uncomfortable confronting death and often avoid mourners, and so reinforce their loneliness. Similarly, it is very important at a *shivah* that those attending talk to the mourners and try to comfort them, and do not just speak to others present. Members of the local community are strongly encouraged not only to attend the funeral and *shivah*, but also to visit the bereaved at other times. Even though they may feel lost for words, it is much better to be with the mourner inarticulately than to absent oneself and deprive them of human warmth. The common greeting, "I wish you long life", is derived from a phrase in the blessing for a new month. It typifies the Jewish belief that despite present troubles there is always hope for the future, and that one should look forward rather than concentrate on the past. Refreshments are usually served after the prayers, although most Rabbis recommend that drinks should be tea or coffee rather than alcohol, so as to preserve the sober nature of the occasion and to prevent any distraction from the need to comfort the mourners.

After the *shivah*

The Jewish way of mourning is a series of stages, each of decreasing intensity, which accompany the mourners from the first moments of grief and gradually return them to the stream of everyday life. Following the intensity of the *shivah* comes the *sheloshim* (thirty days), the remainder of the first month after the funeral, in which mourners go back to work but maintain their distinctive status by avoiding places of entertainment or arranging a marriage. Some follow the tradition of letting their beard grow as an external sign of their loss. After that one enters the stage of the rest of the first year, during which it is customary to say *Kaddish* at the weekly Sabbath services. It is not viewed as necessary to say it on a daily basis, although some choose to do so at those Reform synagogues which have a daily evening service. There are no rules as to how often one should visit the grave; much depends on the mourner and whether such visits are a source of comfort. Regular visits are appropriate, although they should not be so frequent that they

---

1 Idem
2 Idem
3 Idem

prevent the mourner from adjusting to life without the person they have just lost.

Stone-setting

The original purpose of a tombstone was to protect the grave from being disturbed by wild animals. Later it became a way of recording the life of the person who died with biographical details and tributes, whilst the stone itself was, and still is, often extravagantly large and lavishly embossed. The author suggests that just as coffins are required to be of plain and inexpensive wood (and without inner linings or outer handles) so as not to distinguish between rich and poor, so tombstones should also be of uniform size and of decorous design. The wording on the stones varies according to individual preferences, but usually includes the name of the deceased, date of birth and either date of death or age, along with a scriptural verse or personal inscription. There is no objection to the text and dates being in English, although use of some Hebrew and the inclusion of the Hebrew name is encouraged. It is more important that the stone speaks of the deceased rather than lists all the relatives. The stones may be horizontal or vertical, depending on the cemetery regulations. The Orthodox tradition in Britain of waiting a year before a stone is erected is merely one of many customs; in Israel it is often erected after the *sheloshim*. In Reform synagogues it can be at any time (although usually after a minimum of three months so as to allow the ground to settle), and can be chosen according to when family and friends are most likely to be able to attend or when the weather conditions may be favourable. The stone-setting can be accompanied by a short service which emphasises particularly the needs of the mourners and contains the words[1]:

> As they gather round this stone in times to come, may it remind them of the love and affection that do not fade. May it draw them even closer to their families. When they see it, may it remind them not only of the dead but also of You, God of everlasting life. In their sorrow You are with them, may they remember You in the trials and temptations of the world. Teach them that love does not die, and that death is swallowed up forever in eternal life. O Lord, in You we put our trust.

Rabbis often emphasise in their address that while mourning has its place, it

---

1 *Funeral Service*, p.34

should not be excessive. The stone-setting should mark the end of one's mourning period and lead to a renewal of life. It should be noted, however, that such services are not obligatory and are a relatively new tradition; until recently one was simply informed by the stonemason when the stone was ready and went to visit it privately. This is still an option today. There is a danger that some stone-setting services can become 'second funerals' with emotional reunions which reawaken grief rather than assuage it. The author suggests that it may sometimes be more appropriate for the stone-setting to be for close relatives and friends only. Others should visit, and spend time with, the mourners during the year itself. This would be much more helpful than appearing merely at the stone-setting and greeting them briefly.

Yahrzeit

On the *yahrzeit* ('time of year') marking the anniversary of a person's death, it is customary for mourners to light a memorial candle at home in the evening. Appropriate prayers are to be found in the Reform prayer book, including (for a woman)[1]:

> Today I remember with love ..... who has gone to everlasting life, and I honour her memory. As this light burns pure and clear, so may the thought of her goodness shine in my heart and strengthen me, Lord, to do Your will. Amen.

One can also say *Kaddish* in the synagogue, either on that date or the preceding Sabbath, as well as visit the person's grave. Traditionally the date of the *yahrzeit* corresponds to that according to the Hebrew calendar. However, many Jews today have no knowledge of when the Hebrew date occurs and feel that it bears no relation to them, whereas the secular date upon which the person died will always stay fixed in their mind. Some Reform synagogues therefore allow use of the secular date if the mourner so chooses, and they regard it as preferable to the observance of *yahrzeits* decreasing altogether. In addition many Reform synagogues send out letters reminding congregants of a forthcoming *yahrzeit* and that the name of the deceased will be commemorated before the *Kaddish* at the relevant Sabbath service. Other synagogues will only call out the name if the family of the deceased is present at the service. This reflects the fact that the *Kaddish* is primarily for the mourners – a declaration

---

1 *Forms of Prayer*, Vol I, p.301

by them affirming the value of life, and is not, as is sometimes mistakenly thought, a prayer of intercession for the dead affecting their passage in the afterlife. If, however, the deceased were members of the community, their names are remembered whether or not the family are able to attend.

In the years following the bereavement it is customary to observe the *yahrzeit* annually and to say *Kaddish* for the deceased person both then and during the *Yizkor* service at *Yom Kippur*. It is also appropriate to visit the cemetery periodically, particularly at special occasions such as before the High Holy Days or on the person's birthday, wedding anniversary or *yahrzeit*.

9. WHY IS CREMATION PERMITTED BY REFORM?

The question of cremation arouses much controversy, as do many aspects surrounding the emotional subject of death, yet the issue is a simple one. The original method of disposing of a dead body in Jewish tradition was that of burial. However, there was nothing distinctively Jewish about this and it merely reflected a contemporary practice. Thus the patriarchs were buried above ground, as was the custom then, in the family tomb of *Machpelah* (Genesis 23.1-20). This tradition later changed to burial below ground, whilst another, much later development was that instead of the body just being wrapped in a shroud, it was put in a coffin so as to conform with civil law.

Cremation has been the normal practice in certain parts of the world for several thousand years. It occurred in the land of Israel in biblical times, although only in special circumstances, as in the disposal of the remains of King Saul, and in times of plague (1 Samuel 31.12-13, Amos 6.10). It was only in 1884 that it was legalised in Britain. Since then it has become increasingly common, and today cremation accounts for 70% of all funerals. There are several factors for its popularity: it is considered more sound environmentally than burial, as it does not use up land; (in Britain, for instance, it is estimated to save 200 acres of land a year)[1]; it is preferred by those worried about the future upkeep of their grave, particularly if they have no family or their relatives live far away; it is less expensive than burial, largely because it does not involve the cost of purchasing land; it is felt by some to be a more fitting way of dealing with one's grief at the death of a

---

1 Audit Commission, March 1989

loved one. These reasons will not appeal to everyone but are considered important by many people, and Jews often express a desire for cremation too.

Orthodox authorities are opposed to cremation and forbid it. This is partly because it is not traditional and is seen as an imitation of a gentile custom; partly because it is regarded as akin to mutilating a corpse, which is forbidden in Jewish Law; and partly because it involves the destruction of one's body and would therefore prevent physical resurrection of the dead with the coming of the Messiah. Reform synagogues, however, consider that all of these are insufficient arguments to deny cremation for those who so wish. The fact that its general use is a modern development is not necessarily an automatic disqualification, otherwise many other aspects of life today would be forbidden to Jews. Mutilation does not occur in the sense of maliciously destroying a body, for cremations are conducted with the utmost solemnity and reverence. The opposition of Jewish tradition to the burning of a body was based on the assumption that it was a disgrace. It did not envisage a situation in which it was the specific wishes of the deceased. Indeed cremation merely speeds up the natural process of the body turning to dust and ashes. Few Jews today believe in physical resurrection of the dead, with most subscribing instead to a belief in an afterlife for the soul. Even if one does accept resurrection literally, it would be only logical that in miraculous times new life could be given to ashes as much as to old bones, many of which would have crumbled into dust themselves. It has been advanced more recently that sensitivity to the appalling use of crematoria in the Holocaust is grounds for avoiding them today. However, thousands of Jews also died in the Holocaust by being forced to dig their own graves and were then shot beside them, whilst mass burials were common too. Another argument, albeit psychological rather than specifically Jewish, is that burial is more helpful for the grieving process because mourners are physically involved in the ceremony (eg following the coffin, filling in the grave) and are therefore better able to come to terms with their bereavement. It can also be comforting to have a grave to visit at the *yahrzeit* and at other times. Nevertheless, this is a matter in which the wishes of the person concerned should be respected fully. It is therefore the policy of Reform synagogues to regard cremation as a legitimate option and a matter of individual choice. All Reform Rabbis will conduct a cremation service if requested, and in many congregations cremations are as common as burials.

The service used at a Jewish cremation is exactly the same as that at a burial and is conducted by a Rabbi. It can take place at any crematorium, for in Britain most are owned by the local civil authorities and are non-denominational. (The crucifix often displayed at a crematorium is always removed or covered for Jewish services.) If live or recorded music facilities are present, and it is the wish of the family, one may have music upon entry, exit or during the committal stage[1]. As well as the standard repertoire of music for such occasions, there is no reason why the mourners cannot select other music that was particularly appreciated by the deceased, and thus make the ceremony more personal. Full mourning rites occur, just as after a burial, such as a *shivah* and reciting the *Kaddish*. The ashes are disposed of in one of several ways: they can be buried in a Jewish cemetery with a headstone as a marker; they can be placed in an urn in a Wall of Remembrance (also known as a Columbarium) with a plaque; or they can be scattered, either at a special section of a Jewish cemetery (eg rose garden) or according to the person's wishes in a place that held great significance for them. However, some Reform Rabbis discourage scattering, as they feel it is more helpful for mourners if they have a specific spot as a focus for their grief and as a memorial to the deceased person[2]. It should be noted that the Burial Society of the United Synagogue (Orthodox) permits the burial of cremated ashes in an Orthodox cemetery along with a normal burial service, even though it will not officiate at the cremation itself[3].

10. WHAT HAPPENS IN SPECIAL CASES SUCH AS STILLBIRTHS, MISCARRIAGES AND SUICIDES?

Stillbirths

In the past children born dead or who died under 30 days old were not regarded as having been fully developed as persons (*Ketubot* 20b, *Shabbat* 135b). This is still the attitude of Orthodox synagogues today. It is held that there is no point in keeping alive the memory of someone who never properly lived. The child is buried in someone else's grave without the parents being present. There is no funeral service or *shivah*, and no mention of the child on the stone. The procedure was designed to save the family any distress, and was based on two factors: that infant mortality was high and was accepted as natural; and that parents had large families and there would be enough surviving children for them not to mourn those that died so young.

---

1 eg Assembly of Rabbis, 11th July 1962 and 29th April 1982
2 Assembly of Rabbis, 3rd June 1959 and 11th December 1973
3 Laws and By-laws of the Burial Society of the United Synagogue, F. 14, p.61

Reform synagogues, however, recognise that these factors no longer apply. Medical advances have meant that child death is comparatively rare, while modern families are very small. As a result, each pregnancy is much more important to today's parents and is expected to result in a healthy offspring. Death on, or shortly after, birth is highly traumatic and the grief is compounded by feelings of guilt and a sense of failure. In addition it is now recognised that despite the shortness of the child's life the mother already has developed a strong bond with it, which was formed during the months it was in her womb. She therefore feels bereaved and suffers all the differing emotions of a mourner. It would be wrong, therefore, to act as if nothing had happened, and deny the mother and her husband the means of expressing their grief and coming to terms with it through mourning rituals.

It is clear that a new situation exists and that it requires a new attitude and policy which can take account of the death without confusing it with that of a fully grown person. Parents who wish to forget as soon as possible what they consider to be a 'mishap' follow the traditional procedure, although the Rabbi will be aware of the shock and hurt that they will still face, and give them full pastoral support. Parents who wish to acknowledge formally the death that has occurred are permitted to do so. The child has its own grave and there is a simple funeral service, although usually for immediate family only. The service voices the pain and confusion of the parents and also helps them to let go of that which they had so briefly. A shortened *shivah* can take place according to the situation; a small stone is erected with the name of the infant or, if unnamed, with the inscription "Child of ......". It is not usual to observe the *yahrzeit* or to say *Kaddish* every year. Unless the death was due to a hereditary disease or a gynaecological problem, the parents are often encouraged to have another child, albeit waiting a minimum of three months for the mother's body to rest and for both parents' emotions to recover. The author suggests that when a subsequent child is born, parents consider giving it the additional Hebrew name of Hayyim (for boys) or Hayya (for girls) – meaning "life" – so as to both acknowledge the previous loss and rejoice in the new child.

Miscarriage
Miscarriages happen much more frequently than is commonly imagined for they are often not known about by those other than the immediate family and are rarely mentioned unless the pregnancy has continued to such an extent that it is physically obvious to outsiders. Nevertheless, they can be highly traumatic for parents who had every expectation of a successful pregnancy. It is

particularly distressing for the mother who not only carries the foetus but very often is aware that all is not well before the miscarriage occurs. In keeping with past tradition, Orthodoxy does not have any form of mourning ritual, whereas the Reform recognise that the parents may need to give expression to their hurt. In Britain the foetus is legally the property of the hospital where the miscarriage takes place, and it is disposed of by the hospital authorities. No funeral takes place, therefore, but some Rabbis will conduct a service at the home of the parents if requested. Special prayers have been written for those who have experienced a miscarriage, amongst which the following gives expression to the feelings involved[1]:

Lord our God,
For a time you gave us the hope of a new life,
Placed in us the expectation of a new awakening.
    Now, in Your wisdom,
    You have taken that hope from us,
    have delayed, for reasons known only to You
    the arrival of that new soul into our world.
Lord, we thank You still for the hope You gave us,
And pray that You may renew in us that hope in time to come;
    though the pain of our disappointment is real, and deep
    we acknowledge still that You are our God,
    You renew Life beyond Death,
    You give, and take away,
    You hold all our souls in the palm of Your hand.
May it be Your will to give us, once more,
    the chance to share with You
    in the bringing of new life to this our world;
May it be Your will that we shall be strengthened,
    both by our hopes
    and our disappointments,
    and learn to love the more deeply, that which we have.
Blessed are You, Lord, who shares the sorrow of Your creation.

Some parents may wish to follow the custom mentioned above regarding a stillbirth, of giving a special additional name to a subsequent child.

---

[1] Composed by Rabbi Walter Rothschild of Leeds Reform Synagogue

Suicide

Suicide has always been regarded as a heinous offence in Judaism and as akin to murder (*Baba Kamma* 91b). It is a denial of the goodness of the world and a surrender to despair. It also usurps God's prerogative of giving and taking life, which applies as much to one's own life as to that of any other person. As a sign of condemnation and as a deterrent to would-be suicides, severe restrictions were placed at the funerals of those who had committed suicide: they were buried in a separate section of the Jewish cemetery and there were no mourning rites. However, such penalties have little effect nowadays, and it is recognised that much more powerful factors are at work in the mind of someone contemplating suicide. Moreover, mourning rituals are primarily intended for the benefit of the surviving family and, in the case of a suicide, they are often needed even more than in other circumstances. The bereaved are usually traumatised, having not only undergone a sudden loss but also suffering from enormous guilt, wondering whether the death might not have occurred if they had acted differently. Reform synagogues are equally opposed to suicide but regard the needs of the relatives as paramount. Thus funerals of suicides are conducted in the same way as other funerals and full mourning rites (*shivah*, stone-setting, *yahrzeit*) are observed. Recently, perhaps influenced by the Reform approach, some Orthodox Rabbis have adopted a more lenient attitude to the matter by declaring that no reasonable person commits suicide, therefore they must have been deranged at the very moment of suicide, therefore they are not responsible for their actions, therefore a normal funeral can take place. Despite its good intention, this is merely a legalism designed to circumvent the posthumous penalties against suicides which are still held to be in operation. In addition it distorts the reality of the situation in which suicides are often pre-meditated and carried out rationally; denying this is not necessarily helpful to the family concerned. It should be added that anyone acquainted with a person who is in a state of depression, or who talks about suicide, should befriend them or refer them to those who might be able to prevent a tragedy taking place.

11. CAN NON-JEWISH RELATIVES PARTICIPATE IN ANY OF THE CYCLE OF LIFE CEREMONIES?

Non-Jews have always been welcome to attend Jewish religious ceremonies. In biblical times Solomon asked God to hear and respond to the prayers of non-Jews who worshipped in the Temple (I Kings 8.41-3) whilst they were also allowed to bring sacrifices for the Temple altar (*Menachot* 73b). Similarly today non-Jews are permitted to attend synagogue services if they so desire, whilst non-Jewish clergy or teachers are encouraged to do so because of its educational value and the greater harmony between Jews and non-Jews that it can bring. If the non-Jews concerned are relatives of a member of the synagogue then their attendance is considered even more welcome. Non-Jews can participate in the service in general ways such as standing when the congregation rises and joining in the reading of the prayers in English. They are not given any of the usual *mitzvot* in services such as reciting the blessing over the *Torah* or lifting the scroll. When a close family celebration takes place, many synagogues permit non-Jewish relatives to participate in certain special roles which are not connected with the general running of the main service itself.

In the case of a circumcision, the ceremony usually takes place in the parental home, or in hospital if the mother is still there. The declaration and blessings recited by the father would not usually be appropriate for a non-Jew and might be recited instead by a Jewish relative or the Rabbi. The roles of the *kvatter* and *sandek* are purely functional, bringing and holding the baby, and could be done by a non-Jewish father or grandfather if they so desired. It should be noted that although *kvatter* is usually translated as 'godfather', the position does not carry any religious responsibility for the child's future as it does in the Christian tradition.

In the case of a baby blessing for the child of a Jewish mother and non-Jewish father, the father is permitted to come up in front of the Ark with his wife and child for the ceremony[1]. Some Rabbis permit him to also open the Ark or to read the special prayer in English recited by the father, if he has declared his willingness to support his wife in providing a Jewish home and upbringing for the child.

In the case of a *bar/batmitzvah* where the father has shown similar support, he is permitted by some Rabbis to stand by his child during the *Torah* reading. In synagogues where the parents open the Ark for the special prayer recited by their child, a non-Jewish father may be allowed to participate too.

In the case of a wedding, the non-Jewish parents of a proselyte bride or groom may stand under the *chuppah*, as parents normally do[2]. Some Rabbis permit other roles, such as the non-Jewish father of the bride escorting her

---

[1] eg Assembly of Rabbis, 2nd May 1963
[2] eg Assembly of Rabbis, 31st October 1962

into the synagogue. There is no objection to the bridesmaids not being Jewish as they have no religious standing in the ceremony and are a non-Jewish custom that has been introduced in recent centuries. The same applies to the best man, although for practical reasons it is preferable if he is Jewish and familiar with Jewish weddings so as to be of greater help to the groom.

In the case of a Jew who dies leaving behind a non-Jewish spouse, two issues are involved: the mourning rites for the departed Jew and the status of the surviving spouse. In the first matter a normal Jewish funeral and *shivah* occurs, as is the right of any Jew, assuming that it is requested by the spouse or other members of the family. In the second matter, although civil marriage is not valid according to Jewish religious law, it is recognised that in real terms the couple were husband and wife[1]. Thus even though the non-Jewish spouses have none of the obligations of a Jewish mourner, they are considered mourners from a pastoral point of view. The Rabbi conducting the funeral and *shivah* will be specially sensitive to their different religious background, and the awkwardness that they may feel at Jewish rituals and prayers. Both out of respect for the deceased's partner and for humanitarian motives, the comfort and support normally extended to a mourner by Rabbi and congregation will be extended to them too, if so desired.

In the case of the death of the non-Jewish spouse of a Jew, there arise questions concerning both the place of burial and mourning rites. It is sometimes requested that non-Jewish spouses who had no religious faith of their own and who identified more with the Jewish community of which their spouse was a member, should be buried in the synagogue cemetery. In keeping with the strong Jewish tradition of having a separate cemetery for Jews, it is not permitted to bury a non-Jew in a Jewish cemetery[2]. A Rabbi may, however, officiate at the funeral of a non-Jewish spouse in a non-denominational cemetery that is under the control of the local civil authority. A Rabbi may officiate in such a service also at a crematorium; some communities permit the ashes to be scattered in the Jewish cemetery afterwards, whilst others do not[3]. These permissions conform with a long-standing tradition to act helpfully towards non-Jews, including arranging their burials when necessary (*Gittin* 61a). Jewish mourning rituals for a non-Jewish spouse are not considered necessary according to the Orthodox interpretation

---

1 eg Assembly of Rabbis, 14th July 1959
2 eg Assembly of Rabbis, 27th March 1963; see also 27th April 1983
3 eg Assembly of Rabbis, 13th January 1965

of Jewish Law. Reform Rabbis take the attitude that such rituals are largely intended to be a comfort to the mourner and therefore can apply just as much to a Jew whose non-Jewish spouse has died. Thus it would be entirely appropriate to say *Kaddish*, sit *shivah* and observe the *yahrzeit* if the surviving spouse so desired. This would also be the case when proselytes lose their parents or siblings.

CHAPTER FOUR

SERVICES

Sing to the Lord all the earth
Serve the Lord with joy,
Come before Him with singing

Psalm 100.1-2

1. WHAT IS DIFFERENT ABOUT THE STRUCTURE OF THE REFORM PRAYER BOOK?

(Discussion of prayers in English, the role of women, triennial reading of the *Torah* and use of music is dealt with independently in subsequent chapters.)

It has been said that the Bible is God's gift to humanity and that the prayer book is humanity's gift to God in return. The saying highlights the fact that the prayer book is a product of human endeavour and, although revered, is not sacred. It is to be treated with respect but is open to revision, for it is a continuous process to which each generation wishes to contribute. Indeed this has been the case historically, for the prayer book has developed considerably over the centuries, with new prayers being written, different structures used, and considerable regional variations. Even individual prayers have changed, as in the case of the *Amidah* which took several centuries to coalesce from a variety of versions to its current form.

The constant revision of the prayer book is not only an historical fact but is also essential to its purpose if it is to remain a living work rather than become a museum piece. A successful prayer book serves many functions: it is the attempt of individuals to communicate with God and is an expression of their deepest thoughts and emotions; it reflects the reality of life and people's everyday concerns, and yet also helps them rise above them and attain spiritual fulfilment; it caters for individuals, and yet also merges their identity with the rest of the community; it is an affirmation of Jewish faith and historical experiences, and yet also gives voice to one's own personal search and Jewish identity. In order to achieve these tasks, the prayer book must be a bridge between the vast storehouse of Jewish tradition and the circumstances of modern life, blending the two together without dismissing the value of the former or compromising the integrity of the latter. The changes made to the services in the Reform prayer book, *Forms of Prayer*, have been undertaken in this spirit and fall into three main categories: theological, historical and structural.

Theological

One of the problems with the development of the prayer book in the past was that although each generation added a prayer, they hesitated to delete any existing passages. This even included those which referred to conditions long since past and of no religious significance today, such as the prayer still said in Orthodox synagogues for the scholars of Babylon who ceased to exist several centuries ago. This continuous process of accretion meant that the size of the prayer book grew immensely and the length of the service increased correspondingly. In Temple times the service probably lasted less than an hour, whereas in modern Orthodox synagogues it can last up to four hours. The result is that many prayers are said at an extremely fast rate to complete them in a reasonable time, while many people attend synagogue for only part of the service, arriving up to two hours late because they find the full service too long. It is clearly impossible for those present throughout the service to maintain concentration for such a lengthy time, while those coming late are a constant interruption and destroy any decorum. As with a bush that has become hopelessly overgrown, the Reform have pruned back the prayer book to a size that is now more in keeping with its original length. It prevents weariness and allows one to give full attention to the service. The average Sabbath service lasts about one and a half hours, and congregants are present from beginning to end.

The desire to shorten the service coincided with another tenet of Reform thinking: that the liturgy should express sentiments to which the community subscribes, so that one means what one prays. Prayers which totally contradict one's beliefs encourage dishonesty or indifference, and should be omitted. As a result, a number of prayers have been removed, such as those relating to sacrifices. Passages that express highly negative attitudes to non-Jews, reflecting previous periods when hostile relationships existed, have been removed also, such as parts of the *Aleinu*. So too are those that, whatever benign interpretation is given to them, disparage women. Hence the omission of the morning blessing in which a man thanks God for not making him a woman. On other occasions slight alterations have been made so that the prayers correspond better to modern thought. Thus in an age when Jewish, Israeli and British law have all abolished the death penalty, the twelfth blessing in the *Amidah* has been changed from calling for the death of slanderers to calling for an end to slander. Similarly references to the arrival of the Messiah have either been omitted or changed to the coming of the Messianic Age, which corresponds more to Reform thinking and emphasises the qualities of an era of peace rather than the person of the Messiah. Thus the translation of the first paragraph of the *Amidah* speaks not of bringing "a redeemer" but of bringing "rescue" to future generations. For the same theological reasons, references to the physical resurrection of the dead, to which Reform thinking does not subscribe, have been amended to life after death. Thus the translation of the second paragraph of the *Amidah* no longer ends "Blessed are You, Lord, who revives the dead" but "who renews life beyond death". It should be noted that although references to physical resurrection of the dead in the *Amidah* have been changed in the English translation, it remains in the Hebrew original; this was an attempt by the editors of the prayer book to strike a balance between the development in modern thinking and the traditional Hebrew format of the liturgy.

Other principles employed in editing the liturgy are as follows: prayers that are repeated several times in one service, such as the *Kaddish*, lose their impact through repetition and so are limited to one recitation. Prayers that are in Aramaic are either omitted or translated into Hebrew, as it is a language unknown to most Jews today and without the historical significance of Hebrew. The only exception in the Sabbath service is the *Kaddish*, which is retained in its original form because of its special character. The large collection of Psalms which occupy a considerable part of the Orthodox service have been reduced to a few of the most appropriate ones. However a Psalm Anthology at the back of the Reform prayer book means that they are always available for individual use or as a substitute for those printed in the main service.

Whilst several parts of the service have therefore been deleted, new prayers have also been composed so as to address the particular concerns of this generation. It is in keeping with Reform theology that God speaks to humanity in each age, and therefore each age has insight that could be added to the liturgy. Thus the Sabbath evening service includes[1]:

> Lord of all creation, You have made us the masters of Your world, to tend it, to serve it and to enjoy it. For six days we measure and we build, we count and carry the real and the imagined burdens of our task, the success we earn and the price we pay.
> On this, the Sabbath day, give us rest.
> For six days, if we are weary or bruised by the world, if we think ourselves giants or cause others pain, there is never a moment to pause, and know what we should really be.
> On this, the Sabbath day, give us time.
> For six days we are torn between our private greed and the urgent needs of others, between the foolish noises in our ears and the silent prayer of our soul.

---

1 *Forms of Prayer*, Vol I, p.17

On this, the Sabbath day, give us understanding and peace.

Help us, Lord, to carry these lessons, of rest and time, of understanding and peace, into the six days that lie ahead, to bless us in the working days of our life. Amen.

The object is not to value modernity above all else but to seek out that which speaks to modernity. Thus at the same time selections from the wisdom of previous generations that were never included before have been introduced, ranging from Biblical passages to Rabbinic literature to mystical poetry to *Chasidic* sayings. They include prayers from both the *Ashkenazi* and *Sephardi* liturgy, ignoring the artificial divisions of Jewish life, and emphasising the unity of the Jewish people and their common heritage.

Historical

In the last fifty years the Jewish world has changed almost beyond recognition. It has witnessed the murder of six million Jews, and the impenetrable cloud of the Holocaust still haunts us and affects our lives and attitudes. There has also been the rebirth of the State of Israel, a centuries-old dream come true, which has brought a miraculous flowering of Jewish identity and achievement. The prayer book – the autobiography of the Jewish people – has to take account of both these momentous events. The Holocaust is commemorated by a special Memorial Service for the Six Million which mourns "the genius and the wit that died, the learning and the laughter that were lost"[1]. The prayer book also has the unique feature of several illustrations, particularly of European synagogues that were destroyed in the Second World War and whose inclusion not only decorates the prayer book but also ensures that their memory is kept alive. The State of Israel is acknowledged in a new *Yom Ha'atzma'ut* (Israel Independence Day) Service that celebrates "the hope that was born out of suffering, the springs that came to the dry, sad valley, the rose that blossomed in the desert"[2]. In addition, there is a new prayer for the State of Israel during the Sabbath morning services, reflecting both the hopes and worries associated with it. It asks that "peace may reign on its borders and tranquillity in its homes. May the spirit of friendship and understanding remove all fears and heal all wounds"[3].

---

1 Ibid, p.256
2 Ibid, p.260
3 Ibid, p.161

The prayer book also recognises a further change in Jewish life: that an age of faith has given way to an age of secularism, in which there is much doubt and confusion as to religion, while prayer itself, once automatic, is often problematic for many people. This, too, has been acknowledged[1]:

> There are times when it is hard to hear You, and times when it is hard to follow You; and I know that this is my loss. In the quietness of this Sabbath I turn my thoughts to You. Help me to hear Your voice, to find Your image in my soul, and to be at peace.

Prayers such as that quoted above allow expression of these uncertainties, and thereby help those who feel them to stay within a religious framework. The special selection entitled 'Meditation before Prayer' contains material which also speaks to those with questions of faith[2]:

> I believe in the sun even when it is not shining.
> I believe in love even when feeling it not.
> I believe in God even when He is silent.

Structural

Every prayer book can suffer from being so familiar that prayer becomes routine and mechanical. In an effort to maintain a regular structure yet add freshness to it, the Sabbath evening service has four alternative introductory sections, each containing a different prayer, song and psalm. The Sabbath morning service has six different opening sections, each with a different theme: Tradition, Life and Death, The Future, The Just Society, The Community and The Family of Israel. It is left to individual synagogues whether they use them in rotation or prefer some more regularly than others. Similarly it is up to each synagogue whether prayers are sung, read together, read responsively or said silently. Each congregation has its own *minhag* (custom). Another structural change is that, unlike the Orthodox prayer book which starts with the daily services, the Reform prayer book begins with the Sabbath services. This is in recognition of the fact that, for most Jews, communal prayer occurs on the Sabbath. Home prayers and mid-week prayers are, of course, also included, as are a considerable number of prayers relating

---

1 Ibid, p.65
2 Ibid, p.6

to personal circumstances, such as prayers for a journey, during sickness, and before an operation. Entirely new, and again reflecting contemporary life, is the prayer for an anniversary (be it birthday or wedding anniversary) which, whilst not an official ceremony in Jewish tradition, is a significant occasion for most Jews today. Part of the prayer declares[1]:

> On this day I come before You with my private memories and thank You for my own experience, and for companionship and love. Whatever the future brings, may this day always renew my spirit, giving me happiness on my journey through life.

Several congregations encourage their members to read the prayer in synagogue on the nearest Sabbath to their anniversary. It can also be said at home privately.

Among other innovations that reflect the realities of Jewish life is a prayer for committee meetings which not only introduces a moment of religion to discussions that often concern very secular matters, but also helps establish an atmosphere appropriate for synagogue business[2]:

> Let us listen to each other with respect, and treat each other with wisdom and generosity, so that we witness to the master whom we serve, and justify His choice of us. May none of our controversies rise up, like those of Korach, from ambition and self-seeking. Let them only be for the sake of heaven, like those of Hillel and Shammai.

Special prayers have been composed for interfaith meetings and for international understanding which echo the moves towards religious and political harmony in the world. In addition there are three anthologies at the end of the prayer book – a Study Anthology, Psalm Anthology and Song Anthology – which are available for private or communal prayers. They can be used as supplements or alternatives to the existing prayers, and they also serve as an educational facility, bringing a treasure chest of Jewish tradition and learning into one's hands.

---

1 Ibid, p.292
2 Ibid, p.296

2. WHAT IS DISTINCTIVE ABOUT THE REFORM HIGH HOLY DAY PRAYER BOOK?

The High Holy Day prayer book – the *machzor* – contains many of the features of the Daily and Sabbath prayer book in its blend of tradition and modernity. One crucial difference, however, is that as *Yom Kippur* is a day-long service, there is no need to shorten the liturgy. However, considerable revision has been made so that one does not just 'get through' the day but is able to say the prayers with conviction and sincerity. Prayers that are considered theologically obsolete in Reform thinking (mention of sacrifices, physical resurrection of the dead, a personal Messiah) are omitted, as are those which lack religious appeal for today. In their stead a vast range of material has been substituted, both ancient and contemporary. A readiness to accept religious insights from any Jewish source – Rabbis, poets, psychologists – has been the key principle. As the Introduction declares: "In the confusion of our times, the word of God has come to us (as perhaps it always has) in unexpected ways and through unexpected people ... We find our spirituality in the diaries of an adolescent girl, in the records of ghetto doctors and in the honesty of modern Jewish writers"[1]. New prayers specially composed for the *machzor* have also been included, such as that in the *Yizkor* (memorial) service[2]:

> We live restlessly, confusing things of eternity with things that pass ...
> We struggle for goals we can never attain and only with death do our struggles cease. Like children falling asleep over their toys, we let go our grasp on our possessions, and death overtakes us.

In addition each section of the High Holy Day Services is introduced by a series of meditations that evoke the special feelings of the moment and express the deepest thoughts of those present, such as that before the *Yom Kippur* Afternoon Service[3]:

> As this quiet time ends, I look back on the year, and recall as well the good things it gave me:
> I remember the friends I made and the jokes I heard and told.

---

1 *Forms of Prayer*, Vol III, p.x
2 Ibid, p.608
3 Ibid, p.534

I remember the times when I was able to put up with fools, and people who were irritating or ungrateful.
I remember the times when they were able to put up with me.
I remember the occasions when the strength of my own courage and generosity surprised others as well as myself.
I remember the times when I dared to think for myself, and found I could be alone.
I remember all that was spontaneous and uncalculating in me, when I seemed to recover the innocence of childhood.
I remember the illnesses from which I was spared, the disasters which never occurred, and my worries about things which never happened.
I remember the moments when I knew I had a soul.

Another special feature of the *machzor* is its recognition that many Jews come to the High Holy Days unprepared and then find it very hard to summon up the concentration and spiritual energy that they demand. The *machzor* therefore has a Calendar of Repentance containing short readings for each day of *Elul*, the month preceding *Rosh Hashanah*. The passages are designed to help preparation by raising the themes of self-examination and repentance, and by building up a sense of anticipation. They culminate in a newly written *Selichot* service which combines traditional passages with modern composition. The service – omitted from the Reform liturgy for many years, but now restored – is usually held once before *Rosh Hashanah*, whereas numerous *Selichot* services are held in Orthodox circles. There is another Calendar of Repentance for each of the days between *Rosh Hashanah* and *Yom Kippur*, so that the religious momentum is sustained throughout the Ten Days of Penitence. The readings include passages from the *Talmud* as well as those by twentieth century writers such as psychiatrist Victor Frankl[1]:

What was really needed was a fundamental change in our attitude toward life. We had to learn ourselves and, furthermore, we had to teach the despairing men in the concentration camp that it did not really matter what we expected from life, but rather what life expected from us.

A further item is that not only are the *Torah* and *Haftarah* portions for *Rosh Hashanah* and *Yom Kippur* included in the book, but they are accompanied by a rich variety of commentary on both the individual verses and their

---

1 Ibid, p.4

general themes. These can be read privately before the services, or during them, and serve to illumine one's understanding of the texts and highlight their relevance to the High Holy Days. A Study Anthology at the back of the *machzor* provides additional material on the major themes such as sin and repentance and their application to a wide range of situations including malpractice in business, the wrongs of jealousy and the difficulty of repentance.

The *machzor* also caters for events surrounding the High Holy Days that take place at home – be it the *Kiddush* at the dinner table, blessings over the children or the correct Hebrew greetings for the specific days. It emphasises that prayer and holiness are not limited to the synagogue but can accompany people wherever they are, and should permeate the home.

---

3. WHAT IS THE REASON FOR HAVING ENGLISH PRAYERS IN THE SERVICES, AND HOW DOES INCLUSIVE LANGUAGE AFFECT THE TRANSLATIONS?

If prayer is to be meaningful, it has to be intelligible to the person saying the prayers. The argument that all Jews should be able to read and understand Hebrew is an admirable ideal and one to which Reform Rabbis heartily subscribe; yet it does not reflect the reality that many Jews cannot read Hebrew at all, and even if they can, few know what it means. An all-Hebrew service would leave many praying by rote only, with others feeling totally excluded. It seems only sensible, therefore, to include some prayers in the vernacular and to encourage Jews to feel at home in the synagogue service. Moreover this 'innovation' is in fact merely a return to a much older tradition. Translations of the *Torah* readings had to be made even in biblical times when the people returning from Babylon were unfamiliar with Hebrew (Nehemiah 8.8). As Aramaic continued to be more popular than Hebrew for everyday speech, the Rabbis of the *Mishnah* and *Talmud* permitted the *Shema*, *Amidah* and grace after meals to be recited in the vernacular (*Sotah* 7.1,32b), a decision confirmed by other authorities who suggested that private prayers be said in Hebrew and communal prayers in the vernacular (*Shulchan Aruch, Orach Hayyim* 101.4) – contrary to modern Orthodox custom which advises the reverse. It should be remembered that some of the most familiar parts of the liturgy were actually composed in Aramaic, the then vernacular, such as *Kaddish, Kol nidrei* and *Chad gadya*. In Israel today, where everyone can comprehend Hebrew, Reform synagogues hold the service totally in Hebrew.

The Reform prayer book has the format of Hebrew prayers being on one side of the page with the English translations opposite. The English text is thus available to everyone for private use. It is employed, too, in communal prayer. As a very broad generalisation, there tends to be a balance of 60% Hebrew and 40% English in services, although this does not necessarily apply to every synagogue. Each community has its own custom both as to what percentage is used and as to which prayers are said in which language. Many synagogues avoid a fixed routine, but vary the prayers said in English from week to week so as to encourage familiarity with both the Hebrew version and its meaning. In most cases, though, the better known prayers are said regularly in Hebrew – the *Barchu*, *Shema*, *Amidah*, *Aleinu* – while the intermediary passages and psalms are recited more frequently in English. The songs are always sung in Hebrew.

Whilst Reform is adamant that English is both permitted and helpful in a service, it is equally insistent that the use of Hebrew be retained. It is the language in which the prayer book was composed and, as with all literature, it is best read in the original wherever possible. It is also the language of the Bible and the Children of Israel, and therefore has acquired a special significance. It is the language of modern Israel, now the centre of the Jewish world, and has undergone a revival that links the ancient tongue with modern life. It is also a universal language, common to all Jews, that acts as a bond between those who live in totally different environments yet share a unique heritage. Every effort therefore is made to promote Hebrew. Reform religion schools have adopted new methods of teaching Hebrew so as to enable children to learn it better, while most Reform synagogues run courses to improve the Hebrew literacy of adults. Comprehension is regarded as being as important as reading skills.

The English translation used in the Reform prayer book has changed in recent years. Until 1977 'old English' was used, with words such as 'thee' and 'thou', and phrases such as 'Thy beneficent mercies' and 'vainglorious deceits'. However, despite the sentimental attachment of many who had grown up with such prayer-language, it was felt that there was no point in having a translation which was almost as confusing as the Hebrew. Modern language is needed for modern people and they can pray best in the language in which they think. The translation used in the current Reform prayer book therefore reflects contemporary English, although care has been taken to avoid clichés and fashionable phrases, and it is in a style that flows naturally. On certain occasions the translation is inspired by theological considerations rather than being a literal rendering of the Hebrew. Thus the blessing that concludes the second paragraph of the *Amidah* reads "who renews life beyond death", which does not correspond exactly to the Hebrew but is more in keeping with a modern understanding of its meaning.

At the time of writing, there is one particular aspect of the translation, and indeed of the Hebrew text itself, that is exercising considerable attention. It is clear that throughout the ages prayer books were written by men with fellow men in mind. Virtually all the imagery is male-orientated. However, some 50% of those who use prayer books are women, many of whom now feel that exclusively male language is inappropriate. It can be argued that male terms are intended to be neutral and all-encompassing, such as the word 'mankind', but the reality is that they are often not seen as such by women. This is not a matter of 'trendy feminism' which seeks to replace masculine terms by female ones, but it is a general awareness in the community that the liturgy should seek to include all who pray. In the new edition of the festival *machzor* serious attempts are currently being made to introduce 'inclusive language' – language that can apply to both sexes equally and can include everyone. Thus instead of the opening paragraph of the *Amidah* speaking of "our God and God of our fathers" it refers to "our God and God of our ancestors"; in addition an alternative version of the second paragraph of the *Amidah* includes the names of the matriarchs – Sarah, Rebecca, Rachel and Leah – alongside those of the patriarchs – Abraham, Isaac and Jacob[1]. Instead of the second paragraph of the *Aleinu* talking of "all mankind shall speak out in Your name" it has "all humanity ..."[2]. Instances of "every man" have been replaced by "every person".

The policy of avoiding specifically male terminology applies also to descriptions of God. This is in keeping with the traditional view that God is incorporeal and without sexual attributes, although the tendency has always been to use masculine imagery. This is not only unwarranted but can often be limiting and unhelpful. New Reform liturgy, therefore, employs neutral terms. The description of God as "king" has often been changed to "sovereign", while "master" has become "ruler". In all such cases the essential meaning of the word has been retained but the gender problem has been

---

1 *Forms of Prayer, Shavuot* (Experimental Edition), p.17
2 Ibid, p.31

removed. Some people may miss phrases with which they were familiar, but it is felt that the need for language to be as inclusive as possible is a far more important principle.

4. WHAT IS THE ROLE OF WOMEN IN REFORM SERVICES, AND WHAT HAS BEEN ITS EFFECT?

It is a cardinal principle of Reform Judaism that men and women are equal. This is not to ignore the differences between the sexes but rather to state that these have no significance as far as religious activities are concerned. In an age where women are prominent in all spheres of public life, and have become leaders of countries, it seems inconceivable that full rights should not be extended to them in synagogue rituals too. There is no balcony or division between the sexes as in Orthodox synagogues, and so men and women sit together in Reform services. Women may participate in all aspects of the services, although some of the practices mentioned below do not apply to all congregations, for each one is autonomous with the right to decide its own customs. Nevertheless, in many Reform synagogues, women may lead the prayers, perform *mitzvot*, and be responsible for the reading from the *Torah*. When a *minyan* is counted women are included in the number needed to form a quorum. As full participants in the service, women are also given the opportunity to carry a scroll during the numerous processions at *Simchat Torah*. (In this context it should be noted that it is a common but mistaken assumption that women are not allowed to touch the *Torah* lest they 'defile' it because of their menstrual cycle. However, even according to the strictest view this is not the case, as the sanctity of the scroll is regarded as such that it cannot be made 'unclean' (*Berachot* 22a) and can only be rendered unfit for use if the lettering fades or a mistake in the text is discovered.) The *batmitzvah* ceremony for girls takes the same form as *barmitzvah* for boys, and the marriage service gives an equal role to women. Women can also become Rabbis, and several serve as ministers to Reform congregations. These developments are not seen as concessions but as the natural rights of women which were denied to previous generations. They are part of a complete re-evaluation of the role of women, and arise from a desire to remedy the disadvantages under which they were placed previously. Thus women are also given equal rights in matters of status such as divorce proceedings, and are freed from the bonds of being an *agunah*, undergoing *chalitzah* and being prohibited from marrying a *cohen* if a divorcee. They are regarded as fully competent in legal matters and, for instance, can act as witnesses on a *ketubah*.

None of these innovations are to be found in Orthodox synagogues, even though it is clear that in earlier centuries women occupied a more active role in religious affairs. Thus the *Talmud* declares that a woman is eligible to be among the seven people called up to the *bimah* for the *Torah* reading during a Sabbath service, although it advises against it out of "respect for the congregation" (*Megillah* 23a). However, two Rabbinic ordinances limited the religious involvement of women in subsequent centuries. One was the ruling that women were exempt from positive commandments needing to be fulfilled at a specific time, such as putting on *tefillin* and living in a *sukkah* (*Kiddushin* 1.7). There is a practical reason for this in that women with young children often find that their children's demands have to take precedence over religious duties. Yet this does not apply to all women all the time, for there are a considerable number of women who either have no children or whose offspring are grown up. The exemption was not a prohibition, but it came to have the same effect, so that women never participated in synagogue life and what was intended as a benefit became a restriction. The other ruling was that women, although allowed to study *Torah*, were not obliged to do so (*Sotah* 3.4). This resulted in a general neglect of women's education, including knowledge of Hebrew, so that they were often unable to follow the service. It was inevitable, therefore, that women's role in synagogue became passive even though there was no actual ban on much greater involvement. Indeed, when Orthodox Jewish women recently pressed their Rabbis for the right to lead prayers and read from the *Torah*, this was granted, albeit in services for women only. By way of compensation for their limited synagogue role, Orthodox authorities often declared that women reigned supreme in the home and that a balance of power was therefore achieved between the sexes. However, this was not entirely true, for most domestic rituals – *kiddush*, *havdalah*, grace after meals – generally remained in the hands of men, while all decisions as to domestic practices were inevitably left to the superior knowledge of men. This is not to infer that women did not occupy a position of great respect and honour in Jewish life, for they were highly esteemed in both biblical and Rabbinic literature in the role of wife and mother. Indeed it can be said that Reform has merely brought their low status in religious matters into line with their high position in family life, and raised the former to match the latter. Of course, the new rights of women also involve new responsibilities. Women in Reform synagogues are expected to keep the commandments and perform all rituals, including the positive ones connected with time, as much as men.

The first difference noticed by someone who has never been to a Reform synagogue before is the mixed seating, and it can seem very strange to those not used to it. However, once the initial surprise has worn off, it seems perfectly logical and loses its novelty. Nevertheless, it has a profound impact on communal life, affecting not only the women themselves but also the rest of their families. An obvious result is that the typical ladies' section, upstairs or at the back of the synagogue, with nobody interested in the service and everyone chatting amongst themselves, is absent from Reform synagogues. Instead women are with the men in the centre of the synagogue; they feel much more involved in the service (and much more valued) and respond accordingly. The decorum is high, and women join in the prayers as much as the men. A natural development has been that women are expected to know as much about synagogue life and be as familiar with Hebrew as men. Education of girls in religion schools is thus exactly the same as boys so that they too are fully equipped to play an active role in synagogue. Adult education courses often find themselves catering to women from Orthodox backgrounds who never learned such skills in their childhood. A higher ratio of women than men at such courses reflects the need, and the desire, of women to take advantage of the opportunity for Jewish knowledge now presented to them. An increasing percentage of adult women who never had a *batmitzvah* in their childhood wish to do so now they are members of a Reform synagogue, and to rectify what they feel to be a missing part of their Jewish heritage. They learn to read from the *Torah* and have a public ceremony at an appropriate date.

Female equality extends to all other areas of congregational life. No synagogue activity is limited according to sex and many women sit on councils, serve as wardens or chair the community. Conversely, catering committees and guilds are still predominantly organised by women, although not exclusively, and they are open to men too.

The growing participation of women has also influenced their husbands, many of whom prefer attending services when they can sit together with their wives. Those families who are used to praying together at home find it only natural to do so at synagogue too. Strong involvement of women can have a very positive effect also on children when they see that both parents take their Jewish commitment seriously. Moreover, a mother who is immersed in synagogue affairs and in Jewish knowledge will help provide a much better education for the children. This is particularly so for girls, whose role model for many years is their mother and whose pattern of Jewish life usually imitates that of the mother both in their childhood and when mothers themselves.

5. WHAT EXPECTATION IS THERE CONCERNING THE RITUAL WEAR OF MEN AND WOMEN IN SYNAGOGUE, AND OF CLOTHING IN GENERAL?

Most types of ritual wear, such as *tallit*, *tefillin* or *arba kanfot* have been associated traditionally with men. This is because they are regarded as positive commandments connected with a specific time, obligatory for men but from which women are exempt (*Kiddushin* 1.7). Thus for women *tallit* and *tefillin* were optional and could be worn or not according to the preferences of the person concerned. However, as was seen in the previous section, force of custom militated against such practices, turning the exemption into a virtual prohibition, and it is almost unheard of for women to wear a *tallit* or *tefillin* in an Orthodox synagogue in Britain today. The Reform practice is to return to the original position in Judaism whereby ritual wear is open to both men and women, with it being standard for men and optional for women. Whilst this attitude may appear to contradict the principle of complete equality between the sexes, it is a balance between this principle and the reality that many women come from Orthodox backgrounds and are so unused to ritual wear that enforcement would be counter-productive at present and might put them off synagogue attendance. Moreover, the public emergence of women who desire to wear items such as a *tallit* is a very new phenomenon that only developed in Britain in the 1980s. It is therefore felt to be wiser to publicise the option and encourage those who wish to take it up, with the result that with time and education a new habit may become the norm and women will feel as comfortable with ritual wear as do men. Discussion of the various types of ritual wear will therefore apply equally to both sexes, even if they are not taken up equally by women at present.

Arba kanfot

The biblical command that one should wear *tzitzit* (fringes) on the four corners of one's garments (Numbers 15.38; Deuteronomy 22.12) is based on the fact that four-cornered garments were the typical dress at that time. When the wearing of such garments became rare, the *arba kanfot* (four-cornered vest) or *tallit katan* (small tallit) was introduced by the Rabbis as a way of still fulfilling the command to wear the *tzitzit*. Strictly speaking it is not necessary to wear the *arba kanfot* as the command is to have *tzitzit* only if one is wearing a four-cornered garment in the first place. It is more in the nature of an added piety for those who so desire, although it has come to be regarded as compulsory in Orthodox communities. The Reform policy is to leave it up to individual choice. As far as can be ascertained, the vast majority of Reform Jews do not wear the *arba kanfot*, although there are individuals who do consider the custom important and who wear it on a daily basis. The author suggests that it be more widely encouraged, for amongst its merits is the fact that it is put on when getting dressed and so establishes a Jewish 'moment' first thing in the morning; as it is worn until nightfall, it also carries a Jewish awareness throughout the day.

Tallit

The *arba kanfot* was an unobtrusive method of wearing the *tzitzit* throughout the week, but a much more public and resplendent four-cornered garment became customary for Sabbath services: the *tallit*. Originally signifying a gown, it has come to have the meaning of 'prayer shawl' and has led to a considerable variety of traditions concerning its use amongst the Orthodox: being worn by all males regardless of age, or only by males over thirteen years old, or only by married males. Some people tend to prefer those which are blue and white and made of silk (the *Sephardi* custom), and others that are black and white and made of wool (the *Ashkenazi* custom). It is clear from the *Talmud* that women were permitted to wear a *tallit* and may have done so in those times (*Menachot* 43a). However, the exemption based on positive time-bound commandments meant that they were not obliged to do so and therefore tended not to wear a *tallit*. In Reform synagogues it is generally the custom that all males over thirteen are obliged to wear a *tallit* while boys under thirteen often tend to do so. Women are eligible to wear a *tallit*, but it is left to one's personal discretion. In some Reform synagogues women are obliged to wear a *tallit* if they perform a *mitzvah* such as opening the ark or reading from the scroll. There are a growing number of women in Reform synagogues, albeit still a small minority, who wear a *tallit*. Many had considered the idea privately for some time, but the catalyst was the public example of women Rabbis ordained in the late 1970s and early 1980s who not only wore a *tallit* themselves but who also stimulated female congregants to explore their religious heritage in greater depth. Their experiences indicate that far from being a declaration of feminism, the wearing of a *tallit* is a rediscovery of Judaism[1]:

> It took a long time before I was able to wear a *tallit*. Quite a lot of the reason, I think, dates back from my early teens when I was a member of an Orthodox community. I went to *shul* every week and gazed down from the balcony at the lucky boys who were able to be actively involved in the service. It never occurred to me that that could be me one day. I knew my place!
>
> For several weeks (my) *tallit* bag accompanied me to *shul* on the *Shabbat* mornings. Tentatively I clutched and squeezed it but could not bring myself to put it on.
>
> I began to wear a *tallit* to further my expression of belonging and sharing in the community, to state my position as a healthy and positive member of the *kehillah* (congregation), prepared to wear the *tallit* as a cloak of responsibility with pride and joy. Over the past seven years that I have worn the *tallit* it has come to symbolise many more things to me. To wear a *tallit* with a group of others is to visually unite, to lose concerns over dress, to merge as a whole with one voice. A bringing together of mind and body to the oneness of prayer – a loss of ego. Wrapping myself up in a *tallit* concentrates my mind, it is a constant reminder throughout the service of my purpose. The *tallit* is like a cocoon, allowing for the possibility of a deeper change from within, whilst separating off from the outside world. It makes me feel special, as I believe it could for anyone who wears it with true *kavvanah* (concentration), totally irrespective of the sex of the wearer.

In view of this gradual development, it may be a very appropriate present to give a girl a *tallit* for her *batmitzvah*.

In recent years it has become possible to buy a *tallit* with colours other than blue or black, such as multi-coloured ones which have been marketed in America and Israel. These are acceptable for synagogue use for a *tallit* is

---

1 Barbara Borts, *Women and Tallit*, pp.20, 18, 23

merely a four-cornered garment with fringes on each corner and the colour of the garment is irrelevant. Nevertheless the element of unity with the rest of the congregation referred to in the above quotation may be lost, while it would be wrong for the *tallit* to become a fashion item.

Tefillin

The wearing of *tefillin* is based on Deuteronomy 6.8 which later constituted the first paragraph of the *Shema:* "Hold fast to them (the words of God) as a sign upon your hand, and let them be reminders before your eyes". This was interpreted literally with the result that leather prayer boxes containing passages from the *Torah* are worn on the left arm – the right arm for those who are left-handed – and on the forehead. Traditionally, they are not worn on the Sabbath and festivals but only at the morning services of ordinary days by males over thirteen years. In Reform communities it is not seen as an obligatory ritual, and many prefer the interpretation first made by Samuel ben Meyer in the twelfth century that the verse should be understood figuratively: that one's actions and one's gaze should always be guided by the precepts of the Bible. Nevertheless, laying *tefillin* is recognised as an option for those who so wish, save that it is open to all over thirteen years, including women. Those who wish to lay *tefillin* but belong to congregations that do not hold daily morning services, can do so when saying prayers at home. A meditation before putting on *tefillin* and the appropriate blessings are provided in the Reform prayer book at the start of the morning service[1]. Both the theory and practice of *tefillin* are taught at religion schools as part of general Jewish knowledge.

Shatnes

The ban on wearing articles of clothing that contain both wool and linen derives from the Bible (Leviticus 19.19; Deuteronomy 22.11) but has no obvious reason. Some commentators have attempted to provide explanations: according to Maimonides it was to avoid the practices of heathen priests; according to Nahmanides it is sacrilegious as it suggests God's handiwork can be improved upon. Nevertheless, traditionally, *shatnes* is seen as a law that will only be understood in the Messianic era. In Reform thinking it is regarded as being a rite that had some significance in biblical times but which has lost all meaning today and need not be maintained.

---

1 *Forms of Prayer*, Vol I, pp.213-215

Head Covering

The subject of head covering has been left towards the end because, although the best known Jewish ritual wear, it is the only one not to be based on any command in the Bible. Originally it was a custom that applied in certain limited situations, such as part of the priest's uniform (Exodus 28.4) or as a sign of mourning (2 Samuel 15.30). It became associated with males at prayer in *talmudic* times but was still only an option (*Nedarim* 30b, *Shabbat* 118b, *Berachot* 60b). Gradually it became obligatory for the person leading the service to have their head covered, then for all those saying prayers, and it was later extended to covering one's head at all times. The covering of a married woman's hair dates from biblical times (Numbers 5.18) and was seen as a sign of modesty so as not to appear attractive to other men. The custom is maintained today by Orthodox communities, with the women wearing permanently either a *sheitel* (wig) or a *tichel* (headscarf) after marriage. Women who choose not to cover their heads normally are still required to do so in Orthodox synagogues with a hat or scarf. The Reform policy is that it is mandatory for all males to cover their heads in synagogue and at other times of prayer; no distinction is made between types of head covering, eg a hat or a *kippah*. A head covering is not regarded as necessary at other periods during the day, although some people do cover their heads when studying sacred texts. Covering one's hair is not regarded as having any relevance to a woman's marital status and women are not obliged to do so after marriage, either generally or when in synagogue[1]. Instead, covering one's head in synagogue is viewed as an option for all females, of whatever age or status. As a result, some women (a small but growing number) choose to wear a *kippah* during prayer or another form of head covering that is kept specifically for times of worship (eg a beret set aside for that purpose). Thus the reason for women covering their heads has changed, no longer being a sign of modesty but an act of reverence similar to that practiced by men. Again the influence of women Rabbis, most of whom wear a head covering of sorts, is partly responsible for the emergence of this new trend.

General Clothing

There is also the larger question of one's general clothing. The biblical injunction that "A woman shall not put on man's apparel, nor shall a man wear woman's clothing" (Deuteronomy 22.5) has been interpreted by

---

[1] Assembly of Rabbis, 31st October 1962

Orthodox authorities as applying to all forms of wear and includes a ban on unisex clothing. In Reform circles, however, the command is seen as referring specifically to transvestism and limited to cross-dressing. Wearing apparel common to both sexes is permissible, and there is no objection, for instance, to women wearing trousers. In addition, Reform does not support the notion that one needs to cover every single piece of one's skin, as some Orthodox circles insist. However, there is still a certain level of modesty to which one should adhere in one's appearance.

---

6. WHAT IS THE PRACTICE CONCERNING THE *TORAH* AND *HAFTARAH* READINGS IN REFORM SYNAGOGUES?

In Orthodox communities today, the whole of the *Torah* is covered in one year through the weekly readings on Sabbath mornings. As this involves several chapters each Sabbath, the reading is usually done at a fast rate, is incomprehensible to those who cannot understand Hebrew, and is hard to follow even for those who can do so. It also takes a long time and can be very tedious, with congregants losing concentration and chatting during the readings. The constant pleas for silence that are heard in some synagogues are ample evidence of the problem. In order to avoid such difficulties and to restore the respect due to the *Torah* readings, Reform synagogues read a much smaller section each week. It gains in dignity what it loses in length, with congregants being able to appreciate the passage and concentrate on its meaning. Of course with shorter readings it is impossible to complete the whole *Torah* in the course of a year; instead the readings are stretched over a period of three years. This 'innovation' is in fact merely an adoption of the original position concerning the *Torah* readings in ancient Israel, in which the sequence of readings from Genesis to Deuteronomy took three years (*Megillah* 29b), known as the 'triennial cycle'. It was a later Babylonian custom to squeeze the readings into one year, which then became the usual Jewish practice.

The system used by the Reform synagogues is to combine both traditions by dividing each *parashah* (weekly section) of the annual cycle into three parts and reading from each part once every three years. The result is that the same *parashah* is read in Reform synagogues as that in all other synagogues worldwide, albeit a smaller amount. The Reform calendar does not include every single chapter of the *Torah* as it is felt that certain aspects do not necessarily merit public readings, eg genealogical tables (Genesis 36) or dermatological ailments (Leviticus 13)[1]. Occasionally the *Torah* readings in the calendar are out of synchronisation with those in the Orthodox calendar for this country. It arises because the Reform calendar adheres to the biblical definition of the length of festivals (which is also that observed by both Reform and Orthodox in Israel today), whereas the Orthodox calendar outside Israel adds an extra day to many festivals. Thus *Simchat Torah* is celebrated in the Reform calendar immediately after the seven days of *Sukkot*, whereas the Orthodox calendar adds an eighth day to *Sukkot* and so observes *Simchat Torah* a day later.

As there is a shorter weekly *Torah* portion in Reform synagogues, it is not customary to call up seven people as is done in Orthodox synagogues. In some communities there is only one *aliyah* (call-up) while others have the custom of three *aliyot*; this is reminiscent of the tradition that three people are called up when the *Torah* is read at morning services on Mondays and Thursdays (*Megillah* 4.4). Everyone in the community who is over the age of 13, male or female, is eligible for an *aliyah*. The person given an *aliyah* recites in Hebrew the blessings before and after the *Torah* portion[2], and the *Torah* portion is read by the Rabbi. However, those who are able to read the portion themselves are encouraged to do so, as was originally the case before general knowledge of Hebrew decreased and the task was allocated to specialists. Several Reform synagogues have classes to teach those who wish to learn to read *Torah*, while those who have had their *bar/batmitzvah* in recent years are sometimes asked to re-read their portions when they re-occur so as to re-utilise their skill and remind them of their new role in the community.

It is not customary to have a *mi-sheberach* (blessing) after an *aliyah*, as the honour is considered sufficient in itself, whilst the practice often leads to a tedious lengthening of the service in other synagogues. The Reform have also abolished the custom of *shnoddering* whereby either financial bids are made for the honour of a *mitzvah*, or a charitable donation is promised by recipients of a *mitzvah* and publicly announced. It was an effective way of fundraising that may once have been necessary, but the practice is considered inappropriate for a service today, diverting attention onto financial matters

---

1 Jonathan Romain, *Calendar of Torah and Haftarah Readings*, p.3
2 *Forms of Prayer*, Vol I, pp.156-158

and excluding poorer members of the community from having a *mitzvah*. The same principle of making no distinction between rich and poor amongst the congregation was the reason for abandoning the custom of buying seats in synagogue – still common amongst many Orthodox congregations – with prices graded according to their position. Instead, no seats are owned by any individual, and those attending services may sit wherever they please.

The manner in which the *Torah* portion is recited is dictated by the custom of each synagogue. In a few communities the portion is chanted according to a traditional *tropp* (melody). In most cases, however, the portion is not chanted as it is felt that this distorts rather than elucidates the sense, and it is considered preferable to read the portion. An English translation or summary is usually provided immediately before or after the reading, a practice dating back to the first mention of the public readings from the *Torah* (Nehemiah 8.8). Another custom is to read a verse in Hebrew and then translate it into English, a method designed to give immediacy to the *Torah* reading, particularly for those unable to comprehend Hebrew, and which dates back to *mishnaic* times (*Megillah* 4.4).

The selection of the passages for the *haftarah* (concluding reading) has been extended to cater for the triennial cycle used in Reform synagogues. On a few occasions the date of the Sabbath determines the reading: thus the *haftarah* of the Sabbath immediately preceding *Tishah B'Av* is a condemnation of the sins of Israel, while the Sabbath afterwards contains words of consolation. Usually, however, the *haftarah* has a thematic connection with the *Torah* portion: for *Shelach-Lecha* the spies sent out by Joshua (Joshua 2) parallel the spies sent out by Moses (Numbers 13). In these instances a different *haftarah* is selected for each weekly reading in the triennial cycle, one of which is the traditional *haftarah* from the annual cycle and two of which are new passages. Moreover, whereas the *haftarah* readings in the annual cycle were limited to passages from the Prophets, selections have now also been made from the Writings, thus extending the public reading of the Bible to books such as Job, Proverbs, Daniel and Nehemiah. Once again this is an echo of an older practice, for excerpts from the Writings were used as the *haftarah* in *talmudic* times (*Shabbat* 116b), while complete books from the Writings are still read at festivals, such as Ruth at *Shavuot* and Ecclesiastes at *Sukkot*. A totally new development is the inclusion of a passage from the Apocrypha which is outside of the Jewish canon of sacred writings. Nevertheless, the use of I Maccabees 2.1-28 as the *haftarah* for the second Sabbath during *Chanukah* seems entirely appropriate and much more suitable than the biblical reading stipulated in the traditional calendar (I Kings 7.40-50). In most synagogues the *haftarah* is read in English, with the blessing before and after said or sung in Hebrew[1]. The blessing after the *haftarah* consists of only the last of the four paragraphs used in the Orthodox prayer book so as to shorten the lengthy recitation and to make it parallel to the blessing before the *haftarah*.

7. WHAT IS THE REFORM ATTITUDE TO HAVING MUSIC DURING SYNAGOGUE SERVICES?

There is a variety of musical practices in Reform synagogues. Many have instrumental music at Sabbath services, generally in the form of an organ; others have no instrumental accompaniment (although they might do so on special occasions, such as with guitars or clarinets at youth services). The decision is purely a matter of local custom, unlike in Orthodox synagogues where instrumental music is specifically banned. It is well known, of course, that in Temple times music was an accepted part of the service with a range of instruments in use, including the lyre, trumpet, cymbals, drum and flute. The Psalmist takes them for granted in his "Song for the Sabbath Day" (Psalm 92.2-4):

> It is good to give thanks to the Lord
> and to sing praises to Your name, O Most High,
> to declare Your loving kindness in the mornings
> and Your faithfulness every night.
> With the ten-string lute, with the lyre
> with the gentle sound of the harp

The Book of Chronicles records in detail the singer-musicians in Solomon's Temple who occupied an important role in public worship (I Chronicles 25).

In later times, instrumental music was prohibited from services for several reasons: first, the use of instruments outside of the Temple was considered forbidden according to the laws of Sabbath rest and concern that a broken instrument be repaired on the Sabbath (*Eruvin* 104a); second, the ban was one of the symbols of mourning for the destruction of the Temple (*Shulchan Aruch, Orach Hayyim* 560.3); third, the ban was reinforced by the

---

1 Ibid, p.158

fact that organs became common in Christian worship and there was a desire to avoid imitating non-Jewish practices (based on Leviticus 18.3).

Reform thinking considers that all these objections lack sufficient validity to prohibit the use of instruments in synagogue services today. Playing a musical instrument is not considered 'work' according to the Reform view (see VI.2) but a pleasurable activity in keeping with the spirit of Sabbath joy. The loss of the Temple is certainly recognised as a tragic event and a turning point in Jewish history. It is commemorated in several ways – such as the observance of *Tishah B'Av*, or the transference of various Temple objects to the synagogue (the Eternal Light, the bells and breast plates on the scrolls, the glass smashed at a wedding). These are considered sufficient memorials by themselves. Not only is there no need to add to them through banning music, but also the ban deprives the service of a facility that can contribute much beauty and harmony to it. There are also some who consider that the re-unification of Jerusalem in 1967 has ended the period of mourning, although this is a very recent argument and post-dates the other one. The claim that the use of an organ is imitating church practice is debatable as there is the suggestion that an early form of the organ was played in the Temple (*Arachin* 11a). Moreover, organs are merely artifacts which churches put to certain use. It would be inappropriate to use in synagogue services hymns and melodies that were specifically composed for Christian worship, but organs themselves are 'neutral' and should no more be banned than are stained-glass windows. Indeed the weakness of this argument is evident from the number of modern Orthodox synagogues at which the organ is played at weddings, a practice that originated in the seventeenth century.

Reform synagogues that use an organ tend to have choirs. Synagogues without an organ may also have choirs, although some prefer simply to have congregational singing. In all cases choirs are 'mixed' with both men and women participating. The Orthodox objection to women singing in choirs on the grounds that a woman's voice will arouse licentious thoughts (*Sotah* 48a) is considered to be the product of a misplaced sense of caution and totally unjustified in today's integrated society. The use of non-Jewish choristers is permitted in some synagogues in Britain today, but is not sanctioned in Reform synagogues as it is felt that the members of the choir should be an integral part of the congregation[1]. Even if the vocal ability of small congregations is limited, their enthusiasm can still add more to the service than would a

---

1 Assembly of Rabbis, 31st October 1962

polished performance by those from outside of the community. There are hardly any Reform synagogues that use a *chazan* (cantor), whereas in Orthodox synagogues they still conduct most of the service. Instead, the role has been taken over by the Rabbi who leads the whole service and who is often assisted by a choir. The demise of the *chazan* has not been a deliberate policy but rather an incidental effect arising from a combination of factors – the shortening of services, use of the vernacular, the greater prominence of the Rabbi in services, and the organisation of choirs – all of which have lessened the need for a *chazan*. In addition there has been a desire to abandon the operatic quality of services associated with some *chazanim* and to place greater emphasis on prayers in which the whole congregation can participate.

8. IS THE PRESENCE OF A *MINYAN* STILL REGARDED AS NECESSARY IN REFORM SYNAGOGUES?

Traditionally, personal prayer could always be said at any time and in any place, but some of the statutory prayers required the presence of a *minyan*, a quorum of ten males over the age of 13 (*Berachot* 6a). The figure 'ten' is derived from an interpretation of Numbers 14.27 according to which "this evil congregation" referred to the twelve spies minus Joshua and Caleb, and so a "congregation" consists of ten men (*Sanhedrin* 1.6). It can also be derived from Abraham's plea to God to save Sodom if ten righteous men could be found there (Genesis 18.32). The prayers that need a *minyan* are defined as the *Barchu*, *Kedushah*, the blessings before and after the *Torah* and *haftarah* and the *Kaddish* (*Megillah* 4.3, *Soferim* 10.7). The effect of this stipulation was to lay great stress on communal sharing of prayer, and it emphasised the duty of every individual to help make up a *minyan*. As such, it was a highly beneficial regulation. The only problem with the *minyan* system is that it assumes that Jews live close to each other and are always available for services. This is not always the case in Britain today where many Jews are scattered throughout the country and do not necessarily live in areas of high Jewish population. Synagogues in rural areas, new towns and places of small Jewish settlement often find that they have members who wish to come together for Sabbath services, but who are not sufficient in number to form a *minyan*. In such situations the concept of the *minyan* inhibits rather than assists communal prayer, preventing those who wish to conduct a service from so doing. Moreover, it leads to unfair consequences, penalising those who make the effort to attend synagogue because of those who are absent. In addition, the inclusion only of men in the *minyan* contradicts the Reform principle of the equality of the sexes whereby women 'count' in the service just as much as the men. It can also lead to the ludicrous situation whereby, for instance, a synagogue has nine men present and twenty-five women, but from an Orthodox point of view a quorum of ten is still lacking! In Reform synagogues, therefore, the necessity of a *minyan* for public service has been abolished, and the prayers can be said and the *Torah* read irrespective of the number of worshippers present[1]. It should be noted that this decision to proceed with less than a *minyan* of ten is not unique, but echoes the original practice in Israel which accepted six or seven, according to different schools of thought, as the minimum number necessary. It was a later Babylonian practice to fix the number at ten (*Soferim* 10.7).

Whilst all Reform synagogues agree that Sabbath services can take place without a *minyan*, there is a variety of practice concerning the reading of the *Torah*. Some communities feel that the above principle applies equally to the *Torah* too, perhaps more so in view of its educational value, and so read it however many people are present. Others feel that it is on a different level from the recitation of prayers and should be treated separately. Moreover, on a practical level, the *Torah* service involves a considerable amount of activity – opening the Ark, taking out the scroll, parading it amongst the congregation, undressing it and raising it – which presupposes a minimum congregation of around ten. It is therefore their practice only to hold the *Torah* service if there is a *minyan*, although the counting of the *minyan* includes women and is defined as ten adults. If they find that less than ten adults are in attendance, the weekly portion is either read from a *Chumash* (the printed edition of the Five Books of Moses), or it is read from the scroll but without the usual parade and blessings[2].

Apart from synagogue services, there are various other occasions associated with a *minyan*. One of these is the *shivah* and the services that take place in the home of a person who has just suffered a bereavement. Essentially, these are ordinary daily services which could be held in synagogue but which are transferred instead to the home of the mourner; it is a courtesy arrangement so that the mourner need not leave the house during the mourning period in order to pray, except on the Sabbath when formal mourning is lifted. There is no reason, therefore, why the *minyan* is any more necessary in someone's home.

---

1 Assembly of Rabbis, 23rd July 1952
2 Assembly of Rabbis, 9th July 1985

The Reform policy of conducting a synagogue service, including the saying of the *Kaddish*, if a *minyan* is not present applies also in the case of a *shivah* service. Of course, as with the synagogue service, this permission is based on a situation in which no other option is available. The importance of full communal participation where possible is still strongly emphasised. It is particularly so in the case of a *shivah* where the support of members of the congregation can be of great comfort to a mourner, whether or not they were close beforehand. The responsibility of one Jew to another, including to help form a community of prayer, is still a priority incumbent upon all.

In the case of a funeral, the procedure is the same as that already described: all in the community are encouraged to attend, both as a sign of respect for the departed person and as a support for the mourners, although the funeral service is conducted in full irrespective of the number present. The practice in some circles of forbidding a mourner to say *Kaddish* for a relative if a *minyan* is lacking is considered an unwarranted addition to their distress and contrary to the spirit of Jewish mourning rites.

Another occasion associated with a *minyan* is the *Sheva brachot*, the seven blessings recited at a wedding (*Ketubot* 7b). In most cases there is an abundance of people, with family and friends crowding into the synagogue. However, some marriages occur in which there are less than a handful of people present, such as where there is no family or at a second marriage. In these instances, too, the full wedding service takes place, and anything less would be deeply hurtful to the couple concerned. The Jewish validity of the marriage is dependent on the giving of the ring, oath of marriage and signing of the *ketubah* in front of two witnesses. The presence or absence of a *minyan* is irrelevant to the legality of the marriage in Jewish Law.

A *brit milah* has never required the presence of a *minyan* in Jewish Law; the tradition of having family and friends present is in order to share the joy of the birth and not to guarantee a *minyan*.

9. ARE VIDEOS OR PHOTOGRAPHS ALLOWED AT A WEDDING OR *BAR/BATMITZVAH* IN REFORM SYNAGOGUES?

The advantage of recording a wedding is that one can 'relive' the experience afterwards, particularly the couple themselves, for whom there is so much going on that it is hard to appreciate it all at the time. It can also enable relatives or friends who were unable to attend the ceremony to enjoy the event. However, there are several disadvantages involved. The sound and sight of clicking cameras and flashing bulbs can intrude on the service, while cameramen and photographers trying to obtain a 'good angle' can cause considerable distraction. The presence of a camera lens can lead to self-consciousness, with those attending being more concerned with 'how it will show up on film' than with the ceremony itself. A wedding can become more of a showpiece than a deep, religious act, and lose its special atmosphere.

It is clear that there are arguments for and against the recording of weddings, and there is a variety of practice amongst Reform synagogues[1]. Some prohibit the use of videos during the ceremony; others permit them, subject to certain conditions eg the camera is not placed on the *bimah* but in a discreet position elsewhere in the synagogue, no extra lighting is allowed, and once in position the camera may not be moved. With regard to photographs: no synagogue permits them to be taken during the ceremony itself. Some ban photographs in the synagogue completely, whilst others allow them after the ceremony under the *chuppah* has been concluded (ie pictures may be taken of the couple signing the marriage register and the procession out of the synagogue).

Different criteria apply to a *bar/batmitzvah* in that it is not a private event consisting only of those specifically invited, but is part of a regular public service which is attended by many who have no connection with the family. Moreover, it concerns the statutory prayers for a Sabbath rather than being an 'extra' service. The need to avoid any distraction is even greater, while those present for reasons other than the *bar/batmitzvah* ceremony have a right to privacy and to not be recorded. It is therefore not the practice among Reform synagogues to permit video or photographs at any time during the service. However, in itself taking photographs is not considered a transgression of the Sabbath laws; thus some synagogues will permit photographs of the celebrant and their family to be taken after the service, either in the hall or in the synagogue itself when it is empty.

The variety of practice in these two issues reflects the autonomy of the congregations and their right to develop their own customs. The policy of one community cannot by itself be cited as justification for another community to change its stance.

---

1 Assembly of Rabbis, 28th March 1989

CHAPTER FIVE

DAILY AFFAIRS

These words which I command you today shall be upon your heart ... talk about them when you sit in your home and when you walk in the street; when you lie down, and when you rise up.

Deuteronomy 6.6-7

1. WHAT HAPPENS IN THE ORDINARY DAY OF A REFORM JEW?

(The subjects of *kashrut* and Sabbath observance are covered elsewhere.)

According to the Jewish sage Simon the Just, "Civilization is based on three things – on learning, on prayer and on good deeds" (*Avot* 1.2). The saying provides a guide for the conduct of daily life that is as useful today as it was in the fourth century BCE (Before the Common Era). It sets priorities and helps instil purpose to one's time. The normal bustle of everyday affairs must proceed apace and cannot be avoided, yet it can be directed in such a way as to distinguish between a meaningless rush, largely preoccupied with oneself, and a fulfilling lifestyle that is also of value to others. All three goals outlined by Simon the Just can easily become part of one's day if they are given careful thought, along with the determination to put them into practice.

Learning
There is an old adage that an ignorant Jew cannot be a good Jew. Clearly that is not to be taken literally, for there are many Jews who are uneducated through no fault of their own, yet whose moral standards make them examples to all. However, the underlying intent of the saying holds true – it is only through learning about one's Jewish heritage that one can fully appreciate its value; that one can determine the best way to conduct oneself in everyday life; that one can say "I am a Jew" with confidence in its meaning; that one can successfully pass on the tradition to the next generation; that one can explain the significance of Judaism when asked by non-Jews; that one can defend Judaism when it is libelled or misquoted. An ignorant Jew can be a good person, but an educated Jew has a much better chance and is also more likely to enjoy being Jewish. In practical terms Jewish learning has always been regarded as a lifelong activity. It means that there are no time limits. There is nothing to exclude those of whatever age who have not yet begun learning, or to constrain those who have already started to learn from deepening their knowledge. Study is best undertaken initially with a teacher, either individually or as part of a course. It makes one part of the chain of tradition that is handed down across the centuries. It also allows for question and discussion, so that Judaism is not just something one knows about academically but it becomes one's own tradition and takes root. If classes are unavailable, then books are a good substitute, although it is important to obtain a recommended reading list (perhaps from the nearest synagogue or a

Jewish library) so as to start at the right level and to cover basic material first. Individuals may have their own areas of special interest later, but the major areas that should be tackled first include: Bible, Hebrew, History, Liturgy, Rabbinic Literature, Rituals and Practices, Sabbath and Festivals. One may not be able to master all areas, but one should have a working familiarity with them and know which books to consult for further information. Scholarship may be limited to a few people but all can have a basic knowledge of Jewish life. The way to ensure this is to set aside a regular time for study, ideally an hour a day or, if impossible, some other achievable daily or weekly amount (eg one evening class a week or a chapter of a Jewish book a day), but at minimum devoting a certain part of the Sabbath to Jewish learning. A regular commitment is all-important and the secret to success. As another *mishnaic* sage, Hillel, declared so rightly "Do not say 'When I have leisure I will study', perhaps you will never have leisure" (*Avot* 2.5).

Prayer

The value of prayer can be different for each person (and it can change during different stages of one's life). It can be a way of communicating with God, of examining oneself, of expressing one's appreciation of life, of voicing one's hopes and fears, of expressing solidarity with others, of reinforcing one's Jewish identity, of creating 'a moment apart', of achieving tranquillity, and no doubt other purposes too. Prayers can be said privately or communally, with each having its advantages. Private prayers can have more spontaneity and flexibility; communal prayer can bring a sense of camaraderie and an uplifting atmosphere. All Jews are urged to attend Sabbath services at synagogue. Daily prayer is encouraged too, although the venue is optional. Those praying at home can follow the regular service in the prayer book for midweek morning, afternoon or evening services. The Reform prayer book contains an anthology of psalms and study passages that can be used for personal reflection. One can also add or substitute personal prayers. In the case of families the time of prayer can be shared by all members of the household. The service can be truncated or adapted if this is more appropriate for children, and with everyone participating in some way. Such domestic prayer can both strengthen the family bonds and educate the children in a living Judaism. The key element is regularly setting aside a few moments and creating time for an act which can enrich the rest of the day. In addition, it should be remembered that despite the structures and regulations that have developed around the services, the act of prayer is at root an intensely personal experience. Spontaneous prayers can always be said whenever, and wherever, the desire arises.

Good Deeds

Much time and thought is often devoted to the ritual aspects of Judaism, but even more important are its ethical features. One shows one's love of God by one's treatment of God's creatures. The biblical injunction to "love your neighbour as yourself" (Leviticus 19.18) means that not only should one avoid hurting others in any way, but that one should also take positive steps to help them wherever possible. Putting Judaism into daily practice includes being honest in business dealings (Leviticus 19.36), treating others with respect (Leviticus 19.17), keeping one's temper under control (Proverbs 14.29), avoiding malicious gossip (Leviticus 19.16), assisting those with a burden (Deuteronomy 22.4), returning lost property (Exodus 23.4), caring for the handicapped (Leviticus 19.14), visiting the sick (*Sotah* 14a based on Genesis 18.1), responding to others in a warm spirit, and generally regarding the rights and feelings of others as being as important as one's own. An additional aspect is giving charity to those in need (Leviticus 25.35) although this should not just be done when a particular request is presented, but one should make regular donations to charity at other times. Jewish tradition declares that even the poor should give to charity, for few have none worse off than themselves. It has long been the custom for Jews to work out in advance a set amount per month or per year that they can afford to give to charity (as well as responding to emergency appeals that arise). In the past it was laid down that it was appropriate for individuals to give one tenth of their earnings to charity (*Shulchan Aruch, Yoreh Deah* 249.1). Nowadays the amount will vary according to the abilities of each individual, although the underlying principle still remains that everyone should give something regularly. Some people prefer to adopt one particular charity, others to assist a variety of different causes. A useful exercise is to obtain the details of several charities, ascertain what are one's main concerns (and make it a family decision if appropriate), allocate a fixed sum to the charity/charities chosen, and review both the amount and the inclusion of other charities annually. Preference might well be given to Jewish charities which depend entirely on Jewish support for their work, and to causes in Israel which rely partly on the assistance of world Jewry to maintain their activities. Nevertheless, there is also a responsibility to the wider society and to consider the needs of all, whatever their religion, race or colour.

2. WHAT IS THE REFORM ATTITUDE TO *KASHRUT*?

It is often mistakenly assumed that Reform adopts a negative approach to the dietary laws. This is not the case, as will be seen below. The truth is that Reform adopts a negative approach only to the exaggerated weight sometimes attached to the dietary laws – whereby the quality of one's Judaism is judged by what one eats rather than by how one behaves, and when gastronomy seems more important than morality. As with most rituals, it should be stressed that meticulous observance is not sufficient by itself; they have to be accompanied by ethical behaviour if they are to serve the purpose of reminding one of the values demanded by Judaism. In the case of *kashrut* it might be said that it is as important to guard what comes out of one's mouth as what goes in. Another cause for concern is the acrimony between *kashrut* authorities which weakens the public confidence and promotes communal divisiveness. Nevertheless, the dietary laws themselves are seen as having positive significance. As well as the familiar rationales for their observance – the beneficial effect of self-discipline and their hygienic value – there can be added the sense of Jewish identification that arises from eating in a Jewish way three times a day. There are many other ways of being Jewish, but few that permeate the home and affect the rhythm of daily life to such an extent. Moreover, certain aspects of *kashrut* have acquired an added historical dimension through the resistance of Jews to those who have sought to destroy Judaism by forcing them to eat pork, from Maccabean times to the Nazi era.

Kashrut affects both private and communal life and there is a distinction in the policy for each aspect.

Personal Observance

In the private domain Reform encourages the observance of *kashrut* and affirms its value. However, it does not specify the particular aspects that should be kept or make a distinction between their merits. It holds to the principle of individual choice in the personal observance of ritual law. It is for each household to decide what degree of *kashrut* is maintained therein. It should be a conscious decision based on a knowledge of the different procedures and a commitment to Jewish life. Thus *kashrut* may vary considerably between Reform households depending on the families concerned. Needless to say there are certain minimum standards, and a Jew who eats pork would be viewed as deliberately flouting a Jewish law universally recognised and sanctified by history. Other forbidden foods such as shellfish and eels – are popularly regarded as less heinous, but they too are discouraged, as are those foods specifically forbidden in the Bible (Leviticus 11.1-47). It is recommended that meat be purchased from a *kosher* butcher, where the animal would have been killed and cleaned in the prescribed way. Although *shechitah* (Jewish slaughter) is occasionally criticised by animal rights groups in Britain, it has been consistently supported by the Government and many leading scientific authorities in recognition of its humane and efficient methods. The RSGB and the Assembly of Rabbis has fully supported the Board of Deputies in its public defence of *shechitah* whenever the issue is raised, and particularly during the unsuccessful attempts in 1987 to rescind it through Parliamentary legislation.

It is largely the post-biblical interpretations of *kashrut* that are regarded as optional owing to the questionability of some of the interpretations that have arisen. Thus the prohibition against seething a kid in its mother's milk (Exodus 23.19) has been extended out of all proportion to the original law. It has led not only to a ban on mixing any milk and meat products but also to detailed regulations concerning separate cutlery, crockery and washing-up utensils. Some Reform Jews see no value in these additions and do not observe them; others feel that they are meaningful and maintain them completely; yet others keep them partially (eg abstaining from eating milk and meat products together but not insisting upon separate cutlery). The latter position is particularly common as it allows a high degree of ritual observance yet does not prevent one from eating at public restaurants or at the homes of non-Jewish friends (where fish or vegetarian meals can be requested), nor does it isolate them from fellow Jews whose homes are not of the same standard. It should be noted that a common argument in favour of *kashrut* advanced in Orthodox circles is that it prevents social relations with non-Jews and consequently lessens the possibility of inter-marriage. This is not a reason favoured by Reform synagogues who are equally opposed to inter-marriage yet see no need to shun non-Jewish company, and who believe that one can enjoy the friendship of non-Jews without losing one's Jewish identity. Another personal decision is the purchase of foods that contain forbidden ingredients, such as animal fats or additives. Some avoid such products, whilst others consider that the principle of *bittul b'shishim* should be extended to apply, whereby if the forbidden food is less than one-sixtieth of the whole mixture it is permitted. In the *Talmud* this refers only to cases of forbidden foods falling accidentally into the mixture (*Chullin* 97b), although it can be argued that the fact of whether it got there accidentally or on purpose cannot affect its actual constitution. There is general agreement that food that is intrinsically *kosher* (eg honey or nuts) does not require a special certificate on it. There is also no need for a *shomer* (supervisor) to be present at the production stages to ensure that forbidden foods are not added accidentally; such an occurrence is extremely unlikely, particularly in view of stringent civil legislation relating to food production and control of ingredients. The same attitude applies at Passover: foods that are normally free of all *chametz* (eg coffee or tea) do not need special '*kosher* for Passover' labels, which only add unnecessary expense to state the obvious.

The practice that is prevalent in some circles of having one set of rules for eating at home and another for elsewhere is regarded as inappropriate. An argument could be made that one is distinguishing between the Jewishness of one's home and the secular world outside, but this is outweighed by two other considerations: first, one's own Jewish observance should be consistent and not limited to a particular place; second, it is confusing for children and can lead to charges of hypocrisy.

In addition to these aspects of *kashrut*, an entirely new question has been raised in Reform thinking: whether the categories of prohibited foods should be extended to include animals bred under methods of modern technological farming that are cruel to animals. Such examples might be battery hens which are unable to walk around and are kept in darkness, or calves fed on artificial liquids that fatten them but still leave them craving for food. Many would consider these practices to be contrary to Judaism's insistence on humane treatment of animals, which includes those to be killed for food (Leviticus 22.28, Deuteronomy 5.14, 22.6-7, Proverbs 12.10). Some Reform Jews therefore choose to abstain from animals raised in 'factory farm' conditions, holding that it offends against Jewish ethics, taking the attitude that "even if a particular animal may be *halachically kosher* it may well still be morally *trefah*"[1].

It is clear that although there is no dogmatic Reform definition of what is *kashrut*, there are two clear principles to serve for individual guidance. First, Reform values the observance of *kashrut*. Second, it recognises that there are different expressions of *kashrut* which can be equally valid; one may not be 'a hundred per cent *kosher*', but that does not mean that one is not *kosher* at all. There is no need to adopt an 'all or nothing' approach, and instead one can follow an acceptable middle path, expressing one's Jewish identity through aspects of one's diet.

---

1 Donald Roodyn, *Alternative Kashrut*, p.4

Synagogue Functions

In the public domain, such as a synagogue or synagogue-organised events, consideration has to be given to wider needs and for the community to be as inclusive as possible. It is felt important that the *kashrut* should be of sufficient level so as to enable most Jews to eat there without qualms and to prevent the dietary laws dividing one Jew from another[1]. Those synagogues that serve meat ensure that it is *kosher* and have guidelines concerning the separation of milk and meat products[2]. Other synagogues permit milk meals only (ie fish or vegetarian). This practice also serves an educational function and provides a model for those unfamiliar with *kashrut* regulations. Non-Jewish caterers may be permitted providing they are under supervision of the Rabbi[3]. The issue also affects the organisation of the Sabbath *kiddush* which often involves sandwiches and/or cakes. Some synagogues allocate the task to a catering committee or a women's guild so as to ensure that the regulations are adhered to; in other synagogues individual members or families provide the *kiddush* on a rota basis and are informed of what is permitted on synagogue premises.

Blessings

It is appropriate not only to consume the right food but also to express appreciation for it, particularly in an age when famine and drought are still regular occurrences in different parts of the world. In addition to the single blessing before a meal, a form of thanksgiving should be said afterwards (in Hebrew, English or both). Options range in length according to circumstances. Thus after the rushed midweek meal one might say a single blessing, *chazan et ha'kol* – "Blessed are You, Lord, who gives food to all" – whereas on the Sabbath one could sing leisurely the long version of thanksgiving after meals[4]. A new, concluding paragraph has been added to the traditional version:

> We have eaten and been satisfied. May we not be blind to the needs of others, nor deaf to their cry for food. Open our eyes and our hearts so that we may share Your gifts and help to remove hunger and want from our world.

---

1 Assembly of Rabbis, 19th January 1955
2 For an example of one such policy, see Appendix 2
3 Assembly of Rabbis, 3rd February 1958
4 *Forms of Prayer*, Vol I, p.331 (See also p.270 for blessings for foods other than bread)

Wine

The situation regarding wine differs radically from that of food: the *kashrut* of food depends on the source from which it came, whereas the *kashrut* of wine depends on who handles it. Traditionally, if a non-Jew was involved in any stage from picking the grape to bottling the wine, it is not considered *kosher*, for all must be done by Jews. These regulations date back to the time when non-Jews were idolaters and used their wine for libation-offerings to their gods. It was important to disassociate Jews from wine that might have been dedicated to heathen deities. Such pagan worship disappeared many centuries ago, but the ban on wine made by non-Jews is still maintained by Orthodox authorities. In Reform synagogues it is generally felt that the law has no validity any more and that although one should observe the laws of *kosher* food, no distinction is necessary between wine touched by Jews or non-Jews. The only exception is in synagogue services where the *kiddush* wine is *kosher* so that all present may be able to participate whatever their level of religious practice. In the case of synagogue social functions, some synagogues allow only *kosher* wine while others permit ordinary wine so long as an alternative drink is present for any who might wish it.

---

3. ARE WOMEN EXPECTED TO GO TO THE *MIKVEH* EVERY MONTH?

The laws concerning *niddah* ('menstruous women') stem from the passage in Leviticus 15.19 "And if a woman has an issue, and her issue in her flesh be blood, she shall be in her impurity seven days". She was not to have any sexual contact with her husband during that time, or even touch him. Later Jewish Law determined that the period of separation should be a total of twelve days (five for the menses itself and a further seven days, during which there should be no bleeding). At the end of that time she was to bathe herself in "running water". Whilst this can be the sea or a river, it is more usually a *mikveh* ('a gathering of waters') which is a small room containing a pool of natural water with a depth of approximately chest height. The woman goes to the *mikveh* after dusk, for the sake of modesty, and the only other person present is a female attendant. The woman removes her clothes and any rings or articles of jewellery before stepping into the water, immerses herself completely by ducking underwater three times, and recites a blessing. She is then permitted to resume marital relations with her husband. The couple are not allowed to have contact if the twelve days have passed but the woman has not been to the *mikveh*.

According to Orthodoxy, monthly visits to the *mikveh* are obligatory for all married women who have not yet reached menopause. A modern *mikveh* will tend to be a tiled, heated pool with adjoining private bathroom/shower, along with hairdrying and other facilities. For the Reform, it is not regarded as obligatory because it is recognised as a highly personal matter that is for each woman to decide for herself and in conjunction with her husband[1]. In an age when the sexual revolution has meant that the subject of sex is no longer a taboo and is openly portrayed and discussed, menstruation still causes embarrassment to some people and many women prefer to deal with it privately. No Reform synagogue has a *mikveh* of its own, and the building of a *mikveh* at the Sternberg Centre for Judaism – the headquarters of the RSGB and the seat of the Reform Beth Din – is motivated primarily by the need for a *mikveh* for proselytes who undergo immersion as one of their conversion rites.

The overwhelming majority of female members of Reform synagogues do not go to a *mikveh* on a monthly basis, although a few individuals do. They tend to be younger wives who have rediscovered the idea of the *mikveh* as one of the consequences of the Jewish feminist movement and the search for distinctively female rituals and customs. The appeal of a *mikveh* is that it acknowledges the bodily and emotional changes that a woman undergoes during menstruation. It also encourages male appreciation of a woman's special sensitivity at such a time. It should be noted that, contrary to popular opinion, immersion in the *mikveh* is not intended to physically cleanse the woman (with the inference that until then she is 'unclean'), for she is required to bathe before entering the *mikveh*. Instead it is seen as having a spiritual significance, symbolising the renewal of the woman's bodily rhythm and celebrating the mystery of her unique productive powers. The notion that a woman is 'impure' in any way is rejected totally. The idea that the couple concerned should abstain from all non-sexual forms of physical contact is also unacceptable. The desire of partners to express themselves through touch need not be dictated by the biological cycle.

One of the more traditional arguments advanced in favour of the *mikveh* is that the period of monthly sexual abstinence contributes to the couple's

---

1 Assembly of Rabbis, 6th April 1966

respect for each other. It also enhances the sexual enjoyment once contact is resumed and maintains the freshness of their relationship. Of course, these benefits can be achieved by those who refrain from sexual intercourse during the menstrual cycle but do not attend a *mikveh* afterwards.

In the Orthodox tradition it is also obligatory for a woman to attend a *mikveh* shortly before her marriage, and the date of the wedding is fixed so as to take account of the most suitable time for her visit. Reform Rabbis often mention the custom when meeting with a couple to discuss the wedding plans, but leave its observance optional. The only occasion when immersion is obligatory for the Reform is as one of the requirements of conversion, in which case it applies equally to men, women and children. Here, too, going to the *mikveh* has a religious significance rather than being to cleanse any physical impurity. It indicates the change of direction in the life of the person converting to Judaism. In some Jewish circles a custom has developed for men to attend the *mikveh* on certain occasions – such as Friday afternoon, before the High Holy Days, and a groom before his wedding. As in the other cases, the immersion has a spiritual symbolism.

---

4. WHAT DISTINCTIVE JEWISH CHARACTERISTICS SHOULD ONE'S HOME HAVE?

An English Jew's home should not be his castle. Castles have the image of keeping people out. A Jewish home should be one that is always open to others and where there is a spirit of hospitality. Hospitality is a concept of which it is easy to approve but is not always put into practice. It means inviting new members or visitors to the synagogue back for a Sabbath meal; it includes ensuring that those who live alone, or who are lonely, are asked to share the warmth of one's home from time to time. A castle usually contains a chapel; this tends to limit religion to one particular room, whereas a Jewish home should be permeated throughout with aspects of Jewish life. Part of this can be achieved through having all, or a selection of, the following articles in a variety of rooms, each of which helps create a special atmosphere.

Mezuzah

The tradition of putting a *mezuzah* on the outside of one's front door stems from Deuteronomy 6.9, which forms the first part of the *Shema*: "Write them (the words of God) on the doorposts of your home and at your gate". It should be placed on the righthand side (as one approaches from the outside), on the upper third with the top leaning towards the door. On one level it is a simple marker that the occupants of the house are Jewish. More importantly it is a positive declaration of identity and a reminder that one is therefore obliged to uphold the traditions and values of Judaism. Having a *mezuzah* on all the living rooms and bedrooms of one's house is not regarded as essential, but it is recommended as it extends the act of identification even further. There is a short ceremony for fixing a *mezuzah*, known as *chanukat ha'bayit* ('dedicating the home'), which contains the appropriate blessings along with the prayer[1]:

> We fix the *mezuzah* to the doorpost of this home to fulfil the command of our creator and to remind ourselves and all who enter that we should love Him with all our heart and all our soul and all our might.
> We ask His blessing on this home and all who live in it. May its doors be open to those in need and its rooms be filled with kindness. May love dwell within its walls, and joy shine from its windows. May His peace protect it and His presence never leave it.

The notion, common in some circles, that the *mezuzah* has protective powers, is a survival of medieval superstitions; unfortunately it has led to totally ridiculous claims that failure to check one's *mezuzah* can bring calamity upon the household. The custom of kissing a *mezuzah* when entering a house is a personal piety adopted by some, although it is not necessary and is rare in Reform circles.

Ritual Objects
Many Jewish ceremonies take place in the home rather than in synagogue, and so the articles necessary for them should be present. They need not be put away in a cupboard, but can be left on a sideboard or windowsill and be constant reminders of festive occasions, such as a *chanukiah*, a *Pesach* plate (which can be hung on the wall), Sabbath candlesticks, *kiddush* cups, *havdalah* spicebox. It should be stressed, however, that these need not be expensive items and can equally well be homemade creations. Their value is in the extent to which they are used, not their financial worth.

---

1 *Forms of Prayer*, Vol I, p.308

Wall coverings

A number of articles can adorn one's walls, such as a *mizrach* – a plaque denoting the direction of east so as to facilitate facing towards Jerusalem during prayer, a custom dating from the time of Solomon (1 Kings 8.44; see also Daniel 6.11, *Berachot* 4.5). Such plaques can be made or bought, plain or decorated. If one possesses an illustrated *ketubah* (marriage document), it can be framed and displayed; one tradition is to hang it in the bedroom. Paintings of Israel or Jewish scenes are highly appropriate.

Books

Books can open a whole world of knowledge and experience. They also add warmth to a room, while a glance at their titles quickly identifies the priorities of the household. The bookshelf should have a number of basic Jewish works, such as the Bible, a set of prayer books (Sabbath, High Holy Day, Festivals) and guides to Jewish life. A variety of other books should also be present – on Jewish history, cooking, folklore, religious life and Israel, as well as Jewish biographies, fiction and children's books. Personal taste will vary considerably, but one should attempt to build up one's own Jewish library over the years. In addition, one may wish to subscribe to Jewish journals so as to keep in touch with communal developments and thinking, such as the 'Jewish Chronicle' (news), the 'Jewish Quarterly' (culture and history), 'Manna' (a Reform journal) and 'European Judaism' (intellectual trends).

Charity Box

Judaism has always emphasised the value of *tzedakah* (charity) as a regular and natural act. A charity box in the home acts as a constant reminder of the needs of others less fortunate than oneself. Many families have the tradition of putting money in the box shortly before the start of the Sabbath or festivals, and so the box is often placed near the candlesticks.

The Kitchen

Whilst there is no one physical mark of a *kosher* kitchen, there are many telltale signs to the experienced eye, such as the absence of forbidden foods and the care not to mix milk and meat products. A distinctive colour scheme is usually employed by those who also maintain separate crockery (very often blue for milk, red for meat).

Relationships

In addition to possessing all the appropriate ritual and other Jewish objects, it is even more important that the quality of relationships within the house corresponds to Jewish values. Trust, respect, kindness, helpfulness and good humour are the ideal hallmarks of a Jewish home. It would be unrealistic to expect no harsh word to ever be heard or temper to be lost, but they should be occasional occurrences only, quickly rescinded and the problem resolved in the best interests of all. A Jewish home is not perfect, but it can aim for perfection and constantly try to better itself.

Location

As well as the inside of one's home, its location also needs consideration. Amongst the many factors playing a part when choosing where to live – proximity to work, schools, shops, transport – the Jewish factor should also be prominent. Living far away from a Jewish community ensures that one is unlikely to have much communal religious life, Jewish social contact, or the availability of Jewish facilities; any children will also be deprived of Jewish friends and religious education. Conversely, being within reasonable access to a synagogue will allow one to participate in wider Jewish affairs and enrich one's personal and family life.

5. HOW DOES REFORM VIEW THE CHANGES IN JEWISH FAMILY LIFE?

Jewish family life has changed enormously in the last fifty years. In general, family members no longer live in close proximity to each other, but are scattered throughout the country; structures of authority have altered, with family leadership often being transferred from the oldest generation to the one that is most successful in material terms; family ties and loyalties have lessened because of the desire for independence and personal fulfilment.

These changes are largely the result of external social and economic factors, the influence of trends operating in society at large; in the eyes of Reform Judaism the value of the family has not changed[1]. It may be under considerable pressure but it still serves many important functions. It provides

---

1 Dow Marmur, *The Jewish Family Today and Tomorrow*, p.1

a stable unit through which a couple can commit their lives to each other, relate to those around them, and bring children into the world. At its best, love, personal growth, emotional security and mutual support are its hallmarks. It is also a vehicle for the practice of Judaism, which is as much expressed through the home and family activities as it is through synagogue life. Those without families can still practise Judaism fully (see VI.4), although there is no doubt that many Jewish observances assume that one is part of a family group celebrating together. In addition the family is one of the main methods of transmitting Judaism to the next generation. There is much truth in the saying that religion cannot be taught, only caught. It is primarily by experiencing the practice of Judaism at home that children grow up to regard it as a natural and vital part of their identity. Seeing Jewish symbols, eating Jewish food, hearing Jewish table talk, enjoying Jewish rituals and learning Jewish values in their formative years is the best way to ensure that Judaism remains part of them for the rest of their life.

The modern pressures to which family life is subjected means that it is important for Reform Jews to take active steps to preserve its strengths: by respecting the wisdom and experience of older members; by keeping in close touch with other relations; by coming together wherever possible on the Sabbath and at festivals; and by valuing the support that it can provide for individual members.

Another major change in family life has been equal status for women. Daughters are increasingly treated in the same way as sons: invested with the same Jewish and general education, given the same independence, and expected to choose their own career and lifestyle. The division of roles within marriage has also altered considerably. In keeping with its belief in the equality of the sexes, Reform does not hold to a stereotyping of roles, but recognises that there are many options possible. One is for women to stay at home after children are born and to concentrate on being mothers and homemakers. It is a full-time occupation that demands as much dedication and creativity as any outside work. Yet other patterns of family life are available too, with mothers having part-time or full-time jobs that can fulfil their aspirations as well as contribute to the financial affairs of the family. Similarly, men face choices as to the extent they work, and can take an active part in household duties and the children's upbringing. It is for each couple to arrange their own domestic life; the main criterion is that all such decisions should be reached by mutual agreement between the partners and allowing both to satisfy their own needs as much as possible. These discussions should occur before the marriage takes place so that both partners are fully aware of the lifestyle they will be sharing. Of course, there will be many unforeseen developments during the marriage and the relationship should be sufficiently caring and flexible to allow changes in personal growth and direction. At the same time being part of a family unit imposes certain limitations upon individual freedom and brings responsibilities that have to be honoured. Fidelity is one of these and is of the highest importance. Infidelity undermines the whole basis of the relationship, breaking both the religious vows taken upon marriage and the personal trust that has been built up. Some traditional roles may have changed, but traditional values such as mutual respect, care, trust and support are still essential parts of marital life.

The above qualities are also vital to provide the right environment in which to bring up children. The command to "Respect your father and your mother" (Exodus 20.17) carries duties on all parties: children to have regard for those who brought them into the world and nurtured them; parents to fulfil the role of a father and a mother and ensure the stable homelife and loving care that children require. This includes recognising the integrity of children as independent human beings with their own needs and rights, and not merely as extensions of the parents. They should be equipped to take their place in society at large, being confident enough of their Jewish identity to maintain its values and lifestyle within it.

When a marriage fails, divorce has always been permissible, although regrettable, in Judaism. In modern times the sharp rise in the divorce rate nationally has affected Jewish marriage patterns too. The result is that there are many single parent families within the Jewish community as well as second, or even third, marriages. No stigma is attached to those in such situations and the involvement of either partner in synagogue life is not affected. On the contrary, a special effort is often made to give communal support, and Reform Rabbis consider it part of their pastoral duty to help those experiencing the emotional trauma of a divorce. The needs of any children involved will also receive attention, for they are particularly vulnerable and are sometimes exploited by either or both parents. In addition, there may be practical problems that need to be dealt with – such as children missing religion school because of access arrangements, seating plans at a *bar/batmitzvah* where the parents are divorced, or having *seder* meals with different sets of families and step-relatives.

Another scenario which is becoming more common is couples who live together before marriage. It is a relatively new phenomenon that forces re-assessment of traditional attitudes. Reform values the institution of marriage and the act of two individuals making public vows to each other. Indeed, when a baby boy is circumcised, the prayer is offered that he may "enter into the blessings of *Torah*, of marriage and of good deeds"[1]. Yet Reform also acknowledges that many couples living together have a loving and responsible relationship. Most Reform Rabbis do not condemn such a union and there is no attempt to ban them from participation in synagogue life[2]. The question of sexual intercourse needs to be seen in perspective. It is an important part of a marital relationship, but it is not the only factor in a marriage, and so it should not be the sole criterion in judging an unmarried couple living together. The quality and stability of the relationship are important too. There are advantages to postponing sex until marriage – and many Reform Rabbis would urge such a course – but it is recognised that pre-marital sex can be a legitimate expression of a caring and enduring relationship[3]. Nevertheless, it is hoped that eventually the couple will feel it is right to affirm their togetherness, formally and publicly, by entering into 'the holy covenant of marriage', as in fact usually does happen. However, this stance does not sanction promiscuity or casual sexual relationships which are matters of convenience or exploitation rather than commitment.

6. WHAT RELATIONSHIP SHOULD JEWS HAVE WITH GENERAL SOCIETY?

Ever since Jews have lived outside the Land of Israel there has always been the question of how far they should be part of their host society. Sometimes they did not have any option, with the climate of hostility around them determining that they remained totally isolated from the surrounding social and cultural life. At other, more tolerant times they faced a major dilemma: stay too apart and they would be branded as separatists and viewed with mistrust; become too involved and they would lose their identity and no longer be Jews.

The dilemma is particularly acute today where the welcome presented by an open society is so powerful that it not only allows assimilation by those who seek it, but also encourages assimilatory trends amongst those who value

---

1 *Forms of Prayer*, Vol I, p. 313
2 Dow Marmur, op cit, p.7
3 Jacqueline Tabick and others, 'Sex and What Should I Tell My Teenager?', *Manna* (Winter 1990)

their Jewish identity. One response, favoured in ultra-Orthodox circles, has been to turn one's back on general society and to recreate both a physical and mental Jewish ghetto. Reform rejects this attitude as much as it opposes that of the assimilationists. It believes that it is possible to be loyal to one's Jewish heritage yet also participate in British life. More than that, Reform considers it the desirable and right course to pursue. Modernity has many faults but it has much to commend it as well; to dismiss both aspects together would be a gross lack of discrimination. It would also be doing a disservice to Judaism to deprive it of the artistic creativity, psychological insights and scientific advances that have resulted from contemporary life. At the same time, energy is needed to resist its less desirable features, such as its materialism, destructive capacity and many forms of personal abuse. Given such caveats, there is no reason why modern Jews cannot be modern and Jewish, enjoying both cultures that they inhabit and bringing them into harmony. The key word is 'integration', whereby one's roots and lifestyle are firmly Jewish, but without precluding other involvements.

It has to be emphasised that intention and action do not always correspond, particularly in this case where there is a thin dividing line between integration and assimilation. The many attractions offered by society at large can mean that less time is given to Jewish communal life, home celebrations and personal study. It is vital to maintain all three areas if there is to be a real synthesis between one's Jewish life and one's wider interests; anything less would be a form of self-deception and gradually erode the Jewish element. Being part of a minority culture is not easy and requires much commitment to maintain it. This is particularly true of Reform Judaism, which does not have a rule for every conceivable situation and which gives religious responsibility in many areas to individuals themselves. The saying "It is harder to be a Reform Jew because you have to think for yourself" may be an over-simplification but it does contain a certain truth. At the same time the tension between the different aspects of one's life can be very creative – providing different layers of perception, forcing individuals to order their priorities, and presenting daily challenges as to the best way to conduct oneself. Reform Judaism is very far from being 'convenient' as some critics allege; instead, it epitomises the literal meaning of the word Israel ('one who wrestles with God') and is a constant attempt to combine the highest ideals with everyday mundanities, whilst living Jewishly in society at large.

Among many practical issues that arise, the following are to the fore most often (other aspects of which are mentioned elsewhere as indicated):

Dress

There is no specific Jewish dress. The *streimels* and long black coats worn by the *Chasidim* were typical seventeenth century Polish garb that have become associated with Judaism simply because the *Chasidim* are the only people to have maintained it. They do so to deliberately emphasise their group identity, separate both from other Jews and from non-Jews. Reform sees no need for such physical distinctions. One's Judaism should be evident through the lifestyle and code of conduct one follows. The sole commanded Jewish garment is the *arba kanfot*, which is generally worn under one's clothing; although invisible to the public, it can have an important personal significance and its use is recommended (see IV.5). The only other distinctive Jewish wear is a head covering. Most Reform Jews consider it necessary only for the purposes of prayer, although some also cover their heads when studying Jewish texts. A very small number choose to cover their heads at all times, although others wear less traditional signs of their Jewishness, such as chains with a *chai* sign or a *magen David*.

Food

Reform Judaism values *kashrut* and believes that observing the dietary laws, wholly or in part, can act as important reminders of Jewish identity. Within this general principle it leaves the specific degree of *kashrut* followed to the individuals concerned, as a matter for their own judgement (see V.2). In areas of high Jewish settlement there are *kosher* butchers who can provide for communal needs. In towns which do not have a *kosher* butcher, many Reform synagogues run their own '*kosher* shop', stocking fresh or frozen *kosher* products so as to facilitate the observance of *kashrut*. Recent changes in eating habits nationally have meant that there are countless vegetarian restaurants or ordinary restaurants with vegetarian options on the menu. As the *kashrut* observance of many Reform Jews centres on the food itself rather than on the plates and cutlery, it is not difficult to eat in public places whilst at the same time maintaining one's own standards. When invited by non-Jewish friends for dinner (or Jewish friends that do not keep *kosher*) one can easily explain in advance one's dietary limitations – as do those who are fully or partially vegetarian or who have certain dietary problems. Jewish identity and social intercourse need not conflict.

Christmas

The problem of being Jewish in a non-Jewish society is characterised by the annual Christmas question. With high street shopping, television programmes and office decorations all geared towards Christmas months in advance, it is very hard for Jews to escape its impact. The debate is over to what extent they should participate in or shun the festivities around them. A clear distinction can be made between the religious and social aspects of Christmas. According to Christian teaching, the day commemorates the birth of Jesus, the son of God and Saviour. It is therefore inappropriate for Jews to be directly involved in religious ceremonies or other forms of celebration, such as nativity plays or carol singing. It is also inappropriate to bring Christian symbols into one's own home, such as a Christmas tree. Despite arguments that it is only a modern innovation that was originally devoid of any Christian significance, there is no doubt that it has become associated with Christmas and should not be done. There can be no objection, however, to social activities that take place around Christmas but without any religious overtones, such as office parties and get-togethers with neighbours. There is much to commend the goodwill and charity that emerges at that time of year. Indeed, many Jews will feel no hesitation in giving donations to carol singers collecting for a worthy cause. The concern voiced by some Jewish parents that their children might feel they are 'missing out' by not having Christmas festivities at home and resent their Judaism, is best resolved by celebrating *Chanukah* so positively and fully that it is an enormously enjoyable family experience which makes all else pale in comparison.

Schools
Amongst many factors that determine parents' choice of schools for their children, the religious aspect should also be present. Schools that promote a rigidly Christian message are inappropriate and can lead to confusion or confrontation (see VIII.5). Jewish schools are an option to be considered, although there are many ordinary schools in both state and private sectors that teach a broad religious perspective, are tolerant of religious differences, and include multi-faith studies in their curriculum. Confessional situations should be avoided where possible, such as a weekly church service or carol concert. Parents who feel that Judaism is being ignored or misinterpreted in school life should approach the head teacher and make positive suggestions to rectify the situation. Most Reform Rabbis spend time giving talks on Judaism at local schools or hosting guided tours around the synagogue. It is seen as an important part of their work, leading to greater knowledge and appreciation of Judaism amongst non-Jewish children and teachers; it also helps reinforce the religious identity of Jewish children in those schools.

Civic Duty

Alongside the responsibility to their Jewish roots, Jews also have a duty to society around them. It is not only permissible but also right that Jews should be involved in welfare work, human rights activities, ecological concerns, famine relief efforts, local issues, and any other causes that promote the general good (see XII.5). The prayer for the Royal Family in the Reform prayer book, read every Saturday morning, not only asks God's guidance for the rulers of the country but also reminds individuals of the role they have to play in the wider community[1]:

> May He give us all the strength to do our duty, and the love to do it well, so that justice and kindness may dwell in our land ... so that every community of our nation may meet in understanding and respect, united by love of goodness and keeping far from violence and strife. Together may we work for peace and justice among all nations ... so may this kingdom find its honour and greatness in the work of redemption, and the building of God's kingdom here on earth.

Jews who live in Britain today can expect to be faced with constant challenges to their identity. Yet the struggle to be the heirs of the covenant with Abraham as well as full participants in the life of this country can be achieved by those genuinely devoted to both.

---

1 *Forms of Prayer*, Vol I, p.159

CHAPTER SIX

THE SABBATH

The Children of Israel shall keep the Sabbath, observing the Sabbath throughout their generations as a timeless covenant. It is a sign between Me and the Children of Israel forever.

Exodus 31.16-17

1. HOW DOES ONE KEEP THE SABBATH 'HOLY'?

The Sabbath is central to Jewish life. Many Jews mistakenly consider that the High Holy Days are more important and therefore should command greater attention; but despite their enormous significance, they are 'one-off' episodes within the Jewish year, whereas the Sabbath forms the very structure of the Jewish calendar. Its theme of rest – physical and spiritual – is as relevant in today's world of intense pressure as it was in ancient times of strenuous labour. Technology and increased leisure time have brought many benefits, but they often mean that we do more rather than less. In addition, they do not address the question of one's inner calm, and they have not lessened the need for personal renewal.

The Sabbath should be celebrated in one's home with one's family or friends and also in the synagogue with the community at large. The command concerning the Sabbath makes clear that it is to be observed both by doing certain things and by not doing others: "Remember the Sabbath day to keep it holy. You have six days to labour and do all your work, but the seventh shall be a Sabbath to the Lord your God. That day you shall do no work" (Exodus 20.8-10). A Rabbinic comment on the two different versions of the command – "Remember the Sabbath day" (Exodus 20.8) and "Observe the Sabbath day" (Deuteronomy 5.12) – uses the divergence to emphasise that the Sabbath is celebrated in both positive and negative ways.

The word 'holy' often puzzles people and they imagine that it represents something full of awe, so marvellous that it is way beyond their attainment, and this discourages them from pursuing it. However, one can better express the meaning of the Hebrew word for holy – *kadosh* – by substituting terms such as 'special' or 'distinctive'. To make the Sabbath special lies within the ability of everyone, and members of Reform synagogues are encouraged to pursue the following steps to achieve this goal[1].

Preparation
One cannot simply enter the Sabbath and expect it to be meaningful unless one has prepared for it in advance and created the circumstances which will make it sufficiently different so as to be special. Friday afternoon (and Thursday evening for those working the whole of Friday) is thus a time of hyperactivity: ensuring that all shopping is completed, bills paid, tasks seen to

---

1 Dow Marmur, *Remember the Sabbath Day*, pp.6-8

(such as filling up the car with petrol or buying flowers/presents for visits); all urgent professional work should be settled so it is not necessary to do anything (or worry about it) during the Sabbath; the home should be thoroughly cleaned, special meals prepared for Friday evening dinner and Saturday lunch, the table laid with Sabbath requisites and adornments (two *challot* covered by a cloth, salt, wine, candlesticks, white table cloth, fresh flowers) – with all members of the household contributing in some way; preparing oneself by having a bath or shower, dressing in special clothes (if only a fresh shirt, especially a white one), settling any quarrels or bad feelings in the family (and with others), giving to charity (many homes have a charity box beside the Sabbath candlesticks for making donations just before the candles are lit). Of course, the many other demands on one's time – work, children, or even unexpected phone calls – can ruin one's best intentions; yet they should not stop one from making the attempt, for it is in such ways that what could have been 'just another day' becomes a special experience.

Sabbath Eve

The Sabbath is welcomed on Friday evening – *Erev Shabbat* – by the lighting of candles and, where appropriate, blessing the children, singing *Shalom aleichem*, and reading the passage praising the woman of the house (*Eshet chayil*)[1]. The author suggests that women who wish to respond can recite Psalm 112 or 128, both of which are in the psalm anthology at the back of the prayer book; alternatively, the second chapter of Song of Songs can be read. Such a response serves to recognise the contribution of both partners and to express mutual appreciation. The meal is preceded by the making of *kiddush*, with the blessings over the bread and wine. The traditional division of roles between males and females can be maintained or inter-changed (see VI.4). Those unable to say the blessings in Hebrew should say them in English rather than omit them, although they are also encouraged to make efforts to learn Hebrew through adult education classes or other methods. The Sabbath meal should be distinctive with regard to the food itself, such as having an unusual dish, produce from Israel or something different from midweek meals. Equally important is the atmosphere in which it is eaten. It should be consumed leisurely, table talk should include matters of Jewish interest, *zemirot* (Sabbath songs) can be sung in-between courses, *Birkat hamazon*

---

1 *Forms of Prayer*, Vol I, pp.312-18

(thanksgiving after meals)[1] should be recited (it should be said after all meals, but on the Sabbath it could be the longer version and new tunes can be introduced). The quality of the evening can be increased immeasurably if it is shared with others, by inviting family, friends or new members of the community to join one. This also fulfils the *mitzvah* of giving hospitality to others, particularly those who are strangers or who are without a family. Attendance at synagogue is also important, although the timing of local services will affect whether this is before or after the meal. In either case personal and domestic arrangements should be made so that synagogue-going will not detract from the home celebrations. Those who do not attend synagogue can say the service at home by themselves, either before the meal or, as one tradition suggests, at the same time as the synagogue service starts so as to show one's identification with the rest of the community.

The Sabbath Day
Shabbat morning should be spent in synagogue. Mindful of the need to cater for those with special interests or without a family to celebrate with, many Reform synagogues periodically provide activities additional to the service itself, such as a *Torah* breakfast which examines the weekly *Torah* portion over coffee and beigels, a children's service geared to their level, a communal lunch or an afternoon study group. The Sabbath lunch largely follows the pattern of the Friday night meal, albeit with a different *kiddush*[2], and it too can be enhanced by the addition of guests from the synagogue invited back for a meal. Sabbath afternoon and evening services are provided in the prayer book, and although few synagogues hold services then, the prayers can be used by individuals privately. The rest of the Sabbath is unstructured and can be filled with a variety of activities – ranging from having a sleep to visiting family and friends, from going for a walk to reading a Jewish book. Study of Jewish texts is especially appropriate. It might also include pursuits that are not allowed according to Orthodox interpretation but are deemed permissible according to Reform thinking, such as attending a concert or working in the garden, if they constitute restful activities in keeping with the Sabbath spirit for the person concerned. In order to maintain the distinctiveness of the Sabbath, its end has to be marked and a separation made between it and the onset of the ordinary days. Thus the short ceremony of *havdalah* should be

---

1 Ibid, pp.330-38
2 Ibid, p.320

performed by all Jews in their homes, closing the special time begun twenty-five hours earlier by the ceremony of *kiddush*. Blessings over the wine, spice-box and *havdalah* candle are recited[1]. When a communal event takes place in synagogue on Saturday night, it is often preceded by *havdalah*, notwithstanding the fact that the Sabbath may have ended much earlier, because of its educational value.

Two Caveats
It is easy to regard the Sabbath as *the* Jewish day of the week and to disregard any Jewish practices on other days. The Sabbath is certainly very important, but is merely one of seven days in what should be a totally Jewish week. As is described earlier (V.1), each day contains several opportunities for Jewish observances, whilst the need to speak and act according to the highest ethical considerations applies to every day of the year.

Those who are unable for some reason to observe the Sabbath for the full twenty-five hours should not feel that the only alternative is to abandon it altogether. Whatever one's situation, one can still have a partial Sabbath and celebrate 'Sabbath moments'. Thus any one of the various component parts of the Sabbath described above can be observed – be it the Friday evening home atmosphere or the Sabbath morning synagogue attendance or the Sabbath afternoon recreation – so that every person at least has one Sabbath moment and will be able gradually to expand it as circumstances allow.

2. WHAT ACTIVITIES DOES REFORM CONSIDER FORBIDDEN ON THE SABBATH?

The command to observe the Sabbath is accompanied by the injunction not to do any work (Exodus 20.9). However, the meaning of 'work' is not defined and there are only a few scattered examples in the Bible of activities that were forbidden. Subsequent Rabbinic literature noted that a repetition of the prohibition against working on the Sabbath was immediately followed by instructions concerning the building of the Tabernacle (Exodus 35.4); from this it was deduced that the type of work forbidden on the Sabbath was that which was required for the Tabernacle (*Shabbat* 49b). Thirty-nine different categories of work were enumerated and any activity related to them was also

---

1 Ibid, p.326

deemed to fall under the Sabbath ban (*Shabbat* 7.2). These formed the basis of traditional Sabbath observance and became guidelines for judging any new activity. Thus turning on an electric light is forbidden as it activates an electric current, and is held to come under the category of kindling a fire; opening a letter is forbidden because it is considered akin to the prohibition against cutting any material. The logic by which many traditional prohibitions have been derived today is so far-fetched as to have no connection to the original meaning of the Sabbath. Thus turning on a television to watch a programme on Israel is prohibited under the ban on kindling a fire. In Reform synagogues it is recognised that the nature of 'work' has changed considerably over the centuries and that the *talmudic* bans sometimes have no relevance to modern conditions. A redefinition of work permitted or forbidden on the Sabbath has been undertaken[1]. The object is to preserve the original spirit of the Sabbath command – a day of pleasurable rest and spiritual refreshment which is marked by refraining from normal work. In some instances the traditional prohibitions still remain in force, such as the ban on commerce, as it clearly contravenes the fourth commandment regarding Sabbath rest. In many other instances, actions forbidden by Orthodoxy are permitted by Reform, such as turning on a light as it enhances rather than detracts from the Sabbath. Sometimes the permissibility of an activity depends on its purpose, as in the case of travelling by car, which is seen as involving no real work and merely serves a particular end. Thus driving on the Sabbath is allowed if it is used to attend synagogue or visit relatives, but not if it is to go shopping. For certain other activities the permissibility will vary according to subjective criteria, as in the case of gardening, which can be a burdensome chore for some people and therefore should be avoided on the Sabbath, whilst it can be a restful delight for others and therefore an ideal recreation for their Sabbath afternoon. Writing – usually associated with work – may also be regarded as permissible in various circumstances, such as wardens jotting down names to be called up for an *aliyah* in the service, children answering a quiz in a creative service, or making notes in a book one is reading.

In practice, therefore, there has been a substantial departure from traditional interpretation of Sabbath observance, with many activities that were prohibited previously now being permitted fully. In principle, though, the same concern remains – that the Sabbath be a day that is distinctive from the other days of the week and which allows everyone to rest and be refreshed.

---

1 Dow Marmur, *Remember the Sabbath Day*, pp.10-12

This takes into account the enormous changes that have occurred in lifestyle since the *Talmud* was written, and it acknowledges that different people relax in widely differing ways. Thus there can be divergent expressions of Sabbath observance which are equally valid. Clearly this approach puts much emphasis and responsibility on individuals to observe the Sabbath meaningfully – a situation that requires both knowledge and commitment. It is typical of the Reform position in many other areas. It is, of course, open to neglect but then those who lack commitment will also ignore a much more rigid system of observance.

Some specific guidelines as to work that should be avoided on the Sabbath have been recommended as follows[1]:

Employment

As a fundamental general principle, all acts and activities related to one's gainful employment should be avoided. Members are urged to refrain from all business and commerce on *Shabbat* as much as possible. This includes dealing with personal and family financial matters. It is recognised that in the contemporary situation it may be almost impossible to avoid deriving financial benefit from commercial enterprises in which one has an interest and which function on *Shabbat*, such as partnerships, stocks and shares. Unless one is participating personally at the time, these need not be considered breaking the Sabbath. Those who cannot avoid working on the Sabbath can at least ensure some aspects of it are celebrated.

Money

Since money is, above all else, the symbol of business and commerce, we should avoid handling it in most instances on *Shabbat*. Our emphasis lies in removing acquisitiveness as well as matters relating to one's livelihood from *Shabbat*. The use of money to pay for travel to *Shabbat* services and visiting relatives may well be appropriate. Shopping should be avoided where possible. Some will regard purchasing refreshments and entrance tickets to recreational activities as appropriate. Payment for prescriptions may be dealt with by the theory of hierarchies – namely that being able to enjoy *Shabbat* in health and comfort overrides the prohibition against using money in this instance.

---

1 Ibid, pp.10-17

Domestic Chores
Household and family chores, actions which may 'feel' like work – cleaning, decorating, car care – are to be considered work and should not be undertaken.

Synagogue Business
According to the *Talmud*, "Scripture forbids 'your business' but 'God's business' is permitted" (*Shabbat* 150a). God's business appropriate to *Shabbat* would include educational activities, hospital and sick visiting. Administrative and organisational meetings are not included, nor is it appropriate on *Shabbat* to deal with matters relating to the financial and business side of the synagogue.

Hobbies
Personal relaxation may be particularly appropriate for *Shabbat* afternoon provided that the positive aspects of *Shabbat* are not neglected, a hobby is not exercised in a selfish way which neglects others, and it does not clash with attendance at *Shabbat* services, study and family.

Home Help
Jewish baby-sitters should not be engaged on *Shabbat* to facilitate attendance at services. Where non-Jews are employed in the household, they should not be asked to carry out work which is inconsistent with the maintenance of *Shabbat*, although their role in helping the family observe *Shabbat* should not be curtailed. Every opportunity must be given for them to celebrate their own Sabbath.

Travelling
As mentioned above, travelling is not forbidden providing it is for a purpose in keeping with the Sabbath. This applies to all people and not just to those who are too infirm or who live too far away from their destination. Nevertheless, it is also pointed out that travelling is often associated with tension, be it crowded buses, running out of petrol or being delayed in a traffic jam, whereas walking can be more peaceful. Choosing to walk might also be a way of differentiating the Sabbath from other days of the week, and so for these reasons (rather than the traditional one that turning on the ignition creates a spark and so desecrates the Sabbath), walking should be considered as an option where appropriate. However, this does not undermine the orig-

inal principle that in Reform thinking there is no intrinsic objection to travelling by car. Moreover, there is no merit to the claim sometimes voiced that it is better to park one's car round the corner, hidden from sight, when going to synagogue than to drive there openly. The assumption is that this form of practice at least acknowledges the validity of the Sabbath prohibitions, even if they are not kept in practice. Yet it is clear that if one takes the prohibition seriously, one must abide by it, and to do otherwise is not only hypocritical but also undermines the authority of the Jewish Law one is supposed to be upholding. Furthermore, it provides an appalling example of double standards to children who can only learn from it a disrespect for Jewish tradition. It is far better to introduce moderate and intelligible reforms to aspects of the religion that seem to have become obsolete, with the result that one has a Judaism to which one can subscribe honestly and whose demands can be met in good conscience.

Use of Electricity

Use of electrical appliances is not seen as 'work' and is permitted where it is in harmony with the Sabbath being a day of light, warmth and joy. Thus one may use the telephone to contact relatives and friends, although not for business purposes. Those who do not wish to be distracted by incoming calls can make it clear to others or use an answerphone. One may watch television and listen to the radio, particularly in the case of cultural programmes or items of Jewish interest, although not if it causes other members of the family to be neglected. Major cooking should not be done on the Sabbath as it involves much personal time and effort, although it is permissible to 'cook' small items, such as boiling a kettle for some tea or heating up some soup which will involve no real work but will add to the enjoyment of the Sabbath, particularly on cold days. Turning on lights, using a lift, and taking advantage of other helpful services provided by electricity are seen as being in consonance with the Sabbath. Many synagogues with large buildings that require sound amplification for the services will use a microphone. There is also no objection to installing special loops for those who have hearing difficulties and would otherwise be unable to enjoy the service.

The synagogue itself has an important function as a role model: it presents ways of observing the Sabbath by offering services, study groups and communal meals and by not organising committee meetings, outings and fund-raising activities. At the same time private lifestyles may differ from the synagogue model. General parameters are set within which individuals can exercise their own discretion. It is deemed quite acceptable that there may be a variety of personal practices. The positive observance of the Sabbath – home ceremonies and synagogue services – are sufficiently strong to give communal cohesion to the individual pluralism.

3. WHEN SHOULD THE SABBATH BEGIN AND END?

Traditionally the Sabbath starts prior to sunset. In Israel this occurs at a reasonably consistent time throughout the year – between 5.00 pm and 7.00 pm – which allows one to finish the working day on a Friday and then enjoy a family meal once the Sabbath has started. However, in Britain sunset can range from 3.30 pm in the winter to 9.00 pm in the summer, and can cause considerable difficulty. In summertime parents with young families whom they wish to witness a Sabbath Eve *kiddush* may feel it is inappropriate to delay it until so late at night. There is a tradition that it is permissible to start the Sabbath two hours earlier than it officially commences, a precedent of which they may wish to take advantage (although the two hours need not be literally adhered to). In winter those at work or school will find that their day continues after sunset on a Friday. Where possible, it is recommended that one should try to leave early so as to be home to celebrate the Sabbath in full[1]. However, when one is not able to do so, various options are available: another member of the family can light the Sabbath candles at sunset, with the *kiddush* and meal taking place when everyone else has returned home; alternatively the lighting of the candles can be delayed until the whole family is present. This violates the traditional ban on kindling lights after sunset, but may be justified by the more important aspect of the family being together for the inauguration of the Sabbath. Some develop this principle into a more flexible, less solar-oriented definition of the Sabbath, and determine that the family will always gather together and start the Sabbath at, for instance, 6.00 pm whatever the time of year.

The times of the Sabbath evening services vary considerably amongst Reform synagogues, although each one usually has a constant time which is kept throughout the year. Some begin at 6.00 pm or 6.30 pm and cater for those who wish to have an early service and then return home for the *kiddush*

---

1 Dow Marmur, *Remember the Sabbath Day*, p.10

and family meal; others start at 8.00 pm or 8.30 pm and cater for those who have already welcomed in the Sabbath at home and prefer to attend services after their meal. Several congregations have the custom of lighting the Sabbath candles at the beginning of the service, a rite which traditionally belongs to the home but which is now often done in synagogue both for educational reasons and to create a Sabbath atmosphere. As this would involve lighting them after sunset in wintertime, some synagogues kindle them at sunset so that they are already burning by the time the service commences; others prefer to light them at the beginning of the service, irrespective of the season.

The Sabbath ends with the appearance of three stars, making the Sabbath last a total duration of twenty-five hours. This was due to the Rabbinic addition of some time immediately before and after the 'real' twenty-four hour Sabbath so as to prevent accidental infringements at the beginning or end of it. The exact time of the conclusion is provided in Jewish diaries and in the Jewish press. However, those families who bring in the Sabbath later than sunset should be careful to end it at a similar time and thereby maintain the full length of the Sabbath period[1]. In all cases the departure of the Sabbath should be marked by the ceremony of *havdalah* which is performed at home and which brings the special Sabbath conditions to a formal end.

4. HOW DOES ONE CELEBRATE THE SABBATH IF ONE IS WITHOUT A FAMILY OR FINDS NO SUPPORT AMONGST ONE'S FAMILY?

The previous three discussions on the Sabbath have all assumed that one celebrates it with the rest of one's family. Indeed most of the Sabbath rituals are orientated towards being with others and sharing certain activities, such as the *kiddush* and a special meal. Yet in today's society where families live apart, be it in the same town or scattered across the country, there are many who are by themselves, covering all ages and either unmarried, divorced or widowed. Students, visitors and newcomers may also lack company with whom to share the Sabbath. Even those who have a partner but who know few others locally – such as young couples without children or elderly couples without a family – may find it hard to celebrate the Sabbath fully with just the

---

1 Ibid, p.18

two of them. Difficulties can also be experienced by one-parent families, by those with non-Jewish partners and by individuals the rest of whose family are disinterested in Sabbath traditions. Lighting candles by oneself can sometimes be so depressing that people prefer not to do it at all. Thus there are many categories of people who, for a variety of reasons, do not fit into the 'normal' pattern of a large Jewish family happily celebrating Sabbath together.

In most Reform synagogues the Rabbi or someone specifically concerned with 'Community Care' will endeavour to find families in the congregation who wish to offer Sabbath hospitality to those who would appreciate it. Many synagogues now have a network of local groups operating within the community based on the different areas in which members live. These each have their own social and/or welfare co-ordinator, one of whose tasks is often to ensure that those by themselves on Sabbaths and festivals are invited to someone else's home. In addition many synagogues encourage their members to organise communal Sabbath activities supplementary to the services. These might include a Friday night meal or discussion, *Shabbat* lunch, or Saturday afternoon study group; they take place either in the synagogue itself or in people's homes on a rota basis. The food is provided either by a committee or, as more often happens, by each person contributing something themselves. These events are open to the whole community, but they are often particularly important for those without families of their own. In these ways the community can act as an extended family, bringing people together, and can create a Sabbath atmosphere and camaraderie that would be impossible to obtain individually. It is also an option for anyone by themselves to invite others to their home for the Sabbath and thus take the initiative in making sure that they have company. Inviting those who are also alone is particularly appropriate as it serves to enhance their Sabbath too.

It should also be noted that although various Sabbath rituals have been allocated by tradition to one particular sex, such practices are merely custom and need not be adhered to rigidly. Thus a man can light the Sabbath candles whilst a woman can recite the *kiddush* blessings. This applies to families as a whole, but is particularly relevant to those by themselves or sharing *Shabbat* with members of the same sex.

CHAPTER SEVEN

FESTIVALS AND FAST DAYS

These are the festivals of the Lord, holy convocations which you shall proclaim in their appointed season.

Leviticus 23.4

1. WHAT VARIATIONS ARE THERE IN REFORM OBSERVANCE OF THE FESTIVALS?

Most of the familiar observances traditionally associated with the festivals are maintained in Reform synagogues. However, some additions and omissions occur which are listed below.

Permitted Activities

As far as Orthodoxy is concerned, all the activities that are banned on the Sabbath are also prohibited on festivals, save that one is allowed to cook food that is to be consumed on the same day. However, Reform considers that, as in the case of the Sabbath, it is necessary to re-evaluate these regulations in the light of modern conditions. Reform holds, for instance, that travelling by car or using electricity no longer constitute 'work', and therefore need not be prohibited on festivals. On the contrary, such activities can often facilitate attendance at services or enjoyment of the festivals. The guidelines as to what should and should not be done at the festivals are the same as those suggested for the Sabbath (VI.1-2). Another difference from Orthodox practice is that as Reform synagogues generally celebrate the first day of the festivals and thus do not have two consecutive festive days (save for those which observe two days *Rosh Hashanah*), the need to prepare food on the day of the festival itself is lessened. The author therefore suggests that this 'permission' need no longer apply, and that festival meals should be cooked before the festival begins.

Rosh Hashanah (New Year)

The blowing of the *shofar* on *Rosh Hashanah* is commanded in Leviticus 23.24 and has become a distinctive part of the service. Traditionally the *shofar* is not blown when *Rosh Hashanah* falls on a Sabbath. However, this is not because the actual blowing of the *shofar* is prohibited but rather to avoid the danger of carrying the *shofar* in the public domain on the Sabbath, which would contravene the laws of Sabbath observance (*Rosh Hashanah* 29b). In Reform synagogues, where the traditional ban on carrying in public has been abandoned, this 'danger' is not regarded as an act that would violate the spirit of the Sabbath. It therefore does not justify the silencing of the *shofar*. Moreover, as some Reform synagogues celebrate one day of *Rosh Hashanah* only, if the date fell on the Sabbath and the *shofar* was omitted, it would deplete the festival of one of its most impressive features. Thus the *shofar* is blown in the normal way whether or not *Rosh Hashanah* occurs on a Sabbath.

The ceremony of *tashlich* ('you shall cast') involves the symbolic casting away of one's sins by emptying the dust of one's pockets into a river or sea (Micah 7.19, *Shabbat* 153a). Additional interpretation is that just as the fate of the fish is uncertain, so is the fate of humanity; or that just as the fish never close their eyes, so is God's watchful care ever present. The rite is performed individually during the afternoon of *Rosh Hashanah*, but is not a widely practised observance. In some Reform synagogues this custom has been revitalised and has become an organised communal act. Members of the synagogue meet at a specific location, cast away their sins and have a short service that might include Psalm 130 and a prayer specifically composed for the occasion, one example of which is[1]:

> As we stand here on the banks of the river we see the waters rushing by. They have a motion of their own and head relentlessly to their destination. Our life is rushing by, although we do not know where it will lead to or when it will end ... We cast out not only our crumbs but also our thoughts for the future. May the New Year come for good – for us, for our families and for those around us. The hurts and wrongs committed last year – by us or against us – may they not be repeated again, and may the thoughtlessness and selfishness that caused them slip away and not return ... May our souls feel cleansed afresh and let us approach the New Year with gladness and with trust.

The *tashlich* is often followed by a study session and communal tea. Part of the new popularity of the ceremony is the informality of the occasion. It is also a rare opportunity to have a service in the open air and be in touch with natural surroundings. (For examination of High Holy Day liturgy see IV.2.)

Yom Kippur (Day of Atonement)

The custom of *kapparot* ('expiation') involves swinging a live cock three times around one's head and reciting a prayer urging that any punishment of the person's sin should fall on the bird instead. It is then killed and given to the poor. The ceremony is never performed in Reform synagogues, being regarded as a primitive and unwholesome rite. However, the principle of giving charity to the poor is strongly encouraged, as is inviting the needy and the lonely to break the fast at one's home. The custom of not wearing leather is left to individuals to decide for themselves. Rabbis wear a *kittel* and although it is rare

---

1 *Tashlich Service* (Maidenhead Synagogue)

for the members of the congregation to do so, it is an option open to all. It is not usual for mass prostration to take place during the afternoon service, as happens in Orthodox synagogues, in emulation of the practice in Temple times. Reform acknowledges the historic importance of the Temple but does not necessarily want to perpetuate the rituals that accompany it.

A tradition that has developed in some Reform synagogues is to have a communal breaking of the fast immediately after the end of *Yom Kippur*. It usually consists of tea and cake. The object is to further the communal spirit by sharing food and greetings together after having spent so many long hours of prayer side by side, particularly as many of those attending are not present at regular synagogue services. It also serves to provide sustenance for those with long journeys home.

Sukkot (Tabernacles)

The *lulav* is not waved in Orthodox synagogues on the Sabbath owing to the ban on carrying in the public domain (*Shulchan Aruch, Orach Hayyim* 658.2). Reform synagogues do not regard this as a criterion for Sabbath observance and hence see no objection to waving a *lulav* on the Sabbath. Congregants are encouraged to obtain their own *lulav* so as to fulfil the *mitzvah* themselves.

Most Reform synagogues erect a *sukkah* on their premises so as to provide an opportunity for those without a *sukkah* of their own to fulfil the *mitzvah* of dwelling in one; it also serves to enhance communal celebration of the festival. In addition, several Reform synagogues have instituted an annual '*sukkah* crawl' during the festival as part of a bid to encourage congregants to build a *sukkah* in their own garden. It consists of an organised tour of different homes and visiting their *sukkot*, with a short study session or activity at each stop, along with light refreshments. Highly enjoyable, the event adds another dimension to the festival as well as serving to educate those unfamiliar with erecting a *sukkah* and enabling them to do so in future years.

The tradition of holding a short *Yizkor* service at the end of the three pilgrim festivals to commemorate the departed is observed in many Reform synagogues. Others, however, do not do so on *Shemini Atzeret/Simchat Torah* or on *Shavuot*. This is partly because the mood of such prayers is considered contrary to the joyous nature of those two festivals, and partly because it is felt that two *Yizkor* services a year, at *Pesach* and at *Yom Kippur*, are sufficient.

Simchat Torah (Rejoicing of the Law)

A novel custom that has developed in a few Reform synagogues is that one of the *Torah* scrolls is unwound completely in the synagogue, with members of the community standing in a large circle to support the different sections. As well as being a joyous celebration of the *Torah*, it also has the educational value of allowing members to hold the scroll and examine it at close quarters, many of whom have never done so before. Women participate in this and in dancing with the scrolls, in keeping with the Reform principle of equality of the sexes. It should be noted that the common assumption that women are not allowed to touch a scroll lest they are menstruating and impurify it, is completely untrue and has no basis in Jewish Law. The sanctity of a scroll is such that it cannot be made impure (*Berachot* 22a).

Pesach (**Passover**)
It is usual not only to abstain from eating *chametz* (leaven products) during *Pesach* but also to remove all *chametz* from one's home (Exodus 12.19). Most householders will prepare for this by running down their stocks of *chametz* products as the festival approaches. The home is thoroughly cleaned before *Pesach* and any unopened *chametz* products might be given away to a local charity or old age home. Special cakes, biscuits, and other foods are bought that are suitable for the festival but it is not considered necessary to obtain specially labelled ('*kosher* for Passover') items that are normally totally free of *chametz* (such as eggs, tea or sugar). These precautions are overzealous in view of the fact that such foods do not contain any grain capable of becoming leaven; in addition, modern production controls mean that the possibility of any *chametz* being accidentally mixed up with them is extremely unlikely. The supervision necessary for the special Passover labels to be issued merely serves as an unnecessary expense to intrinsically suitable items. Some households choose to have separate crockery for Passover; others use their normal set but ensure it is thoroughly clean in readiness for the festival.

Removing all *chametz* sometimes presents great difficulties, such as when one has substantial supplies at home or if *chametz* is used for business purposes. In these instances Reform synagogues do not consider it necessary to sell the *chametz* to a non-Jew for the duration of *Pesach* as is obligatory in Orthodox circles (*Pesachim* 2.1). The practice is regarded as a legal fiction that is entirely inappropriate. A preferred solution for leaven products at home is to put them in a box, seal it and store it in a place where it is away from normal domestic use, eg garage, cellar, attic or garden shed. Many Jews tend to be most aware of *Pesach* at the beginning of the festival because of the *seder* celebration, but it is important to observe the full seven days. The avoidance of eating *chametz* should be consistent throughout the festival and apply not only to home meals but also to lunches at work, school dinners, and social engagements.

A custom pioneered amongst Reform synagogues that has spread to other communities is the holding of a communal *seder* in synagogue, usually on the second evening of *Pesach*. This is not meant to distract from home *sedarim* which are regarded as the best way to celebrate the festival. Instead the communal *seder* is intended for those living by themselves who might not otherwise be able to attend a festive meal, and for those who do not know how to conduct a *seder* themselves but who could learn from the experience and organise their own in future years. The idea has proved very successful, and communal *sedarim* are also held by Orthodox and Liberal synagogues. There is no Reform edition of the *Haggadah* and the traditional version is used. In practice, many Reform households edit the recitation of the text as it is felt to be too long and contains passages that are no longer appropriate. It is likely that a Reform *Haggadah* will be produced in due course. As well as omitting some current passages, it will also contain new material, additional songs, and a revised translation.

Yom Ha'atzma'ut (Israel Independence Day)
Unlike some Orthodox circles who do not recognise the addition of *Yom Ha'atzma'ut* as a new festival, Reform synagogues consider it an accepted part of the Jewish calendar. Local synagogues often join together for a joint *Yom Ha'atzma'ut* service, while a special prayer is recited in each congregation on the preceding Sabbath[1]. It expresses both the miraculous re-emergence of the State of Israel and the hope that it will be a source of peace. It concludes[2]:

> We praise You for the wonders our eyes have seen: the hope that was born out of suffering, the springs that came to the dry sad valley, the rose that blossomed in the desert. In the troubles of our time we have heard the message of Your prophets and seen the fulfilment of Your word. Again You have redeemed us, Lord of truth. Give us courage to complete Your work, and bring redemption to mankind. Amen.

---

1 eg Assembly of Rabbis, 23rd April 1958
2 *Forms of Prayer*, Vol I, p.260

Shavuot (Feast of Weeks)
Shavuot celebrates the time when Israel received the *Torah* on Mount Sinai and when the Jewish people pledged their allegiance to God (Exodus 24.7). Despite its thematic importance, the festival lacks the same popularity as *Pesach* and *Sukkot*, perhaps because it has less ritual associated with it and is not as home-based as the other two. As a way of reinforcing its significance it has been chosen by some Reform synagogues as an appropriate time for children of 15/16 years who have been studying in a post-*bar/batmitzvah* class to make a public demonstration of their commitment to Judaism. They take part or all of the service themselves and might sometimes also introduce additional creative passages, based on the concept of revelation or reflecting the Jewish studies they have undertaken. A separate development is that the tradition of studying Jewish texts throughout the night of *Shavuot* (*Tikkun Leil Shavuot*) has been revived. Many Reform synagogues organise late-night study groups accompanied by refreshments, or hold all-night sessions culminating in breakfast and a dawn morning service.

The book of Ruth contains many themes applicable to the festival quite apart from its harvest background: Ruth's attachment to Naomi and her faith is a symbol of Israel's acceptance of God and the *Torah*; the willingness of Judaism to welcome sincere proselytes; and the religious journey of the non-Jew who enters the community of Israel with the ringing words "your people shall be my people, and your God my God" (Ruth 1.16). The importance of these themes is emphasised in Reform synagogues by using the book of Ruth as the *Haftarah* instead of the traditional readings from Ezekiel and Habbakuk. In Orthodox synagogues Ruth is read at the conclusion of the morning service on the second day of the festival.

The Reform liturgy for *Shavuot* maintains the tradition of including memorial prayers for the departed, although some Reform synagogues do not recite them for the reason mentioned above (see section on *Sukkot*).

2. WHAT IS THE REFORM POLICY ON THE 'SECOND DAYS' OF FESTIVALS?

The Bible clearly states that *Pesach* should last for seven days starting on the fourteenth day of the first month (Leviticus 23.5-6), *Shavuot* for one day on the sixth day of the third month (Leviticus 23.21), *Rosh Hashanah* for one day occurring on the first day of the seventh month (Leviticus 23.24) and

Sukkot for seven days starting on the fifteenth day of the seventh month (Leviticus 23.34). The exact dates of the festivals depended on the declaration of the new month which occurred every twenty-nine or thirty days and was determined by the sighting of the new moon. This would be reported to members of the *Sanhedrin* (the legislative assembly in Jerusalem) which would then officially announce that the new month had begun and authorise publication of the news. The message was spread throughout the country by lighting beacons and sending messengers. However, speedy communication became difficult when Jews settled outside of Israel, such as in Babylon or in Egypt. It was known that the new moon (and hence any festivals that month) could only fall on one of two days. In order to ensure that they observed the festivals on the correct date, an extra day was added to the festivals with the result that *Pesach* became eight days, *Shavuot* two days, *Rosh Hashanah* two days and *Sukkot* eight days (*Betzah* 4b). Those living in the land of Israel still adhered to the time lengths stipulated in the Bible, save for *Rosh Hashanah*, which was given an extra day as it fell on the first day of the month and so it was difficult to publicise its arrival in time even in Israel.

By the middle of the fourth century CE (Common Era) the Rabbis had established a permanent calendar by means of mathematical calculation. The monthly proclamation of the new moon was no longer necessary and was discontinued. (A relic of the original practice is preserved in the ceremony of announcing the coming month in synagogue on the preceding Sabbath)[1]. However, the observance of an extra day for each festival in the Diaspora, and for a second day *Rosh Hashanah* in Israel, was maintained on the grounds that one should "be careful to observe the customs of your ancestors" (*Betzah* 4b). Reform synagogues consider that as the extra day was introduced for specific reasons that are no longer applicable and that as there is no doubt as to the exact occurrence of each festival, it is appropriate to return to the original biblical observance of their length[2]. Thus *Pesach* is kept for seven days and *Shavuot* for one day. *Sukkot* is celebrated for seven days with the result that *Simchat Torah* which follows immediately after *Sukkot* is on the eighth day. This means that *Simchat Torah* is held a day earlier than in Orthodox synagogues, because the latter observe an eighth day *Sukkot* and consequently *Simchat Torah* takes place for them on the ninth day. This is the only occasion when Reform celebrates a festival on a different day from that

---

1 *Forms of Prayer*, Vol I, p.163
2 Assembly of Rabbis, 22nd March 1972

kept in Orthodox synagogues in the Diaspora, although the Reform date for *Simchat Torah* is exactly the same as that observed in Israel. In both the Reform calendar and that kept in Israel, *Simchat Torah* coincides with *Shemini Atzeret*. The latter is a biblical addition to the festival of *Sukkot* (Leviticus 23.36, Numbers 29.35), whereas *Simchat Torah* is a post-*talmudic* addition, and the two have been amalgamated. Many Reform synagogues do observe a second day for *Rosh Hashanah* so as to be in harmony with the practice in modern day Israel; others prefer to follow the Bible and so observe just one day.

3. WHY ARE SOME OF THE FAST DAYS NO LONGER OBSERVED IN REFORM SYNAGOGUES?

The Bible only mentions one fast day that should be observed by all Jews, namely *Yom Kippur*. However, various other fast days arose in the Jewish calendar connected either with historical incidents or religious themes. The tenth of *Tevet* commemorates the day that Nebuchadnezzar, the king of Babylon, laid siege to Jerusalem leading to its eventual conquest and the beginning of the first exile. The seventeenth of *Tammuz* relates to the day when the Babylonians succeeded in breaching the walls of Jerusalem, at which point the fall of the city became inevitable, even though the defenders managed to hold out for another three weeks. Neither of these fasts is observed in Reform synagogues, as both events are only aspects of a much larger catastrophe, the destruction of the Temple in Jerusalem. This is commemorated by *Tishah B'Av* (the Ninth of Av) which includes both the first and second destructions. As *Tishah B'Av* services are observed in Reform synagogues, it is felt that it is not necessary to have any additional fast days. The reunification of Jerusalem in 1967 and the extension of Jewish sovereignty over the city once again has provided further justification for this decision, and has led to calls for the abrogation of the extra fast days in some Orthodox circles too.

Mourning the destruction of the Temple does not imply that Reform Jews would wish to see its restoration. Reform considers that the Temple, the sacrificial cult and the priesthood were valid in their time, but are no longer appropriate for today. The significance of *Tishah B'Av* is that it recognises the enormous Jewish suffering that occurred during both destructions, with loss of life, national subjugation and exile. The fast also marks the major consequences arising from the fall of the Second Temple, both in the course of Jewish history and in terms of religious development. *Tishah B'Av* has also come to commemorate other black events in Jewish history that occurred on the same date, such as the expulsion of the Jews from England (1290) and from Spain (1492). Some Reform synagogues also commemorate the victims of the Holocaust, thereby adding a modern tragedy to those of previous centuries.

The Fast of Gedaliah on the third of *Tishri* marks the assassination of Gedaliah, a Jewish aristocrat who had been appointed Governor of Judea after Nebuchadnezzar's conquest. His benign rule rejuvenated the demoralised people, arousing the fears of the neighbouring Amorite king that Israel would become a threat to him, and so he arranged the death of Gedaliah. The Fast of Esther on the thirteenth of *Adar*, the day before *Purim*, recalls the fast that Esther undertook before approaching King Ahasuerus and putting into action her plan to cause the downfall of Haman. Both fasts are omitted from the Reform calendar, for they are regarded as of little consequence beside the main observances of *Tishah B'Av* and *Purim* respectively.

There are two 'religious fasts' which are limited to specific groups of individuals. On the day before *Pesach* all firstborn are expected to fast in order to remember the deliverance of the Israelite firstborn when the Egyptian firstborn were killed. The author suggests that it is also appropriate to remember the fate of the Egyptian firstborn at whose expense the Israelites finally gained their freedom. This is in keeping with the legend that God rebuked the angels for rejoicing over the death of the Egyptians in the Red Sea because they too are "the work of My hands" (*Megillah* 10b). It is therefore not appropriate to seek ways of avoiding the fast, as is customary in Orthodox circles, by attending a *siyyum* at which eating is obligatory and over-rides the commemoration. Another fast is that of a bride and groom on the day of their wedding until the ceremony. The intention is to emphasise the specialness of the occasion, atone for one's faults prior to that moment, and greet the beginning of a new stage in one's life. Both fasts are regarded as optional in Reform synagogues.

It was also traditional to fast on occasions of misfortune or danger such as during a famine or when a community was threatened by danger. This custom has continued in a different guise in modern times, no longer an act of prayer but a form of protest, as in the case of private and communally sponsored fasts to heighten awareness of the plight of Soviet Jewry, Arab Jewry or other causes.

The decision not to maintain many of the minor fasts means that the traditional ban on holding marriages on those days no longer applies in Reform synagogues. Of course, the fact that the Reform community at large does not observe such fasts does not preclude individual members from adhering to them if they so wish.

4. HOW IS THE HOLOCAUST COMMEMORATED IN REFORM SYNAGOGUES?

The Holocaust was one of the most traumatic events in Jewish history, witnessing the death of six million Jews, a third of the total Jewish population at that time. The appalling loss of life and the destruction of whole communities was rendered even more shocking by the terrible way in which it occurred. The names of the extermination camps – such as Auschwitz, Sobibor, Treblinka – have become etched into the Jewish consciousness as monuments to a time when madness and inhumanity reigned supreme. The thought of killing one out of every three Jews simply because they were Jews is still too horrific to comprehend. Even today, fifty years later, it is difficult to come to terms with the Holocaust or adequately to explain it. The scale of the tragedy necessitates it being commemorated communally and incorporated into the religious calendar.

The actual date on which the victims of the Holocaust are remembered varies in Reform synagogues as it does in the general community because two possible occasions present themselves. Many synagogues observe it during *Tishah B'Av* as:

(a) It too is a '*churban*' (destruction) and it ranks alongside the other shattering events, the first and second destructions of Jerusalem.
(b) *Tishah B'Av* has become a magnet for terrible events in Jewish history in which the Holocaust is yet one more.
(c) The impact of the Holocaust is no different for our generation than the impact of previous tragedies was for those who experienced them.
(d) It serves to invest *Tishah B'Av* with the contemporary relevance which it otherwise lacks.

Other synagogues prefer a different date, partly because *Tishah B'Av* falls at a time when many people are usually away on holiday, while it is also felt that the Holocaust was so unique that it merits a separate day of memorial. Thus they commemorate it on *Yom Ha'Shoah* which was proclaimed by the Knesset in 1951 as Holocaust Remembrance Day in Israel and which occurs on the twenty-seventh of *Nisan*. The date was chosen because it is close to the end of the Warsaw Ghetto Uprising (which started on the first day of *Pesach*) and also because it occurs during the traditional mourning period of the Counting of the *Omer*. The choice of *Yom Ha'Shoah* has the advantage of being in harmony with the practice in Israel today, although some consider that identifying the Holocaust with the ghetto resistance is unrepresentative of the general situation of the victims who were murdered before they realised what was happening or were able to resist.

It was decided initially by the Assembly of Rabbis that *Tishah B'Av* was the most appropriate day for commemorating the Holocaust, although later the growing impact of *Yom Ha'Shoah* was recognised and the choice left to individual congregations[1]. Whichever date is selected, most services begin with the lighting of a memorial candle or, more commonly, of six candles representing the six million Jews who lost their lives. The service usually includes a reading concerning the Holocaust and the experiences of those who suffered in it. A prayer specially composed for the occasion is read[2]:

> We remember our six million dead, who died when madness ruled the world and evil dwelt on earth. We remember those we knew, and those whose very name is lost.
> We mourn for all that died with them; their goodness and their wisdom, which could have saved the world and healed so many wounds. We mourn for the genius and the wit that died, the learning and the laughter that were lost. The world has become a poorer place and our hearts become cold as we think of the splendour that might have been.
> We stand in gratitude for their example of decency and goodness. They are like candles which shine out from the darkness of those years and in their light we know what goodness is – and evil.
> We salute those men and women who were not Jews, who had the

---

1 Assembly of Rabbis, 14th July 1986
2 *Forms of Prayer*, Vol I, p.256

courage to stand outside the mob and suffer with us. They, too, are Your witnesses, a source of hope when we despair.
Because of our people's sufferings, may such times never come again, and may their sacrifice not be in vain. In our daily fight against cruelty and prejudice, against tyranny and persecution, their memory gives us strength and leads us on.
In silence we remember those who sanctified His name on earth.

The service often includes the recitation of the names of family members who died in the Holocaust whilst many Rabbis precede the final memorial prayer with the words "we say *Kaddish* for all those who died in the Holocaust because of their Judaism – both those we knew and those we did not know but who have no-one else left to say *Kaddish* for them". As a parallel form of domestic observance, some Rabbis recommend members of their congregation to light a *yahrzeit* candle in their home at that time.

As well as an annual service, many Reform synagogues have permanent memorials to the victims of the Holocaust such as plaques or sculptures, whilst there is a memorial garden at the Sternberg Centre for Judaism. In addition many have one of 'the Czech scrolls' – 1500 scrolls which were discovered in Prague after the war. They had been collected by the Nazis after the synagogues to which they belonged had been looted and their members deported to extermination camps. The scrolls were brought to Westminster Synagogue, renovated where possible and given to British and other synagogues. Thus they have a new lease of life as well as being testimonies, often the only survivors, of once thriving Jewish communities.

The memory of Jewish communities destroyed in the Holocaust is also kept alive in the Daily and Sabbath prayer book, a novel feature of which is the use of illustrations. Many of these portray synagogues which were burnt down on *Kristallnacht* or which were demolished later by the Nazis[1]. There are also many passages relating to the Holocaust in the High Holy Day prayer book. They occur throughout the *machzor*, but particularly in the *Yom Kippur* Additional Service in the section on martyrdom. Thus amongst the pages of the prayer books of Jews who survived or were born after the Holocaust are constant reminders of those who perished during that terrible period.

---

1 Ibid, pp.78, 211, 254, 306-7

CHAPTER EIGHT

SYNAGOGUE LIFE

*How full of awe is this place;
this is none other than the house
of God, and this is the gate
of heaven.*

Genesis 28.17

1. WHAT ARE THE REQUIREMENTS FOR MEMBERSHIP OF REFORM SYNAGOGUES?

Joining a synagogue is not just a matter of signing a form, but raises many issues concerning status, belief and commitment.

Jewish Status

Only a person with Jewish status – the child of a Jewish mother or converted by a *Beth Din* – can join a synagogue. The membership form for most synagogues contains a statement requiring a signed declaration that the applicant is Jewish. Some synagogues also require documentary proof, such as one's *ketubah* or that of one's parents. Jews who have married a non-Jewish partner are allowed full membership rights. Their non-Jewish spouses are not eligible to be members of the synagogue, although they are welcome to participate in any activities[1]. Membership of a synagogue does not in itself confer Jewish status.

A Jewish couple married in a Registry Office are permitted to become synagogue members without having a religious marriage under a *chuppah*, although that option is available to them should they so desire[2]. Jews who were married in Church are required to reaffirm their Jewish loyalty and identity as a condition of membership[3]. Jews who have been baptized should first appear before the Reform *Beth Din* and officially declare their renunciation of their adopted faith and their desire to return to Judaism[4]. All cases of doubtful status are referred to the Reform *Beth Din* before synagogue membership can be confirmed.

Belief in God

Belief in God is central to Judaism. However, one is not required to profess any particular belief as a condition of membership. Many Jews today are atheists (do not believe in God), agnostics (do not know if there is a God), or unaffiliated theists (believe in God but do not subscribe to organised religion). Nevertheless, they often still consider themselves to be Jews and identify strongly with the Jewish community. They also largely accept many other beliefs of Judaism – the goodness of life, the fellowship of humanity, the ethical imperative – and observe ritual practices. Judaism has always valued personal conduct above purity of faith, and indeed has rarely asked

---

1 Assembly of Rabbis, 1st February 1949
2 Idem
3 Assembly of Rabbis, 1st March 1965
4 eg Assembly of Rabbis, 9th November 1960

Jews to prove themselves by making declarations of belief. Thus the occasion of a *barmitzvah* – the official entry into Jewish adulthood – is marked by one's ability to read from the *Torah* and show understanding of the text rather than by protestations of faith. Moreover, it has always been considered natural rather than sinful to have times of doubt, as did some of the biblical figures, such as Moses (Exodus 4.10-14) and Gideon (Judges 6.36-39). Throughout the ages Rabbis were able to admit that aspects of Judaism perplexed them, but that did not alter their loyalty to Judaism as a whole. It is clearly preferable if one subscribes to belief in God, but one can lead a religious life even if one has certain theological reservations. Even committed atheists can still participate in, and benefit from, communal life, while they may also wish to be associated with a synagogue for the sake of their spouse and children. It is not hypocritical, therefore, to belong to a synagogue in such a position, for one is not required to engage in pretences. In fact, for some people, joining a synagogue is one way of finding out what Judaism stands for and where one can best fit in; for others, belonging to a synagogue and being part of a community is a statement of identity rather than of faith.

Knowledge and Commitment

No requirement is made as to Jewish educational standards as a condition of membership, although those who have little Jewish background are encouraged to take advantage of the facilities provided by adult education classes and the synagogue library[1]. Certain synagogues seek to limit membership to those who will be committed to the community. They inform applicants that they will be expected to participate actively in communal life and attend services regularly, and that to do otherwise would not be welcomed in the congregation. Most synagogues make no such conditions but emphasise that the new members are welcome to be involved in whatever aspects appeal to them. Nearly all Reform synagogues either have a new members' committee or some other mechanism to ensure that they are introduced to, or visited by, members of the synagogue and made to feel part of the community.

Other Issues

Reform synagogues are generally open to all who approach, recognising that few modern Jews believe and practise in exactly the same way. There is a willingness to accept people 'as they are', and for the community to consist of a

---

1 Assembly of Rabbis, 20th January 1988

wide variety of attitudes. This does not preclude a synagogue from representing certain principles, nor from promoting them amongst the members via adult education classes or council policy. Just as there is pluralism within British Jewry at large, so there can be room for individual differences within each synagogue.

Reform synagogues are all autonomous bodies and totally self-supporting. They do not receive funding from the RSGB or any other central source. They depend entirely on the contributions of members to maintain their activities, and this determines the level of the annual subscription. However, no-one is ever refused membership because of their financial circumstances, and all Reform synagogues reduce the subscription for those without means or experiencing difficulties.

In the past a few synagogues included in their constitution the right to refuse certain classes of people. Thus the original statutes of the West London Synagogue excluded usurers and moneylenders from membership, although this no longer applies. It is not the general policy to refuse membership to those with a criminal record unless it is feared that this will be against the interest of members or harm the community. A previous misdemeanour should not necessarily prevent religious activity or acceptance in the Jewish community; on the contrary, it may be an important means of assisting the person's rehabilitation.

2. WHY CAN WOMEN NOW BE ORDAINED AS REFORM RABBIS?

The first woman Rabbi in British Reform was ordained in 1975 by the Leo Baeck College, the seminary for training the Progressive Rabbinate in Britain. Despite certain initial controversy within the Movement, she was appointed as minister to a synagogue and her ordination was accepted by the Assembly of Rabbis[1]. A number of Reform congregations have appointed female Rabbis since then, as have some Liberal synagogues.

Several arguments have been raised against the ordination of female Rabbis, but all can be refuted. The most common objection is that it is not traditional and is a monumental break with Jewish practice. However, there are several examples of women occupying leadership roles in biblical times, such

---

1 Assembly of Rabbis, 17th June 1975

as Miriam and Deborah, with the latter exercising judicial influence over the whole of Israel (Judges 3.5). Queen Athaliah was the sole ruler of the Kingdom of Judah for seven years (II Kings 11.3), while Salome Alexandra reigned alone during the years 76-67 BCE. In later Rabbinic law, women were regarded as exempt from all positive commands that had to be performed at a set time (eg laying *tefillin* or saying the *Shema*). This was because the necessity of looking after the immediate needs of children was deemed of higher importance and allowed to take precedence over religious duties. However, this did not mean women were forbidden from such duties, which they could voluntarily take upon themselves. With regard to one of the main aspects of a Sabbath service, the reading of the *Torah*, the *Talmud* admits that women may read from the scrolls, although adds the rider that this should not be done "because of the honour of the congregation" (*Megillah* 23a). What acted as a disqualification in the fifth century can serve as a justification in the twentieth century. Modern congregations which respect the equal rights and abilities of women see no slight to their honour in having a woman lead the service, and often feel that, on the contrary, it would be an insult to their reputation if they were to deny women such responsibilities. It should also be noted that the function of a Rabbi has changed considerably over the centuries: whereas previously it had primarily a judicial significance, with the authority to give legal pronouncements on all aspects of Jewish life, today it has more of a pastoral and educational role. Both these areas have traditionally been dominated by women who still provide the bulk of the nursing and teaching professions.

Another objection to women Rabbis was that they would be unacceptable to the Orthodox Rabbinate: any divorce documents signed by them as witnesses would be invalid, whilst any conversions authorised by a Reform *Beth Din* of which they were a member would be null and void. However, this ignores the fact that the authority of all Reform Rabbis is denied by the Orthodox authorities and any document issued by a Reform *Beth Din* is automatically regarded as invalid by them. Whether Reform Rabbis are male or female is a secondary issue and completely irrelevant. It is highly unlikely that this situation will change in the foreseeable future, and so it is no reason to prevent the ordination of women. It could also be argued that it would be wrong to let the religious development of the Movement be arrested for the sake of possible political gain.

A further objection was that the ordination of women would split the Reform Movement, cause internal dissension and lead to mass resignations. In the event none of this transpired. Although many congregants found having a woman Rabbi strange at first, a sight and concept that they were not used to, it was admitted that this was the product of habit rather than conviction. Once the novelty had waned, it quickly became apparent that women Rabbis function as well as their male colleagues. They have proved their ability to fulfil all Rabbinic duties to such an extent that it becomes hard to remember why there had been any controversy in the first place. Individual congregants may still have their personal preference for a male or female Rabbi – as much as for an older or younger one, or for a more liberal or more conservative one – but it is clear that in practice the introduction of women Rabbis has been very successful. It can also be said to have been a beneficial move, for the extra insights of women and their different perspectives in certain areas have enriched both the lives of their communities and the development of the Reform Movement as a whole.

With hindsight the ordination of women was merely the logical outcome of the principle of the equality of the sexes. Once women had been granted an equal role in the religious life of the community, there were no rational grounds for preventing them from qualifying for the Rabbinate and occupying positions of religious leadership. On the contrary, there were many positive reasons for encouraging them to do so.

3. ARE SYNAGOGUE FUND-RAISING ACTIVITIES INVOLVING GAMBLING PERMITTED?

Fund-raising appeals for the erection or renovation of synagogue buildings are endemic to British Jewry. Those responsible for such projects often seek novel ways of obtaining donations, including gambling evenings. It has to be admitted that various forms of 'chance' are to be found in the Bible. Thus the High Priest used to draw lots so as to determine which of two goats should be used for the sin offering on *Yom Kippur* (Leviticus 16.8), while Joshua divided up the land of Israel amongst the twelve tribes by lot (Joshua 15). However, apart from the fact that some would suggest that these acts were an expression of the Divine plan, it is clear that they were methods used in order to make an objective decision rather than to lead to personal gain. The widespread custom of spinning *dreidls* at *Chanukah* might be cited as an example of gainful intent, although it is more in the nature of a pedagogic device and the 'gambling' is usually done with matchsticks, raisins or peanuts. Later Rabbinic literature certainly appears to disfavour games of chance, with the integrity of those who play with dice or who back racing-pigeons being called into question

(*Sanhedrin* 3.3). The Rabbinic objection to such gambling is that it is a form of robbery (*Shulchan Aruch, Choshen Mishpat* 370.2). If this definition is accepted, then not only should Jews not participate in any form of gambling, but also the fruits thereof should not be used for any synagogue project.

Another aspect is that addiction to gambling is a vice that currently plagues society and affects the Jewish community too. It can impoverish families, ruin marriages and destroy individual personalities. Everything should be done to combat it, and synagogues should certainly not be seen to encourage it as an official activity, however benign the cause and however carefully supervised. The nature of gambling is also an issue, for it introduces a competitive edge and a possible cause of friction that is out of keeping with the usual feelings of harmony and common purpose that synagogue life tries to foster. Instead of uniting people in shared activity it divides them into winners and losers. As gambling evenings are not the only method of fund-raising, many other methods can be employed with highly successful results.

Individuals are, of course, free to spend their money as they wish providing it abides by the law of the land. There is a difference, however, between that which people choose to do themselves and that which synagogues publicly promote. A case may be made out for the selling of raffle tickets as it is a practice that is specifically associated with charitable functions and does not correspond to the normal methods of gambling. However, the author suggests that casino-style affairs, 'A Night At The Races' evenings and general gambling practices should not be brought into communal life. Some Reform synagogues already have rulings which ban gambling evenings on synagogue premises or for synagogue fund-raising.

4. IS IT APPROPRIATE TO HOLD APPEALS IN SYNAGOGUE ON *KOL NIDREI*?

The custom of holding appeals in synagogue on *Kol Nidrei* is a widespread phenomenon in British Jewry and is particularly associated with pledge cards for the JIA (Joint Israel Appeal) being placed on every seat at United Synagogue services. Other synagogues allow congregations to choose from a range of options including specific charities in Israel, synagogue projects and local charities. In many cases, part of the Rabbi's sermon is devoted to encouraging the community to give as much as they can, or else a member of the synagogue council will speak separately on the need for donations.

There are many arguments for such a practice. The worthiness of the causes is beyond dispute and no-one could challenge the purpose of the appeals. Indeed their intrinsic merit is recognised by the *halachah*, for although transactions regarding business affairs for personal gain are forbidden on the Sabbath, that which is for the communal good is permitted (*Shabbat* 150a). It can also be pointed out that the High Holy Days, and *Yom Kippur* especially, are closely associated with giving to charity. One of the most familiar refrains in the liturgy is that "repentance, prayer and charity avert the evil decree"[1]. It is regarded as hypocritical merely to recite the words without putting them into practice, and so not only are *Kol Nidrei* appeals in keeping with one of the main themes of *Yom Kippur*, but they offer the means to fulfil it and encourage one to translate prayer into action. Moreover, it is well known that synagogue attendance at *Kol Nidrei* is one of the largest during the year, so the launch of any appeal would have much greater impact and is likely to be more successful than on any other occasion. If one believes the designated charities to be of importance, then it is only fitting to ensure that they receive maximum publicity and are supported as generously as possible.

All these arguments are valid, and several Reform synagogues hold *Kol Nidrei* appeals for a variety of causes. However, there is also a strong case for refraining from such appeals on the grounds that *Kol Nidrei* is a time of prayer, of introspection, of deep emotion and of communal togetherness. It has a very special atmosphere which it is inappropriate to disturb with appeals for money, turning people's thoughts away from religion and repentance and on to their bank balance and monthly income. These are the very things which the liturgy encourages them to put out of mind for a few hours and to concentrate instead on higher matters. In addition it is felt that as many in the congregation only attend once or twice a year, they should not be met with financial demands when they do come. Spiritual enlightenment and personal renewal should be the key themes. Instead, the question of having to respond to a pledge card on one's seat is likely to dominate people's minds for most of the service and to distract from the prayers. Moreover, a stereotype sermon on the importance of giving to charity means that a golden opportunity to explore other avenues of Judaism in a challenging way is missed. It should also be noted that giving to charity is not limited to the High Holy Days but is associated with the Sabbath and other festivals. In fact it should be a regular habit that is part of everyday life (see V.1). There are

---

1 *Forms of Prayer*, Vol III, p.226

other occasions, therefore, when appeals can be made and when they will not interfere with and demean such important days in the Jewish calendar. Reform synagogues which subscribe to this view do not hold appeals in synagogue at *Kol Nidrei* but either send out appeals by post shortly before the High Holy Days or have special campaigns at other times during the year. When an emergency arises, such as a major accident or a natural disaster, it is often mentioned at the nearest Sabbath or festival service along with details of how to channel funds to help the situation. However, money or pledges will not be collected at the service itself.

5. WHAT IS THE REFORM ATTITUDE TO JEWISH EDUCATION?

Home

Traditionally, Jewish education begins in the home. Sociological studies show a strong correlation between an educated, open, happy Jewish home and the maintenance of a Jewish lifestyle by the children of such homes when adults themselves[1]. Conversely, a large percentage of those who have no contact with Judaism as adults often received little Jewish awareness at home during their formative years. For this reason it is often said that 'religion is caught rather than taught'. Children are very adept at ascertaining what is central to their parents' lives and what is irrelevant. They also learn through imitation. A combination of these two factors means that the example of Jewish living established by the home will often be the dominant influence in the child's future appreciation of Judaism. This applies to what is actively seen and the extent to which rituals and festivals are observed. It also includes the attitude to such customs and whether the parents view them as tiresome duties, mere habits done for the sake of the children, or a meaningful way of life that is an integral part of their own life. Equally Jewish and equally important are the moral values that are exemplified in the speech and action of parents: honesty, reliability, communal service and many other qualities should be seen and heard. The parents' own level of knowledge should be sufficient to develop their children's Jewish education until adult-

---

1 A M Bayfield, 'Religious Education: Towards A New Approach', *Reform Judaism* (ed Dow Marmur) p.125

hood. It is not sufficient to rely on others to educate one's children Jewishly. Even if parents lack information in certain areas, they should ensure that their home contains plenty of Jewish books through which they can pursue the answer to questions together with their children. Rabbis are always very willing to discuss how parents can best provide a Jewish background at home and further their own Jewish knowledge.

Synagogue
Another crucial aspect to children's Jewish education is participation in Jewish public life, both by attendance at the services and by involvement in the youth clubs and any other social and cultural activities appropriate to their age. It is only in this way that they will see wider Jewish life in action and come to appreciate a sense of community. Moroever, it will allow the children to mix and make friends with their own Jewish peer group. The more familiar the children are with the synagogue, the more they will be at home and regard it as 'their' synagogue, having a sense of belonging and feeling comfortable in it.

Religion School
All Reform synagogues have a religion school. They normally meet on a Sunday morning, with some having additional classes midweek. Their object is to supplement that which children learn at home and at synagogue, rather than to be a substitute for it. They seek to introduce the child, within the constraints of a short once-a-week period, to the widest aspects of Jewish life – learning not only about the biblical period but also modern Jewish history and contemporary events, not only about Jewish ritual practices but also Jewish ethics and moral standards. Religion schools differ in their approach to Hebrew, with some concentrating primarily on reading and comprehension skills suitable for use in services, whilst others include spoken Hebrew and teach it as a modern language. It is recognised that only a limited amount of the vast heritage of Judaism can be covered or retained, but one of the most important goals is inculcating a love of Judaism and a strong Jewish identity. If this is achieved, the children will continue their Jewish education long after they have left formal schooling. Religion schools generally start with classes for five year olds, although some also have groups for younger children. Most have abandoned the previous tendency to end at thirteen years, and they contain post-*bar/batmitzvah* groups, extending Jewish education till the age of fifteen or sixteen. All children of religion school age are contacted by the Rabbi or school secretary so as to ensure their enrolment. It is highly unusual for

members of a Reform community not to send their children to religion school. In cases where children attend boarding school, arrangements are made for correspondence courses during term-time and special classes in the holidays.

Jewish Day Schools

In previous decades Jewish day schools were limited to the Orthodox community, and only to a small percentage amongst it. Such schools were generally regarded unfavourably because it was felt that they were separatist and were a reversal of the emancipation of the Jews into English society which had once been so strenuously fought for. However, there is currently a change of opinion among both Reform synagogues and British Jewry as a whole, with the benefits of Jewish day schools being more widely appreciated. In 1981 the first Reform Jewish day school, Akiva School, was established which caters for the primary school age range, although it intends to develop facilities for secondary education in due course. The possibility of another Reform Jewish day school is being explored at present, a reflection of the success and high reputation enjoyed by the Akiva School.

The move towards Jewish day schools is based on the realisation that, however dedicated the teachers, the religion school system of two or three hours education a week is incapable of instilling sufficient depth or quality of Jewish knowledge. The system may have worked when it included additional classes four or five times a week and received strong parental reinforcement at home, but in today's situation, when both are usually lacking, once-a-week classes are expected to fulfil unrealistic goals. At a Jewish day school, however, Judaism and Hebrew can be taught on a daily basis; through a combination of regular classes and considerably increased time one can attain a degree of Jewish learning that is much more successful. It also has the advantage that Judaism is taken as seriously by the children as are other subjects, rather than being relegated to religion school where it lacks the same status as 'real work'. The change to day school education also reflects a growth in ethnicity; that whereas previously one's Judaism was a spare-time activity and limited to home life, many Jews now regard their Jewish identity as central to them and want it to pervade the whole of their children's lives. The fear that Jewish day schools would divorce children from British life and culture has been overcome by giving it as much attention as would any other school and seeking to maintain high academic standards in general areas of study. Of course there are still many parents today who prefer ordinary schools on principle. Others argue on pragmatic grounds that when one leaves a Jewish school the transfer from a Jewish environment to a general one at university or at work can be so great a shock that it causes a high drop-out rate. According to this view, it is therefore better to be familiar with an integrated lifestyle from childhood in an ordinary school, with one's Jewish consciousness being developed at home and in synagogue. The issue is entirely a matter of personal choice.

General Schools
Most general schools, whether in the private or state system, have a daily or occasional assembly with some form of religious content. Its nature can vary considerably from exclusively Christian worship to songs and prayers acceptable to all faiths. Some parents choose to withdraw their children from the assembly, but the author suggests that this is not obligatory as it can lead to considerable social isolation for the children concerned, whilst assemblies are often used for non-worship purposes including presentations and general information. Potential problems can often be avoided by full discussion with the head-teacher before the child enters the school, and with the form-teachers after enrolment. Many schools will be amenable to exempting Jewish children from confessional situations (such as a carol service or nativity play). If the religious character of the school is so antithetical to Jewish life that parents are concerned at its influence, it may be better if the child is not sent to that school in the first place. Otherwise the child can attend assembly but not participate personally in any prayers. They will not suffer any religious confusion provided parents inform their children about where Judaism differs, and give them a sound Jewish education.

Withdrawal from religious education lessons is not particularly recommended. It does no harm for Jewish children to learn about Christianity, which is the dominant culture and faith of the land, as long as they have a strong Jewish identity from home and synagogue life. Being familiar with the major beliefs and practices of other religions, especially Christianity, should be part of one's general knowledge. Moreover, many schools include multi-faith studies as part of their religious education curriculum. If we encourage non-Jews to learn about Judaism so as to foster greater harmony and understanding, then we must be ready for Jewish children to learn about other religions too. Knowing about them is not the same as believing in them. If, however, the religious education classes are more in the nature of religious indoctrination then, again, the question of the school's appropriateness should be raised.

6. WHAT IS THE REFORM POLICY ON MIXED-FAITH MARRIAGE?

Reform adopts a two-tier approach to mixed-faith marriage: it distinguishes between the phenomenon of mixed-faith marriage and the situation of individuals within them, with a different approach to each aspect.

Reform, like all Jewish groups in Britain, is opposed to the marriage of a Jew to a non-Jew. (It should be noted that this does not refer to a Jew who marries a convert to Judaism for once individuals have converted, they are regarded as fully Jewish.) The reason for this opposition is based on a variety of negative results that arise from outmarriage. First, it leads to a numerical decline in the Jewish population: if the children of such a union have a non-Jewish mother, they are not Jewish, while even if they do have a Jewish mother they might not be brought up Jewish. As the size of British Jewry, and indeed world Jewry, is comparatively small, a substantial rate of mixed-faith marriage would seriously endanger the survival of Judaism itself. Second, even in those families where the children are Jewish and are brought up as such, the divided religious character of the family and the divergent traditions at home can cause a weakening of Jewish education, identity and continuity. Third, mixed-faith marriages can result in marital difficulties, for although some such marriages are highly successful, others feel the strain of the religious and cultural differences between the couple. Many of these problems are not evident initially but surface later on, triggered off in particular by the arrival of children, or by a desire by one partner to return to their religious roots. Whilst a marriage between two Jews is no guarantee of a successful relationship, it does have a better chance of enduring, for the more a couple have in common, the more stable and harmonious the partnership is likely to be.

Reform Rabbis, therefore, are not prepared to officiate at a mixed-faith marriage, give a private blessing to the couple afterwards, or even attend the ceremony, all of which would be condoning the threat it presents to Jewish life and opposing their own principles. It is one of the rules of the Assembly of Rabbis, the professional body to which all British Reform Rabbis belong, that no member shall participate in any mixed-faith wedding ceremony in any way, whatever the circumstances and wherever the venue[1]. As it happens, civil law also precludes the marriage of a Jew and a non-Jew taking place in synagogue. The 1949 Marriage Act, following previous legislation, allows

---

1 Assembly of Rabbis, 11th October 1972, 22nd November 1979

168 FAITH AND PRACTICE

synagogue marriage secretaries only to register "two persons both professing the Jewish faith". As a way of avoiding the problem of mixed-faith marriage in the first place, Reform religion schools endeavour to provide a thorough and meaningful Jewish education (both before and after *bar/batmitzvah*) so as to give young Jewish adults positive reasons for marrying within the faith and continuing its traditions. They also organise youth clubs, student activities, singles' groups and other events that will enable them to meet and socialise with fellow Jews. In addition, parents are reminded of their responsibilities and are told of the different long-term effect on children of homes that are full of warm, vibrant Jewish life, and those devoid of any Jewish atmosphere or commitment.

Despite the adamant stand Reform takes against mixed-faith marriage, it recognises that it does occur and that it is on the increase. The shortfall of expected synagogue marriages of Jews born in the 1950s and 1960s indicates that the alarmingly high figure of approximately one in three of all Jews are marrying out of the faith[1]. The traditional policy of ostracising those who take non-Jewish spouses has failed to have a sufficiently deterrent effect on mixed-faith marriage. Moreover, in the current situation it may even be counter-productive, for it ensures that the Jewish partner feels no inclination to maintain any contact with the Jewish community, and so they and their children are lost to Judaism. A very different attitude has evolved in the Reform community which feels that the present crisis level demands a more positive response, while still disapproving of mixed-faith marriage. This takes two separate forms, depending on the position of the non-Jewish partner: those whose fiancés or spouses are interested in converting to Judaism are encouraged to do so, providing they are sincere and prepared to undergo the usual period of instruction. In this manner what may have started off as a mixed-faith marriage can become a Jewish family, with both partners conversant with Jewish tradition, the home run according to Jewish lifestyle, and any children being brought up in a Jewish environment.

When the non-Jewish spouses are not interested in becoming Jewish, the majority of cases, the problem of a mixed-faith marriage remains. Nevertheless, Reform regards outright rejection of the couple as not only pointless but also a failure to recognise that many Jewish partners still feel very Jewish, wish to remain part of the Jewish community and want to pass on their Jewish heritage to their children. Whereas mixed-faith marriages once

---

1 Waterman and Kosmin, *British Jewry in the Eighties*, p.12

were signs of rebellion against one's Jewish family, now they are often not motivated by any hostility to Judaism. They arise simply because of chance meetings or mutual affinity with non-Jews engaged in similar pursuits at university or at work. Moreover, just because one falls in love with a non-Jewish person, it does not make one any less Jewish. The general attitude adopted is therefore that although Rabbis will not participate in the act of mixed-faith marriage, they may be involved in the rest of the couple's life and encourage them to maintain their Jewish connection as much as possible. In many synagogues the Rabbi will make a point of trying to meet with a mixed-faith couple when they become engaged so as to discuss the options that face them and possible problems that may occur in their personal or family life.

There is, therefore, no objection to the Jewish partner of a mixed-faith marriage becoming a member of a Reform synagogue and many communities make considerable efforts to encourage them to play an active role[1]. As it is considered undesirable to have two classes of membership, there is no bar on them having a *mitzvah* in a synagogue service[2]. The constitutions of Reform synagogues usually state that membership is open only to members of the Jewish faith, and so a non-Jewish partner cannot join the local congregation. However, they are welcome to attend services and synagogue social events (in practice the former is rare but the latter is common). In this way they become more knowledgeable about Jewish life and are more willing to allow their spouse and children to participate in communal affairs. Some synagogues encourage the non-Jewish spouses to attend 'Introduction to Judaism' classes so as to further their Jewish awareness even though they may not wish to adopt the Jewish faith personally. In addition, many Reform Rabbis extend pastoral services to non-Jewish partners of members, such as visiting them when ill or comforting them at times of bereavement.

Children of Jewish mothers are regarded as Jewish and are encouraged to enrol in the religion school and youth clubs. The children of non-Jewish mothers are not regarded as Jewish. Nevertheless, if both parents wish their children to receive a Jewish education, it is permissible for the children to attend religion school subject to the policy of the local synagogue[3]. When this does occur, it is stressed to the parents beforehand that this does not confer

---

1 Assembly of Rabbis, 1st February 1949
2 Assembly of Rabbis, 27th March 1963
3 Assembly of Rabbis, 30th April 1953

170 FAITH AND PRACTICE

Jewish status on the child, although it would facilitate matters if the mother considered conversion for herself and the children at a later date. For the same reasons, parents of a non-Jewish boy are encouraged to arrange a circumcision shortly after the child's birth.

The efforts to reach out to those in mixed-faith marriage in the manner described above are relatively recent. They arise from a seminar held in 1989 at the Sternberg Centre which was the first to cater specifically for such couples. It pioneered both an outreach campaign towards them, and attempts to compile accurate statistical information on their background and lifestyles[1]. Since then it has received the support of the Reform Movement at large[2]:

> This forty-ninth Annual Conference of the Reform Synagogues of Great Britain, without in any way compromising on its *halachic* position with regard to matters of Jewish status, welcomes the initiatives that have been directed towards bringing those in mixed-faith relationships back to Jewish life, promoting Jewish identity and education, and offering appropriate care to Jews and their families. It urges congregations to support their Rabbis in developing this work both regionally and locally.

---

7. ARE 'JEWS FOR JESUS' CONSIDERED JEWISH?

The 'Jews for Jesus' movement is a recent phenomenon arising in the late 1970s, although in character it is merely a modern version of a centuries-old attempt to convert Jews to Christianity. The only difference with 'Jews for Jesus' is that they claim to believe in Jesus while still retaining their Jewish identity. Thus they observe many Jewish practices such as lighting candles to welcome the Sabbath on Friday evening, reciting the *Shema*, wearing a Star of David and supporting the State of Israel. Despite these outer Jewish symbols, their beliefs are totally in conformity with Christian theology and they accept Jesus as their Messiah and Saviour, as well as doctrines concerning the Resurrection of Jesus and Atonement. They harmonise this inconsistency between practice and belief by describing themselves as 'fulfilled Jews', 'completed Jews' or 'Messianic Jews'. It would seem that this terminology, along with their maintenance of Jewish customs, is a way of

---

1 Jonathan Romain, 'How Can A Jew Remain A Jew', *Manna* (Autumn 1989) p.18
2 Resolution passed at RSGB Annual Conference, 22nd June 1990

assuaging their guilt at adopting Christianity, and is designed to reassure themselves that they have not betrayed their Jewish roots and family. By all objective Jewish standards, however, they have adopted beliefs so alien to Judaism that they must be considered to have left the Jewish faith, even if they genuinely believe otherwise. 'Jews for Jesus', therefore, are viewed as Christians.

A difficulty associated with 'Jews for Jesus' is that they place great importance on missionary work and, in particular, persuading other Jews to accept Jesus. Naturally, everyone is free to follow whatever faith they believe in, and indeed to change their faith, but this should be the result of their own free-will and not from any religious coercion. This means that, although 'Jews for Jesus' are as welcome to attend a synagogue service as any other non-Jews, extreme care has to be taken that they do not take advantage of their welcome to distribute leaflets or influence others. This applies especially to young adults and the lonely. The emphasis on mission is also regrettable because of the harm it could do to the enormous progress in religious dialogue between Jews and Christians that has occurred in recent decades. Such dialogue is founded on a willingness to accept the validity of the other's faith, and is undermined by any attempts at conversion. It is important that Christian authorities stem as much as possible the missionary activities of organisations such as 'Jews for Jesus'; for its part, the Jewish community should recognise that 'Jews for Jesus' are a small minority within the Church and it should maintain inter-faith contact with the mainstream bodies.

Jews who have experienced attempts to convert them by 'Jews for Jesus' or other missionary groups have sometimes been overwhelmed by the 'proofs' that they have been given, particularly quotations from biblical texts. However, like statistics, biblical verses can be manipulated to suit one's own argument. Passages that may seem to point to Jesus fulfilling the biblical prophecies, do not mean that he actually was the Messiah. Many people, for instance, have been born in Bethlehem (Micah 5.1) or have ridden into Jerusalem on a donkey (Zechariah 9.9), but that did not mean they brought the Messianic Age closer. The litmus test of the Messiah is that his arrival is accompanied by peace descending on the world and that an era of universal harmony and love begins. This is clearly not the case at present, and so for Jews the Messianic Age has not yet come, and none of those claiming to be the Messiah, including Jesus, can be accepted as such. It should also be noted that, in the Jewish view, the Messiah will not be a divine figure nor an object of worship (see II.2). It is clear that there are substantial differences between the Judaism and Christianity, which is why one cannot be Jewish and Christian at the same time.

The status of a Jew who joins the 'Jews for Jesus' movement is that of any other Jew who adopts another faith, and questions regarding Jewish involvement are dealt with in the same way. Thus if such individuals wish to join a synagogue, they must first re-establish their Jewish status. This is done by renouncing their belief in Jesus, repenting their departure from the Jewish community and declaring anew their acceptance to Judaism. *Tevilah* might also be required. The same condition applies to those wishing to marry in synagogue. Those who do return to the Jewish community are always welcomed and are regarded as resuming their Jewish status rather than as being converts to Judaism. The children of 'Jews for Jesus' are regarded as Christian, whether born before or after their mother joined the movement. Should such children wish to return to Judaism, they too would be required to make a similar renunciation. They may be required to join a conversion course, depending on their age and level of Jewish knowledge.

In the case of the death of a 'Jew for Jesus', burial in a Jewish cemetery might be permissible in certain circumstances. These might include the last wishes of the deceased, or a request by the rest of the family if they would be distressed by a Christian service. It is possible to adopt a compassionate approach in such cases by regarding the person's death as a cancellation of previous faults, or by applying the *talmudic* principle that even though one has sinned, one is still a Jew (*Sanhedrin* 44a). However, in cases where a Jewish funeral might be taken as a sign of condoning a 'Jew for Jesus' and might encourage the movement, permission should be refused and it be advised that the person be buried in accordance with the beliefs by which they had lived.

CHAPTER NINE

STATUS ISSUES

*Where you go, I will go;
and where you lodge, I will lodge;
your people shall be my people and
your God my God.*

Ruth 1.16

1. HOW DOES THE REFORM *BETH DIN* OPERATE?

The Reform *Beth Din* was established formally on 1st February 1948 and since then has served all communities belonging to the RSGB. It has its seat at the Sternberg Centre for Judaism, the headquarters of the RSGB in North London. Before 1948 cases were dealt with by ad hoc courts, usually held at the West London Synagogue or, if from the provinces, at the local congregations. Theoretically the members of a court need only be learned individuals, but over the centuries it has been customary for Rabbis to be chosen. The Reform *Beth Din* follows this traditional pattern in that any sitting of the Court consists of three ordained Rabbis. Unlike the *dayanim* (judges) of some Orthodox courts, they are not permanent paid members, but are congregational Rabbis who serve on court sittings on a rota basis. This has the advantage that instead of being divorced from the realities of communal life, they are thoroughly immersed in everyday affairs and well aware of the backgrounds and problems of applicants. The overall policy on matters which come before the Reform *Beth Din* is laid down by the Assembly of Rabbis which has debated all the *halachic* issues and established general guidelines. This ensures that the decisions reached at different court sittings are consistent with each other, whilst continuity is provided by the presence at each session of the Convener to the Court, a Rabbi who is a salaried official of the RSGB.

The main cases that arise are conversion and divorce. The procedures in both cases follow the traditional requirements, although when there is a range of options possible, as there so often is in Jewish Law, the Reform *Beth Din* usually prefers the compassionate interpretation rather than the severer restrictions. In certain instances, where it is felt that Jewish Law has become arrested and conflicts with ethical considerations, the Reform *Beth Din* takes upon itself the right to amend details of the law so as to remain in keeping with its spirit. Thus when a husband uses the divorce procedures, many of which were introduced to safeguard the rights of women, to blackmail his wife, the Reform *Beth Din* steps in to prevent such a travesty of justice. Adoption cases also arise, as do status queries, by those whose Jewish status is subject to some doubt and needs clarification. The Reform *Beth Din* is available for questions on all other aspects of Jewish Law, as well as for arbitration in cases of disputes of whatever nature between individuals where both parties ask the court to judge a matter. This facility, one of the most common features of a *Beth Din* in previous centuries, has now been largely transferred to civil courts, although it is still occasionally used by those at odds over a specifically Jewish issue. In all cases the Reform *Beth Din* works closely with the Rabbi of the applicant's synagogue. Much of the ground work is done by the local Rabbi (such as the initial interview and tuition courses for conversion, assistance with the legal requirements and paperwork for divorce and adoption) with the final hearing conducted by the Reform *Beth Din*.

The Reform *Beth Din* is intended primarily for members of Reform synagogues, all of whom have a right to use its services. However, it is often approached by those outside the Reform movement, whether belonging to other synagogues or unaffiliated, who find that the policy of the Reform *Beth Din* is more in accord with their lifestyle and attitudes than that of other courts. Help is extended to them too, although they are expected to join their local Reform synagogue, for the Reform *Beth Din* only hears cases of those belonging to constituent congregations. In the case of converts who intend contracting a Jewish marriage, the Jewish partner must be a member of a Reform synagogue before the candidate can be registered with the Reform *Beth Din*. When requests come from individuals who live in areas without any community nearby, the Convener of the Court either deals with all the aspects involved or makes arrangements for the nearest Rabbi to 'foster' the person concerned.

In all its dealings the ethos of the Reform *Beth Din* is to assist in whatever way possible. As its founder, Rabbi Harold Reinhart, declared, "It is a Court to help people", and emphasis is laid not just on fulfilling set procedures but also on the way people are treated. Whilst there are periodic complaints in the Jewish press concerning the rudeness, evasiveness and lengthy delays experienced at other Rabbinic Courts, such accusations are almost never heard regarding the Reform *Beth Din*. Moreover, the procedures themselves are applied as compassionately as possible and allow for special circumstances. This is particularly important in view of the delicate nature of many of the cases, with divorces often being extremely painful, adoptions involving considerable emotion, and conversions being the result of much soul-searching. Individual problems are seen as situations to be catered for, rather than as reasons for disqualification. Thus those with learning difficulties wishing to convert may be given special assistance if they find the course too demanding. Similarly applicants who have not reached the expected level of knowledge owing to learning problems but whose personal sincerity and practical involvement in communal life have proved exemplary, are judged favourably.

Cases of a special nature involving unusual complications are referred to the Standing Committee before they are dealt with by the Reform *Beth Din*. The Standing Committee is a sub-committee of the Assembly of Rabbis, made up of several Rabbis, who discuss such cases in depth and issue recommendations concerning the best way for them to proceed. Such cases might include a request for conversion by someone married to a non-Jew, or when a woman converts and there is a legal impediment to the conversion of her children from a former marriage.

Full records are kept by the Convener of the Reform *Beth Din*, with a file for each individual applicant, minutes of each Court sitting, and a register of all decisions reached by the Reform *Beth Din*. An Annual Report is issued, providing statistics for the different types of cases heard and a breakdown of specific details, such as the religious background of applicants for conversion, that of any Jewish partners involved, and the type of synagogue in which those applying for divorce had been married.

Fees are charged for those using the Reform *Beth Din* for conversion, divorce and adoption, although in cases of hardship the amount is reduced or waived altogether. As even the full fees are not sufficient to maintain the Reform *Beth Din*, it receives financial support from the RSGB.

Since its inception the Reform *Beth Din* has had an ever-growing number of cases to deal with and the number of Court sittings per annum has increased significantly. This partly reflects the expansion in the number of Reform synagogues and the overall membership of the Reform Movement. The large number of cases that also come from members of Orthodox communities testifies to its growing role in serving the religious needs of British Jewry as a whole.

2. WHAT IS THE REFORM ATTITUDE TO CONVERSION?

In biblical times conversion seems to have been a simple matter whereby non-Jews living in the Land of Israel announced their allegiance to Judaism and assimilated into the community. Ruth's famous declaration to Naomi that "your people shall be my people, and your God my God" (Ruth 1.16) signified her adoption of Jewish status. Conversion was common, as is apparent from frequent references to those "that fear the Lord" (Psalm 118.4) and "foreigners that join themselves to the Lord ... to love the name of the Lord ... keep the Sabbath ... and who hold fast to My covenant" (Isaiah 56.6).

Specific rules of procedure emerged in *talmudic* times, although still allowing conversion and making minimal demands as to prior commitment or study: "In our days when a proselyte comes to be converted, we say to him, 'What is your objective? Is it not known to you that the people of Israel are oppressed, despised, exiled and in constant suffering?' If he says 'I know of this and do not have the merit', we accept him immediately and we inform him of some of the lighter precepts and some of the severer ones ... We should not overburden him nor be meticulous with him ... If he accepts, he is circumcised forthwith ... As soon as he is healed, arrangements are made for his immersion" (*Yebamot* 47a). In later times, however, a more negative attitude became the norm, partly because of the penalties imposed by Christian and Muslim rulers on anyone who converted a member of their faith, and partly because of the increasing hostility between Jews and those amongst whom they were living. The reluctance to accept converts is maintained by Orthodox synagogues today who reject the majority of applicants and insist that successful candidates be strictly observant, study for several years and live in a totally Orthodox environment before being accepted.

The Reform policy is to return to the more welcoming attitude of the *Talmud*: "In accordance with Jewish tradition we recognise the right of gentiles who are able to prove their fitness to be accepted into the Jewish community and we desire, in charity, to give such assistance as we can"[1]. No attempt is made to turn Judaism into a missionary religion, but those who voluntarily seek to become Jewish are helped to do so. The normal procedure is to have an initial interview with the local Rabbi who explains the three conditions for conversion[2]. First the person has to show a sincere desire to become Jewish, be willing to subscribe to Jewish beliefs and practices and wish to identify with the Jewish community. In some cases, particularly when a person has little knowledge of Judaism, it is suggested that they attend services and read books on Judaism for a period before proceeding with the requirements for conversion so as to be sure that their decision is based on a firm foundation. Another interview is then held to re-assess the situation. It should be noted that no objection is raised if the person is engaged or married to a Jew. Reform sees it as a positive factor if the prospective convert has the advantage of a Jewish partner who can act as a support and whose family will provide a structure for Jewish involvement and domestic ceremonies. By

---

1 Assembly of Rabbis,1st August 1956
2 *Current Procedures*, p.1

contrast, the "marriage motive" is considered proof of insincerity and grounds for disqualification in many Orthodox circles.

A second condition is that the candidate attains a competent level of Jewish knowledge, sufficient to feel at home in everyday Jewish life, be capable of carrying out its practices, and be able to pass on the Jewish heritage to any children. The course is usually conducted on a weekly basis at the local Reform synagogue and lasts for a minimum of one year. This allows the candidate to experience the full cycle of the calendar whilst under tuition and gives time to cover the general topics. The syllabus includes the beliefs of Judaism, its differences from Christianity, the synagogue service and practice, home rituals and *kashrut*, the Sabbath and festivals, cycle of life ceremonies, the Bible and Rabbinic literature, Jewish history, the ability to read Hebrew and basic comprehension, the nature of anti-semitism, the significance of the Holocaust and Israel. Candidates who have a Jewish father and a non-Jewish mother, and who were brought up Jewish as children but were not formally converted, have their Jewish background taken into account and may be exempted from the full course. The Jewish partners of candidates have to attend the course with them. This is partly to share in the process of the candidate's journey to Judaism and to give active encouragement; and partly to ensure that their own level of knowledge matches up to that which the candidate will attain. The candidate is also expected to experience Jewish life at first hand through attendance at services, participating in home celebrations and becoming involved in communal life.

The third condition is fulfilling the ritual aspects: circumcision is required for males and it is performed by a *mohel* either with a general anaesthetic in hospital or with a local anaesthetic in his surgery. This is in fulfilment of the rite expected of all born Jews since the time of Abraham (Genesis 17.10). If the candidate was circumcised as a child, this is deemed sufficient, whereas Orthodoxy demands a token second circumcision. Both male and female candidates are required to undergo *tevilah*, immersion in free-flowing water, which can take place either at a *mikveh* (a specifically designed pool) or in a river or in the sea. This ceremony was later adopted by the Church as an initiation rite into Christianity, and it became known as baptism. *Tevilah* usually occurs at the end of the course. It is a physical symbol of the change in the person's life, their new identity, and the new lifestyle in which they are immersing themselves. Some have given the interpretation that the *mikveh* represents the waters of the womb and the spiritual re-birth of a proselyte. The ceremony is totally private, and consists of the

STATUS ISSUES *179*

individuals entering the water, immersing themselves and reciting the appropriate blessing. In addition, a Hebrew name is adopted, which will be used for religious purposes, such as when being called up to the Reading of the Law or on Hebrew documents such as a *ketubah*.

When the course and ritual requirements have been completed, the candidate appears before the Reform *Beth Din* and is interviewed by a court of three Rabbis. The object is to ascertain whether the candidates have reached a satisfactory degree of Jewish knowledge and also to ensure that they have a strong commitment to both Judaism and the Jewish community. If accepted, they are accorded Jewish status and welcomed as a member of the Jewish faith. In keeping with Jewish tradition, a person who has converted is regarded as fully Jewish and no different from a born Jew; they should not be referred to or treated in any other way. For this reason, the second part of the Hebrew name adopted is not necessarily *ben/bat Avraham Avinu* (the son/daughter of Abraham our father) as that immediately identifies the individual as someone who has converted. Instead, it may just be *ben/bat Avraham* or using the name of their actual father, particularly if he himself was Jewish. The certificate presented to the convert declares that the person

> ... has appeared before us this day with a request that we should receive him as a convert to Judaism. He states that he makes this request of his own free will and that he will, to the best of his abilities, fulfil the sacred obligations which devolve upon all members of the House of Israel. He promises that any children that he may have will be trained in the Jewish Faith.
>
> Having examined him, we are satisfied as to the standard of his knowledge of the Jewish Religion and as to the sincerity of his motives. We have accordingly acceded to his request, and admitted him as a Proselyte of Righteousness.

Children who are converting to Judaism with their parents are expected to participate in Jewish life themselves, and to gain a Jewish education by attending synagogue and by enrolling in the religion school. They, too, have *tevilah* and, if male, must be circumcised. They appear before the Reform *Beth Din* with their parents and receive a separate certificate in their own right. Following the *Beth Din* appearance, a short ceremony is also held in the convert's own synagogue, acknowledging their place within the local community in particular, and expressing the hope (in the male form of the prayer)[1]:

> May Your image in him be a light for him and for us. May his love for You and Your teachings grow stronger as the years increase.
> May he be a loyal member of the community of Israel, gaining respect for it in the eyes of the world, and so helping mankind to righteousness and truth.

Couples who are already married civilly often choose to have a *chuppah* and thereby add religious vows to their marriage. It must be stressed that the adoption of Judaism should not entail rejection of one's non-Jewish family. It is important that converts are sensitive to the effect that their change of faith has on their relatives and ensure that they do not feel alienated by it. The command to honour one's parents applies as much to converts as to born-Jews. It often happens that when converts lose a parent they recite the *Kaddish* for them and observe their *yahrzeit*.

On average about one hundred adults convert to Judaism each year via the Reform *Beth Din*. The majority are attached to a Jewish partner, whether a fiancé or spouse, although a number convert without having any Jewish partner. There are also instances of both husbands and wives, and whole families, converting together. The effect of this positive attitude to converts has proved to be highly beneficial. Many of the converts have become very involved in their local synagogue, serving on committees, teaching at religion school, joining the synagogue choir and contributing to communal life in other ways. It has to be said, of course, that others have participated rarely after conversion and joined the ranks of the 'once-a-yearers', although it can be argued that they have won the right to act as do most born-Jews and that they still maintain a Jewish home life. It is extremely rare for anyone to abandon synagogue life completely or to renounce their conversion. Conversely there are many examples of those whose conversion was motivated initially by having a Jewish partner who were divorced several years later and who still maintain their Jewish identity and involvement. The impact on the partners of converts has been extremely positive, leading many who had not pursued Jewish learning or involvement after their religion school days to take an active and regular interest in communal life. It also affects the Jewish

---

1 *Forms of Prayer*, Vol I, p.288

partner's family who often adopt a much greater degree of home observance and synagogue attendance because of the need to set a positive example of Jewish life to the convert. On a wider scale the result has been to lessen the threat to Jewish survival posed by the current high rate of mixed-faith marriages. Instead of Jews who have married out of the faith dropping out of the community, they have been able, where appropriate, to bring their spouse into the Jewish fold and to maintain their own Jewish identity and activity. Similarly, it has also assisted Jewish continuity by ensuring that the next generation is born to two Jewish parents, both of whom are versed in Jewish knowledge and are capable of providing a Jewish home environment.

3. WHAT HAPPENS IN THE CONVERSION OF MINORS AND IN CASES OF ADOPTION?

Minors

A minor is defined as a child under 16 years old, corresponding to the civil definition as to when the age of legal responsibility begins. Anyone over 16 years is considered able to convert in their own right and is treated as an adult proselyte.

The vast majority of conversion cases involving a minor concern children whose mother is undergoing conversion. It is expected that any children will convert with the mother so as to unify the family's religious identity. Indeed it is part of the declaration signed by the convert that they will bring up any children in the Jewish faith. There is no conversion course for children, but they are expected to participate in home ceremonies and attend synagogue services. If the children are of religion school age, they should be enrolled in the religion school so as to receive the same Jewish education as that of any Jewish child. Boys must be circumcised, a procedure carried out under anaesthetic (local or general) unless still very young[1]. If the child has been circumcised at birth, no further ceremony is necessary. (Orthodoxy insists upon a second token circumcision.) Both boys and girls should undergo *tevilah* (immersion) which is usually done at the same time as the mother. The children appear before the Reform *Beth Din* with their mother. Although

---

1 *Current Procedures*, p.3

members of the court may ask minors some gentle questions, they are not examined in their own right but are accepted automatically if their mother is accepted. They receive a certificate recording their conversion and participate with their mother in the acceptance ceremony in the local synagogue.

Some cases of minors involve children of a Jewish father and a non-Jewish mother. In these instances the child is not regarded as Jewish, for Reform follows Rabbinic tradition and recognises the matrilineal line of descent whereby Jewish status is dependent on having a Jewish mother[1]. However, if the father has a strong Jewish identity and the mother lacks a religious involvement of her own, it often happens that such children are brought up in the Jewish faith and consider themselves to be Jewish. As far as the mother is concerned, she usually feels sympathetic to Judaism and is willing to have the children brought up as Jewish although, having no religious convictions herself, she feels unable to convert personally. Clearly it is much more desirable if the mother converts and the whole family becomes Jewish, but it is felt that the genuineness of the mother's position and the de facto Jewish identity of the Jewish children has to be recognised. It is better to respond positively and to build on the Jewish commitment that is clearly present than to pursue a rigid policy of rejection that results only in excluding would-be Jews[2]. Moreover, this accords with the policy in *talmudic* times where conversion of minors was facilitated by the Rabbinic Courts on the grounds that it was to the child's benefit (*Ketubot* 11a).

If the parents request that the children be converted in their own right without the mother, the matter is referred to the Standing Committee of the Reform *Beth Din* which deals with special cases. Various conditions have to be met: the mother has to attend a course in Jewish studies, both parents sign a written undertaking that the children will be brought up Jewish, home ceremonies must be in evidence, attendance at synagogue and religion school is expected, *tevilah* is performed and boys are circumcised. If these requirements are satisfied, the Standing Committee will give permission for the case to go to the Reform *Beth Din* and for the formal acceptance of the children into Judaism. If the mother is unwilling to co-operate for whatever reason, the children remain non-Jewish, although they will still be most welcome at services and other synagogue events. If they so wish, they can acquire Jewish status of their own accord after the age of sixteen.

---

1 eg Assembly of Rabbis, 9th November 1960
2 Assembly of Rabbis, 13th July 1983

It should be noted that cases occasionally occur within such mixed-faith marriages where the mother has died and the children are brought up solely by the Jewish father; alternatively the parents have divorced and the children are in the custody of the Jewish father. If the children are being brought up as Jews and given a Jewish education, and providing there are no legal impediments, they too are enabled by the Reform *Beth Din* to convert in their own right in the manner set out above.

Adoption
There has never been any formal procedure concerning adoption in Judaism, even though there have been many instances of couples bringing up someone else's child. The position is that whilst a child might owe much, and feel greater love, towards those who actually maintained and cared for it, its natural parents remain its only official parents. From a legal point of view Judaism has a system of permanent fosterage rather than outright adoption. Children are not regarded as property, and so no transfer of ownership is possible. Nevertheless, great merit is accorded to those who 'adopt' children, and such children have considerable moral obligations to their 'adopted' parents (*Sanhedrin* 19b). The role of a *Beth Din* in such cases merely confirms the Jewish status of the child, not his relationship to his 'adopted' parents which is a matter governed by civil law. All acts of adoption, therefore, have to be arranged via the state. If the child is known to have been born of a Jewish mother, it has full Jewish status. Nevertheless, the adopting parents are recommended to go to the Reform *Beth Din* to present the evidence and obtain a certificate to that effect for future reference[1]. If the child's background is unknown or is definitely not Jewish, then the adopting parents go to the Reform *Beth Din* and sign a declaration that they will bring up the child in the Jewish faith. Circumcision is required for boys, and *tevilah* is necessary for both boys and girls. Providing there is no legal impediment, the child is accepted into the Jewish community by the *Beth Din* and given a certificate pronouncing his Jewish status. Those over the age of 16 who have been adopted by Jews but never had their Jewish status defined are treated as adult proselytes, although their Jewish identity and education is taken into account and the full course may not be necessary.

---

1 *Current Procedures*, p.4

4. WHAT IS THE PROCEDURE FOR A JEWISH DIVORCE IN REFORM SYNAGOGUES, AND WHAT HAPPENS IF ONE PARTNER IS UNABLE TO OBTAIN A *GET* FROM THE OTHER PARTNER?

Judaism regrets the break up of the marital home, but it recognises the right of a couple to separate. It is necessary to obtain a civil divorce in order to satisfy the requirements of the state. As far as Jewish Law is concerned, divorce is a free-will act between the two partners of the marriage. All that is required is their mutual agreement and then a *get* (Jewish document of divorce) is easily obtained from a *Beth Din*. The *Beth Din* does not effect the divorce but serves merely to ensure that it is executed correctly and recorded publicly. The importance of a *get* is that it acknowledges that the religious bond made under a *chuppah* has now terminated and it cancels the effect of the *ketubah*. If a couple have a civil divorce but do not obtain a *get*, they are not divorced in the eyes of Jewish Law, and neither partner is able to remarry in a synagogue. Couples undergoing a civil divorce should apply for a *get* at the same time; Reform Rabbis will urge divorcing congregants to expedite the matter whether or not a future marriage is contemplated.

A *get* is obtained by one party applying to the Reform *Beth Din*, whereupon both parties are sent forms requesting details of the marriage, civil divorce and their consent to a *get*. The details of the case are then presented to the Reform *Beth Din* and heard by a court of three Rabbis. If the couple already have a civil divorce and both consent to a religious divorce, the Reform *Beth Din* authorises a scribe to write out a *get* by hand in the traditional manner and signed by two witnesses. The couple are invited to attend the court, and the husband hands the *get* to the wife. If divorcing couples do not wish to participate in the ceremony, they can appoint agents (arranged by the court) to act in their stead and need not be present. The *gittin* are retained by the Reform *Beth Din*, but certificates of divorce are issued to the two parties[1]. The *get* states that:

> (Names) ....
> In respect of the above parties, a *get* was authorised by means of this *Beth Din* of the Reform Synagogues of Great Britain on this (date) .... corresponding to the (Hebrew date) .... and duly executed.
>
> The above mentioned parties are free to remarry in our synagogues.

---

1 *Current Procedures*, p.6

Occasionally one of the partners refuses to consent to a *get* even though they have already undergone a civil divorce. This is sometimes done in order to hurt the other partner and to prevent the person from remarrying in synagogue; alternatively it is designed to pressurise the other partner into agreeing to changes in the divorce settlement concerning finances or custody of the children. Thus the original intention of Jewish Law – to protect the rights of both partners – is frustrated by attempts at malice or bribery. However, an Orthodox *Beth Din* is unable to intervene in such instances because it lacks any power to compel the partner to consent to the *get* or to enact the *get* on its own authority. All it can do is seek to persuade the recalcitrant partner by reasoned argument. If that fails, then no *get* can be obtained and the innocent partner is doomed to remain single or forced to marry outside Jewish auspices. In certain limited situations, an Orthodox *Beth Din* will permit a husband to divorce his wife without her consent, whereas a husband can never be divorced unwillingly. The Reform *Beth Din* regards such an impasse as deeply unfair to the innocent partner and contrary to the spirit of Jewish Law. This is particularly so when a civil divorce has already been obtained and the couple are patently not living together as man and wife and may not have been for many years, in which case a recalcitrant former partner has little moral justification for withholding consent. The Reform *Beth Din*, too, tries to persuade recalcitrant partners that they should give their consent. If all efforts fail, however, the Reform *Beth Din* takes upon itself the power to act and to award a *get* if the couple are already divorced civilly. The injustice of the situation is sufficient grounds for the Reform *Beth Din* to take an active role and impose a solution.

A similar problem can occur if a couple divorced each other civilly several years ago without obtaining a *get* and have now lost contact with each other. When one former partner wishes to remarry in synagogue, he/she is unable to obtain the other person's consent for a *get* as their ex-partner's whereabouts are not known. If the Orthodox authorities are unable to locate the missing spouse, no *get* can proceed and no marriage be sanctioned. The Reform *Beth Din* also attempts to find the missing person. However, if this proves impossible, once again the Reform *Beth Din* will assume responsibility for a decision rather than leave the matter in abeyance. It will authorise a *get* if the former partner cannot be found despite all reasonable efforts.

It may also be the case that one former partner has been certified as insane. According to Jewish Law those who are insane are not regarded as responsible and cannot make any decision of legal standing. Consequently they are unable to consent to a *get* even though this prevents the other partner from establishing a new life for themselves. The Reform *Beth Din* considers it vital to remedy the situation and is prepared to intervene. It is of the opinion that if the insane cannot make a responsible decision, they should not be allowed to block the future happiness of others. The Reform *Beth Din* therefore awards a *get* on behalf of the insane person.

Another problem can occur if one of the partners goes missing and is presumed but not proved dead, for example in a sea or air accident, or in a battle. Even though civil authorities may certify that the person is dead, an Orthodox *Beth Din* often requires greater verification of death, such as an actual witness. This is particularly in the case of a woman whose husband is missing, lest the presumption proves false and the wife's remarriage turns out to be a bigamous union and any children from it are deemed *mamzerim* (illegitimate). If no such certificate is available, the woman is an *agunah* (a chained woman) who is still married to an absent husband and unable to remarry. The Reform *Beth Din*, however, is prepared to accept documents that point to the likelihood of death. It considers certificates of presumption of death by the civil authorities sufficient proof to release the other partner from the marriage.

In all such cases, where the free-will nature of a *get* becomes an obstacle and the cause of unjustified distress, the Reform *Beth Din* takes steps to intervene and make a judgement on its own authority. Whilst these powers are a departure from previous practices, there is precedent in cases where a *Beth Din* in the past assumed responsibility for the education of an orphaned minor or acted in the best interests of an adult woman. The main justification, though, is that such action is necessary to resolve an unintentional injustice in Jewish Law and to rescue all those whose lives would otherwise be blighted by it[1]. The concern of the Orthodox courts is that such steps might lead to second marriages that count theoretically as adultery and so render any children as *mamzerim*. Quite apart from the fact that the Reform have abolished the concept of *mamzerut* (see IX.6), it is felt that if there are major flaws in divorce procedures, it is only right that they should be admitted and remedied. Not to do so would be a much greater disservice to Judaism.

The special divorces awarded by the Reform *Beth Din*, like all of its decisions, are not recognised as valid by the Orthodox authorities, a fact that is pointed out to the recipient at the time. However, it should be noted that no

---

1 Michael Curtis, 'The *Beth Din* of the Reform Synagogues of Great Britain', *Reform Judaism* (ed Dow Marmur) pp.130,135

resolution of such cases would be possible via the Orthodox authorities, and so none of the partners would be able to remarry in an Orthodox synagogue anyway. There is therefore little practical disadvantage involved for those concerned in turning to the Reform *Beth Din*, whilst there is every moral justification in so doing.

5. ARE REFORM CONVERSIONS AND DIVORCES RECOGNISED BY OTHER JEWISH AUTHORITIES?

The traditional requirements for conversion are as follows: sincerity of motive, a warning of the risks and responsibilities involved in being Jewish, study of Judaism, circumcision for males, ritual immersion for both sexes, appearance before a Rabbinic court and acceptance of the obligations of Judaism (*Yebamot* 46-47). All of these requirements are fulfilled by candidates before they are accorded Jewish status by the Reform *Beth Din*. As a result both the Conservative and Liberal movements in Britain and abroad recognise the conversions of the Reform *Beth Din*. They permit its converts to become members of their congregations, accept their children as Jewish and regard them as eligible to marry in synagogue.

Orthodox authorities, however, do not accept Reform conversion. This is because they believe all changes of status can only be supervised by a *Beth Din* consisting of three Rabbis who are fully observant according to the *halachah*. As the Reform Movement does not uphold all aspects of the *halachah*, Orthodoxy does not recognise Reform Rabbis as Rabbis and does not regard the Reform *Beth Din* as constituting a valid *Beth Din*. In their view all decisions of the Reform *Beth Din* are null and void, and so its conversions are invalid. Strictly speaking, therefore, it is not that the Orthodox do not accept individual Reform converts, but that they do not accept the authority of the Reform Rabbis who converted them. As far as they are concerned, any such convert may apply instead to an Orthodox *Beth Din* for a conversion under their auspices and gain Jewish status from it. In practice, however, the Orthodox authorities in Britain discourage conversion and it is an extremely difficult and long procedure for the few who are successful. For its part, Reform recognise anyone converted by an accredited *Beth Din* and so accepts both Orthodox and Liberal converts[1].

---

1 eg Assembly of Rabbis, 10th July 1957

188 FAITH AND PRACTICE

The refusal of the Orthodox to recognise Reform conversions is a sad reflection on the disunity and intolerance that exists in certain aspects of Jewish life today. It means that a Reform convert can never be a member of an Orthodox synagogue. Moreover, the children of a mother who had a Reform conversion are not regarded as Jewish by them and will be barred from attending an Orthodox Jewish day school or marrying in an Orthodox synagogue. Nevertheless, there are sufficient Reform and other non-Orthodox synagogues throughout the country to ensure that most areas have a community into which the convert and any children will be accepted and welcomed. In addition, anyone wishing to convert will obviously choose that branch of Judaism which most corresponds to their own outlook. As the approach to Judaism of Orthodoxy and Reform is so very different, the convert will feel drawn naturally to one of them and will be concerned primarily with its expression of Judaism rather than with the attitude of the other groups to it. It should be noted that all prospective converts are informed of the situation at their first interview with a Reform Rabbi and the matter is set out again by the Reform *Beth Din*.

A further aspect of the issue is the situation in Israel. Under the current Law of Return, any Jew automatically has the right to settle in Israel. A Jew is defined as one who is born of a Jewish mother or converted by a Jewish authority. This includes the RSGB *Beth Din* and thus Reform converts are included in the Law of Return. However, since the establishment of the State, all religious affairs have been controlled by the religious parties who, being Orthodox, do not accept Reform conversion. Thus a Reform convert can acquire Israeli citizenship but cannot be married in Israel, nor can the children of a woman converted by the Reform. As there is no civil marriage in Israel at present, they have to hold the wedding abroad. On their return to Israel, the marriage is recognised by the civil authorities, although not the religious ones. It is quite possible that this situation may change in future years, either because the Law of Return may be revised to exclude Reform conversion or because Reform marriages (or civil marriages followed by a Reform ceremony) may be permitted in Israel.

In Britain the status of Reform divorces is exactly the same as that of Reform conversions: they are accepted by other non-Orthodox synagogues, but the Orthodox view them as having no standing in Jewish Law because the authority of the Reform Rabbis is not recognised, and so neither is that of the Reform *Beth Din*. Thus individuals who received a Reform *get* (divorce) would still be seen by the Orthodox as married to their former spouse. They would therefore be unable to remarry in an Orthodox synagogue until a *get* had been issued by authorities acceptable to them. In view of these difficulties, members of Reform synagogues who are undergoing a divorce and might wish to remarry in an Orthodox synagogue are advised that it might be in their interest to obtain a *get* from an Orthodox *Beth Din*. There is a particular complication with a woman who has obtained a Reform *get*, remarried and had children by her second husband. As her Reform *get* is regarded as invalid by the Orthodox, the second marriage is seen as bigamous and any children arising from it are *mamzerim* (illegitimate) in Orthodox eyes. They hold that such children are unable to marry any other Jew, save fellow *mamzerim*. In Israel a divorced person with a Reform *get* could not remarry at all, as all marriages are under Orthodox control at present. Those concerned would have to obtain an Orthodox *get* if they wished to marry in Israel. If the second wedding was conducted abroad, it would not be recognised by the religious authorities in Israel, who would impose the same restrictions on any children of the second marriage, although it would be valid in the eyes of the civil authorities. Although Reform divorces are not accepted by Orthodox authorities, Reform marriages are recognised as valid by them providing there are no status queries regarding the partners (see III.4).

Despite the above complications, most people obtaining a Reform *get* then remarry in Reform synagogues. Thus in practice they themselves face no difficulties, while any children of the second marriage are eligible to marry in all Reform and Liberal synagogues and so need not experience any impediment either.

---

6. WHY HAS THE CATEGORY OF A *MAMZER* BEEN ABOLISHED IN REFORM SYNAGOGUES?

A *mamzer* is someone who is born illegitimate. This does not mean, as it does in English Law, someone whose parents are not married. In Jewish Law a *mamzer* is the offspring of a forbidden relationship – a marriage that could not take place because the mother was not free, or permitted, to marry the father of the child (*Kiddushin* 3.12). This would include an incestuous relationship, such as the union between a brother and sister, or an adulterous relationship between a man and a woman who was at that time married to another man. It does not include a Jewess who is married to a non-Jew, nor does it apply to two single Jews who are living together without being married. Technically, it also does not apply to the child of a married man and a single woman because originally Judaism permitted polygamy, although this has long been abandoned by most Jewish communities. A child, male or female, who is a *mamzer* is considered fully Jewish and can participate in communal life except that a *mamzer* is unable to marry another Jew "for ten generations" (Deuteronomy 23.3); this has been interpreted to mean "for all time" (*Yebamot* 8.3). A *mamzer* may only marry another *mamzer* or a proselyte; in these cases a synagogue wedding is permissible. However, their children would also be *mamzerim* and subject to the same marital restrictions.

The severity of this law was designed to discourage incest, adultery and other forbidden relationships. However, it means that the children from such unions suffer for a fault that was not of their own making. It also seems to contradict the statement a few verses later in the Bible that children should not be held responsible for the sins of their parents (Deuteronomy 24.16) and Ezekiel's declaration that every person is liable only for their own crime and not for those of others (Ezekiel 18.20). It can further be objected that the permission to marry a proselyte casts doubt on the equality of converts and undermines the rule that once accepted, converts are to be treated exactly the same as born-Jews (*Baba Metzia* 4.10). *Mamzerut* can be described as the Jewish equivalent of a caste system.

The offensive nature of the laws of *mamzerut* is evidenced in the numerous attempts by Orthodox authorities to circumvent the law whenever possible and to exempt particular individuals from the taint of such status. There are also numerous reports that in the past some Rabbis would advise a *mamzer* to move to an area where they were not known and thereby 'lose' their status as a *mamzer*. However, these were only partial solutions; they ignored the roots of the problem and, in any case, not all authorities were so lenient. In recent times, rather than replacing the laws of *mamzerut*, some Orthodox authorities have adopted a more rigorous attitude and have spoken of establishing a register of *mamzerim* to prevent any breaches of Jewish Law.

It is clear that whilst the intention behind the concept of *mamzerut* was to combat immorality, its effect was to create another immoral situation. Reform considers that the status of a *mamzer* is so unfair to the children concerned and so out of keeping with the ethics of Judaism that it should be abolished. The Reform *Beth Din* refuses to hear evidence of *mamzerut* and in this way effectively negates any of its possible repercussions. Whatever value it may have had in previous ages, it is no longer appropriate for Jewish life today. Thus while forbidden unions are condemned and adultery is deplored, any children resulting are not stigmatised and do not have special status; nor are there any bars concerning whom they may marry in synagogue[1]. The term *mamzer* is not applied to anyone today by the Reform and it is regarded as a category with historical meaning only.

7. WHY HAS THE POSITION OF A *COHEN* BEEN ABOLISHED IN REFORM SYNAGOGUES?

The role of a *cohen* (priest) was limited to members of the family of Aaron (Exodus 28.1). The priests were the only people able to perform the sacrifices and were in charge of cultic functions. They were assisted by the Levites, other families from the tribe of Levi, who were responsible administratively for the general running of the Tabernacle in the wilderness and later the Temple in Jerusalem (Numbers 3.5-9). Their role lasted until the destruction of the Second Temple in 70 CE, whereupon sacrifices ceased and the main duties of priests and Levites disappeared. Certain minor functions still remained, such as *duchaning* (reciting the priestly blessing from Numbers 6.24-6) which is done during the *Amidah* either at every Sabbath service (in the *Sephardi* tradition and in Israel) or during festival services (in the *Ashkenazi* tradition). A *cohen* is also involved in the ceremony of *pidyon ha'ben* (redemption of the firstborn) according to the procedure described in Numbers 3.44-51. In addition, the *cohen* is given the honour of being called up first to the reading of the *Torah* (*Gittin* 5.8). However, all the restrictions incumbent upon a *cohen* in Temple times remained in force: they were not allowed to be near a dead body, unless a member of their immediate family, and so are limited to certain areas of the cemetery when attending a funeral (Leviticus 21.1-3); they were also forbidden to marry various categories of women, including a divorced woman (Leviticus 21.7) or a proselyte (*Kiddushin* 4.7). These regulations are still maintained in Orthodox synagogues today.

Reform no longer recognises the special role or restrictions regarding a *cohen* and has abolished the categorisation of Jews into Priests, Levites and

---

1 Michael Curtis, 'The *Beth Din* of the Reform Synagogues of Great Britain', *Reform Judaism* (ed Dow Marmur) p.135

Israelites[1]. It has done so for a variety of reasons. First, the role of *cohen* was primarily based upon the sacrificial cult which no longer exists and has not done so for nearly 2000 years. Orthodoxy still looks forward to, and prays for, the day when the Temple will be restored and sacrifices renewed; Reform regards it as neither likely nor desirable. The concept of priesthood is therefore regarded as redundant. Moreover, it is noticeable that although the notion of priesthood was maintained in Judaism after the fall of the Temple, the religious leadership passed to the Rabbis and scholars; thus even within Orthodoxy the religious primacy of priests was abolished. Secondly, the division of Jews into Priests, Levites and Israelites may have had a significance in the past, but today merely resembles a hereditary class system and carries distasteful associations. Thus the privilege of priesthood and its higher degree of purity is accorded by birth rather than by merit, no account is taken of either moral character or level of scholarship, and it deviates from the otherwise democratic nature of Judaism. Thirdly, there is serious doubt as to whether anyone claiming to be a *cohen* is actually a *cohen* and descended from the priestly stock. As no genealogical tables have been kept, there is no record of whether a person's line is from the original family of Aaron save personal memory and the surname Cohen, both of which have limited validity. Even as far back as the second century there was concern over the proven pedigree of someone claiming to be a priest (*Kiddushin* 4.5). In the absence of definite proof since then, many Orthodox authorities describe modern priests as 'presumed priests' (Maimonides, *Yad, Issurei Bi'ah* 20.1-2) and rule that they should not keep the monies given to them during the *pidyon ha'ben* ceremony but return it to the father as they may not be priests and therefore have no right to it (Jacob Emden, *She'elot Ya'abets*, Part 1 Responsum 155). Fourthly, whatever importance it had in the past, being a *cohen* can often be a disadvantage today, particularly if one wishes to marry someone who is a divorcee or proselyte, a situation that is not uncommon and which is strictly forbidden according to Orthodox law. The benefit of being eligible for the first call-up to the reading of the *Torah* is more than outweighed by the penalty of not being able to marry the person one loves. Fifthly, the loss of the position of Levites is of little consequence as their sole role today is to wash the hands of the *cohen* before the latter recites the priestly blessing over the congregation. Their only privilege is to be called up second to the *Torah*.

---

1 Michael Curtis, 'The *Beth Din* of the Reform Synagogues of Great Britain', *Reform Judaism* (ed Dow Marmur) p.135

In Reform synagogues, therefore, all Jews are considered equal and no distinctions are made as to lineage. Many of those from 'presumed' priestly families have relinquished the title *'ha'cohen'* as part of their Hebrew name, although some retain it for sentimental reasons. They may attend a funeral in the same way as any other Jew, and they face no bar on marrying a convert or divorcee. The few surviving roles of priests have been re-allocated as follows: the ceremony of *pidyon ha'ben* is no longer maintained in Reform synagogues and so no substitute for the priest is necessary; those called to the reading of the *Torah* are chosen according to other criteria such as honouring a member of the community, welcoming a guest or acknowledging someone's *yahrzeit*, birthday or wedding anniversary; while the priestly blessing is given by the Rabbi or person leading the prayers, usually at the end of the service. It should be remembered that the blessing, although given originally by the priests, was not their personal blessing but invoked God's blessing upon the community. Indeed, even in the most traditional circles, parents use exactly the same words when blessing their children on the Sabbath. It is thus equally appropriate for others also to invoke God's blessing during services.

8. IS REFORM CAUSING A SPLIT IN THE JEWISH WORLD BY ITS STATUS POLICIES?

Much of the criticism levelled against Reform by Orthodox circles centres upon status issues and the problems to which they can lead. However, as will be seen below, these problems existed in Judaism long before the Reform Movement began and are merely highlighted by Reform policy rather than caused by them.

The changes in Reform services, Sabbath observance and daily practices are matters of which Orthodoxy disapproves but which do not affect them; they only involve the individuals concerned and their own religiosity. Status issues are more controversial, for in Orthodox eyes they may prevent one Jew marrying another. The root of the problem rests in the Reform *Beth Din*. As it is not recognised as a competent Jewish authority by the Orthodox (see IX.5), any decisions made by it are regarded as invalid and are not recognised. Thus in their eyes a Reform convert still has the status of being non-Jewish and is unable to marry a Jew; moreover, if the convert is a woman, any children arising will also lack Jewish status. Similarly, divorces issued by the Reform *Beth Din* are considered invalid, with the result that a woman is regarded as still being married to her original husband, any second marriage is bigamous and any children of that union are *mamzerim* and they have the terrible burden of themselves being unable to marry most other Jews. The Reform abolition of the category of the *mamzer* and the permission for them to marry fellow Jews compounds the problem in Orthodox eyes, as not only are their children also counted as *mamzerim* but it becomes impossible to know who may be descended from a *mamzer* and have inherited such status themselves. Thus it can be claimed that a shadow is cast over all Reform Jews and that they may either not be Jews at all, or they are Jewish but not eligible to marry other Jews. Theoretically, therefore, an Orthodox Jew has to be very wary of marrying a Reform Jew, and in the absence of genealogical records the two groups may be prevented from marrying. In the most pessimistic scenario the danger arises that there will not only be an ideological divide between Orthodoxy and Reform but the emergence of two entirely separate Jewish people.

Despite the genuineness of this problem, there are many important ancillary factors that have to be taken into account, while a solution to some of the problems is possible.

First it has to be stated that Reform has great regard for the concept of *k'lal Yisrael* (the unity of Israel) which regards Jews as one indivisible people with common roots, a shared history, mutual responsibility for each other and a future in which the fate of one Jew will be linked inextricably with that of all Jews. For this reason Reform has always adhered to traditional forms of Judaism as far as possible and has only deviated from it when matters of conscience dictated otherwise. Thus the requirements for both conversion and divorce are followed while the structure of a *Beth Din* with three Rabbis is maintained. Certain aspects that were omitted by Reform originally, such as *tevilah* (immersion) for proselytes, were later re-introduced so as to abide by the practice of Jewish communities worldwide and to preserve the unity of the Jewish people[1]. Full support has always been given to the Orthodox authorities whenever external events pose a threat to Jewish practices, such as the public defence of *kashrut* against attempts in 1987 to introduce legislation in Parliament to limit it. Irrespective of whether the majority of Reform Jews subscribe to *kashrut* in every detail, it was felt that those Jews who did observe *kashrut* must have the right to continue to do so.

However, whilst the concept of *k'lal Yisrael* is highly valued both in

---

1 Assembly of Rabbis, 10th March 1976, 2nd March 1977

theory and practice, it has limitations. Unity need not mean uniformity. Moreover, it cannot be allowed to mask injustices that emerge in Jewish life or abrogate the responsibility to rectify them. Thus it is clearly wrong for a man who has divorced his wife civilly to be able to refuse to divorce her religiously, withhold his consent for a *get* and thereby prevent her from ever marrying another Jew in synagogue. The failure of the Orthodox authorities to remedy this unethical situation has forced Reform to take steps of its own (see IX.4). Similarly unacceptable is the plight of a woman whose husband is assumed to be dead and is recognised as a widow by civil law, yet who is classified as an *agunah* and refused permission to remarry by the Orthodox authorities because there was no witness to his actual moment of death. Here, too, the failure to develop Jewish Law in this respect impels Reform to do so. Equally horrendous is the position of *mamzerim*, innocent children burdened for life with a social stigma and severely limited as to whom they may marry. The decision of the Reform to abolish the category (see IX.6) is motivated by a belief that laws that have lost their validity may be changed, and that in cases where they conflict with Jewish ethics they must be changed. The fact that such changes will arouse Orthodox opposition is regrettable, but it cannot be a reason for perpetuating unethical laws or be allowed to prevent the pursuit of justice. Moreover, it can be asserted forcibly that Orthodoxy bears a grave responsibility for tolerating such ills for so long and for not taking steps within the *halachic* process to ameliorate them. The oft-quoted defence that they sympathise with the individuals concerned but cannot change the overall situation is pusillanimous, for every individual in distress deserves not only sympathy but practical help. In addition, it is open to challenge in view of the radical changes that have been made to all other aspects of Jewish Law that were found unworkable or undesirable, such as the effective abolition of the death penalty, of the ban on charging interest from a fellow Jew, and of the laws concerning loans during the Sabbatical Year.

It should be noted, of course, that similar instances of marital problems between Jews have occurred in the past, as with members of the Samaritan community or the Karaites. In the wider perspective of the history of other religions, there are countless instances of a faith developing different denominations who refuse to marry each other – or even fought wars against each other. Thus although the Orthodox–Reform divide is a disturbing problem, it is not unique in either Judaism or religious history in general. It reflects the power of religious rivalry and the inability to put the common worship of

God and the fellowship of humanity above doctrinal considerations.

Amid all the attention devoted to the problems over Orthodox–Reform status questions, it is often forgotten that there are various solutions. Two possibilities exist: the first assumes that both movements maintain their current procedures. If an Orthodox and Reform Jew wish to marry in a Reform synagogue, no objections are raised by the Reform authorities and the marriage can take place unhindered. If the couple wish to marry in an Orthodox synagogue, there is no problem if the Reform Jew can prove that there is no doubt as regards Jewish status – a situation which applies to the vast majority of Reform Jews in Britain – in which case the marriage can proceed. If a Reform Jew is a Reform convert or descended from a Reform female convert, the Orthodox will refuse to recognise the conversion; the person can either attempt to undergo an Orthodox conversion or the couple can marry in a Reform synagogue. If the Reform Jew is a *mamzer* by dint of being the child of an adulterous union, no remedy is possible vis-à-vis Orthodox synagogues although the same difficulties would exist if it was the Orthodox Jew who was the *mamzer* and irrespective of the existence of Reform congregations. Moreover, the option of a Reform marriage still remains. However, if a Reform Jew is a *mamzer* in Orthodox eyes because the person's mother had remarried with a Reform *get* and then had children in a bigamous union, there is a solution although it may be distasteful to many: several Orthodox Rabbis in the United States, including the late Moshe Feinstein, have declared that if the first marriage was Reform, then it lacked suitable witnesses (as those present did not qualify as witnesses because it is presumed that they did not maintain Orthodox standards of Sabbath observance); therefore it was an invalid marriage and hence did not need a *get*; thus the second marriage was not bigamous nor the children *mamzerim*. Whilst some of these procedures may involve the embarrassment of having to prove one's Jewishness in Orthodox eyes, the end result will ensure that in nearly all cases there will be no bar to the marriage of a Reform Jew in an Orthodox synagogue.

The second possibility would be for Orthodox and Reform Rabbis to seek ways of working together to put an end to the difficulties over status. They could meet together and draw up common procedures in status matters that will allow recognition of each other's decisions. Alternatively, one unified Rabbinic Court could be established that will deal with cases from both groups according to mutually agreed regulations. Both of these might entail certain compromises by each group, although without sacrificing their own principles. Thus Orthodoxy could widen the scope of certain definitions to allow for a more flexible approach to conversion and divorce, whilst Reform could adopt stricter guidelines. Examples of such co-operation between Orthodox and Reform, such as nineteenth century Hungary, pre-war Germany or certain parts of the United States today, indicate that such attempts can be successful if sufficient will exists. British Reform Rabbis have often expressed a similar desire. It has to be admitted, however, that in the current climate of hostility, in which Orthodox Rabbis are unwilling even to sit on the same panel as Reform Rabbis let alone discuss joint policies, positive developments seem unlikely at present.

It is true, therefore, that a major problem over status questions does exist and there remains the difficulty of defining 'Who is a Jew' to the satisfaction of everyone. However, its effects can be very limited in practice, with some solutions available now, and even better solutions possible in the future if the Rabbinate wills it. For its part, Reform has a strong notion of Jewish peoplehood which embraces all Jews, and sees them as part of the same one people.

CHAPTER TEN

ISRAEL

*If I forget you, O Jerusalem,
Let my right hand lose its cunning.
Let my tongue stick to the roof of my mouth,
if I do not remember you,
if I do not put Jerusalem above my highest joy.*

Psalm 137.5-6

1. WHAT IS THE REFORM ATTITUDE TO ZIONISM?

The term 'Zionism' originally referred to the movement for the establishment of a Jewish homeland; since the establishment of the State of Israel it has come to mean supporting the maintenance and development of the State of Israel. Zionism is one of the few issues in which the attitude of Reform has changed radically from outright rejection to total support. The original opposition to Zionism merely reflected the cold reception given to it by the Anglo-Jewish establishment, including leading members of the Orthodox community and the Board of Deputies, the representative organisation of British Jewry. They defined Judaism as purely a religious faith and without any connotation of peoplehood or national entity. There was a strong emphasis on universalism, and it was felt that the world was progressing towards a Messianic age of harmony and enlightenment. They feared that the idea of Jewish nationality would bring charges of dual loyalty and would endanger their hard-won emancipation and social acceptability. As the first minister of West London Synagogue, Reverend David Marks, wrote in the 1850s, "We unequivocally declare that we neither seek nor acknowledge subjection to any land except the land of our birth"[1]. It was also thought that Zionism would distract Jews from the goal of religious perfection and would pervert the nature of Judaism. Nevertheless, there were some Reform leaders, such as Rabbi Joseph Strauss, Minister of the Bradford Reform Synagogue, who openly espoused the cause of Zionism. It should be noted that Zionism was opposed in its early life by many other groups: Jewish autonomists who believed Judaism was a culture that could flourish anywhere and did not require a specific Jewish state; Jewish Socialists who wished to solve 'the Jewish problem' by bringing social and political reform in their own society; while certain religious groups, such as the Satmar *Chasidim*, were and are still opposed to Zionism because they consider it sacrilegious and usurping the role of the Messiah, who alone will be responsible for restoring Jewish sovereignty to Israel.

A more sympathetic attitude began to evolve in the Reform Movement from the 1930s with a growing number of synagogues supporting Zionist activities or organising their own campaigns. The horrors of the Holocaust severely challenged belief in universalism and the ever-improving character of humanity. The need for a Jewish homeland in which Jews could live

---

1 Henry J Cohn, 'Progressive Jews And Zionism Until 1948', *A Genuine Search* (ed Dow Marmur) p.175

without fear of anti-semitism was recognised widely. Once the State of Israel became a reality, many previous anti-Zionists re-evaluated their position, and the establishment of the State in 1948 was followed by the introduction of a prayer for its well-being in the Reform liturgy. The increasing identification of Jews world-wide with the State and the concern over her survival following a succession of wars led to Zionism becoming accepted by Reform Jews generally. Moreover, it was evident that the earlier fears had proved groundless: the existence of Israel was not perceived as diminishing the loyalty of Jews to Britain; the emergence of Jewish nationalism did not undermine the religious faith of British Jews. On the contrary, particularly after 1967 and the Six Day War, it became clear that attachment to Israel strengthened the Jewish identity of many assimilated Jews who previously had no contact with the Jewish community. In 1958 the Assembly of Rabbis had recommended holding an annual *Yom Ha'atzma'ut* service[1]. In 1968 it issued a call in conjunction with the RSGB for the establishment of a settlement of Progressive Jews in Israel[2]; this dream was brought to fruition by the World Union for Progressive Judaism with the founding in 1977 of a Reform kibbutz, Yahel, which is situated in the Negev. A second such kibbutz, Lotan, was established nearby five years later.

In 1975 the World Union, with the full backing of the RSGB as one of its constituent members, applied for membership of the World Zionist Organisation. Acceptance of the application gave formal acknowledgement of the Reform Movement's commitment to Zionism. It has long been the policy of the Movement as a whole as well as individual synagogues to support fundraising appeals for Israel and to lobby on her behalf. There are also strong educational programmes concerning Israel for both children and adults. As a member of the World Union for Progressive Judaism, now affiliated to the World Zionist Organisation, the RSGB expresses its support for the Jerusalem Platform (1968) which upholds:

- The unity of the Jewish people and the centrality of Israel in Jewish life
- The ingathering of the Jewish people in its historic homeland *Eretz Yisrael* through *aliyah* from all countries
- The strengthening of the State of Israel which is based on the prophetic vision of justice and peace

---

1 Assembly of Rabbis, 23rd April 1958
2 Assembly of Rabbis, 23rd July 1968

– The preservation of the identity of the Jewish people through the fostering of Jewish and Hebrew education and of Jewish spiritual and cultural values
– The protection of Jewish rights everywhere

At the RSGB Annual Conference in 1988, a resolution on Israel was passed unanimously which declared:

> Meeting in Annual Conference in the fortieth year of the State of Israel the Reform Synagogues of Great Britain reaffirms its total support of the Jewish people's right to its own independent State within secure borders.
>
> The members of the Reform Synagogues of Great Britain regard the State of Israel as a unique expression of our people's faith and history. It is the homeland of our people as well as home to our spirit and our soul. We are concerned partners in the struggle for its peace, its security and its future.
>
> The RSGB calls upon its constituents to renew and increase their efforts to strengthen the State of Israel, especially through *aliyah* and through support for the Israel Movement for Progressive Judaism. We believe that by strengthening Israel we will also enrich Jewish life in the Diaspora through close contact with the land, the people, the language, the history and the problems of modern Israel; in turn, a strong Diaspora will manifest the universal values of Judaism and constitute the primary source and strength and support for Israel leading to the Diaspora and Israeli Jewry working together in harmony towards the achievement of Judaism's Messianic hope.

For Reform Jews today, Israel has a multi-faceted significance: it is the scene of much of the early religious history of Judaism; its memory has been enshrined in Jewish prayer for the last two thousand years; it is one of the few places in the world that has had a continuous Jewish presence since biblical times; it has witnessed a remarkable re-awakening of Jewish consciousness in modern times; it holds an increasingly large percentage of the world's Jewish population; it is a haven for Jews suffering persecution in any other country; and it has become a centre of Jewish creativity and achievement. Without doubt, it occupies a special place in the hearts of all Reform Jews.

2. IN WHAT WAYS SHOULD ONE SUPPORT THE STATE OF ISRAEL?

General Support
Reform synagogues constantly urge their members to support Israel in a variety of practical ways. One can provide financial support by giving to the JIA (Joint Israel Appeal), the main fund-raising agency for Israel which transfers money to Israel to be used for educational and welfare projects. Alternatively there are organisations catering for specific interests, such as children's hospitals, forestry plantations, development towns, rehabilitation of wounded soldiers and many more causes. One can also assist Israel economically: as a consumer by buying Israeli products such as fruit and manufactured goods, or in commercial life by investing in Israeli ventures or by developing business relations with Israeli companies. This can apply similarly to those engaged in cultural and scientific fields. Another concrete demonstration of support is by taking holidays in Israel and establishing a personal relationship with the people and places of Israel.

The Reform Movement in Israel
At the present time it is an ironic fact that the Reform synagogues in Britain have more rights and religious freedom than do Reform synagogues in Israel. This is due to the political power of the Orthodox parties in Israel which have strongly, and sometimes violently, opposed the Reform Movement there. Thus Reform synagogues in Israel cannot conduct legally valid marriages, have their conversions recognised, or officiate at funerals. Considerable difficulties have also been experienced in gaining land from local municipal authorities for building Reform synagogues. Reform Jews in Britain are part of a world-wide Progressive campaign to rectify this anomalous situation by urging the *Knesset* to allow full religious liberty for non-Orthodox Jews. A number of synagogues have fostered relations with Israeli Reform communities by twinning with them, learning about each other and organising exchange visits. These and other links are promoted by the London-based organisation The Friends of Progressive Judaism in Israel. It also provides financial support to Reform institutions in Israel (schools, new communities, outreach projects) which are often denied the funding that the Israeli Government gives to Orthodox ones. The RSGB has urged members of Reform congregations to affiliate to Pro Zion, the British branch of *Artzenu* (Our Land), the world-wide Progressive Zionist political organisation which,

amongst other activities, lobbies within Israel on behalf of Reform Judaism. It is also a powerful voice in the struggle to prevent any amendments by Israel's religious political parties to the Law of Return. This law was passed by the *Knesset* in 1950 and allows any Jew the right to settle in Israel. For the purposes of citizenship, current Israeli law recognises the Jewish status of those who have been converted by Reform synagogues. This is fiercely contested by the Israeli Orthodox Rabbinate who regularly introduce bills which would limit recognition of the Jewish status of those making *aliyah* under the Law of Return to those converted by Orthodox authorities. As this would disenfranchise many Reform Jews, particularly in the United States, creating two classes of Jews and dividing the international Jewish community, *Artzenu* is pledged to fight to maintain the status quo.

Aliyah
For many years the RSGB has recognised *aliyah* as an option for Jewish living and fulfilment, and has encouraged those who so desire to settle in Israel. It is seen as the most practical support of all, both assisting to build up the State and contributing to its Jewish life. At the same time the Reform Movement asserts the role of Jews living in Britain and works towards the establishment of a dynamic communal life in this country.

Uncritical Support?
A frequent dilemma for many Jews is whether they should express opinions that are critical of certain aspects of Israel's actions or policies. The hesitation is that, as there are many sectors of British society and many nations that are virulently hostile to Israel, it seems disloyal to add to the chorus of complaints and show cracks in Jewish solidarity with Israel. This is a highly individual and controversial subject, with substantial numbers of Reform Jews to be found on both sides of the argument. However, one can be totally committed to the land and people of Israel without being in favour of a particular government at any one time – a situation that is taken for granted in relation to Britain itself. Moreover, if one claims the right to comment on other countries' internal or foreign affairs, as British Jews regularly do concerning the Soviet Union, then the same right should apply to us or fellow Jews with regard to Israel. It can also be argued that if we are unable to concede any fault in Israel, then not only do we lose credibility when defending her but there is a danger of elevating the State into a god and turning nationalism into paganism. It is salutary to remember in this respect that Israel is a democracy

and that in the country itself there is often vociferous opposition. There is little that is said in the Diaspora that matches the severity of critics within Israel. Whilst it may not be easy or comfortable to be both supportive and critical of Israel, one without the other would be a disservice to both the highest ideals of Judaism and the dreams of the State's founding fathers. It is no accident that part of the *Yom Ha'atzma'ut* service in the RSGB prayer book contains a passage by the leading Zionist thinker and theologian Martin Buber which concludes[1]:

> It seems to me that God does not give any one portion of the earth away, so that the owner may say as God says in the Bible: "for all the earth is Mine" (Exodus 19.5). A conquered land is, in my opinion, only lent even to the conqueror who has settled on it – and God waits to see what he will make of it.

The prayer book also contains the following quotation from David Ben Gurion in the Study Anthology section on Israel[2]:

> The State of Israel will prove itself not by material wealth, nor by military might or technical achievement, but by its moral character and human values.

It is clear that one's support for Israel should be whole-hearted but also honest, with the right to speak out against certain policies as well as to praise her many achievements.

Rights and Borders

It is recognised that whilst Jews in the Diaspora have the right to comment on affairs in Israel, policies will be drawn up and implemented by those living in Israel. The RSGB does not make any attempt to identify with a particular political faction – partly for this reason, and partly because the Reform membership encompasses a great variety of political opinion. Nevertheless, there are certain general views that tend to be held by Reform Jews, such as supporting religious pluralism and the need to give equal rights to Reform communities in Israel. Another issue upon which most Reform members

---

1 *Forms of Prayer*, Vol I, p.261
2 Ibid, p.409

agree is that the area of Judea and Samaria – conquered in the 1967 War – need not be retained for religious reasons in the belief that this is territory divinely sanctioned, a view held by many Orthodox Jews. The fact that these territories were part of Israel in biblical times does not mean that they are essential to Israel today and may never be subject to negotiation. Of course, there may be other reasons for keeping them, such as security concerns, but these are open to change and may one day be negated if a comprehensive peace can be achieved. In the meantime, while Judea and Samaria are under Israeli control, every effort should be made to ensure that human rights are respected and that daily life can be as normative as possible despite the current atmosphere of hostility. The calls for freedom and justice that are made concerning other parts of the world (see XII.5) must apply to Israel too. A resolution at the 1988 Annual Conference of the RSGB declared:

> We understand the need to maintain law and order in the occupied territories as long as the occupation lasts, and we know that the task is a difficult and unpleasant one for the Israel Defence Forces. We recognise the extreme provocation and we are saddened that such provocation only contributes to the increase of hatred and brutalises those involved on both sides. This in no way diminishes the ultimate responsibility for upholding Jewish teaching relating to times when war has to be waged and the treatment of prisoners, and which requires recognition at all times of the Divine Image in every human being, Jew and non-Jew alike.

Israel must protect her interests, but the moral health of the nation is also a vital factor. Hopefully, morality and security need not be incompatible but can go hand in hand.

CHAPTER ELEVEN

MEDICAL ETHICS

You have made mankind little less than divine, and crowned him with glory and splendour. You have given him power over the works of Your hands, and put all things under his control.

Psalm 8.6-7

1. WHAT IS THE REFORM VIEW OF NEW METHODS OF HUMAN FERTILISATION AND EXPERIMENTATION?

In recent years there has been an enormous number of medical advances pushing the frontiers of knowledge forward but leaving a trail of moral questions. It is a constantly evolving process in which we have the ability to do many things, but we have not yet decided whether we *should* be doing them. It would be an extremely retrograde step if morality, having striven for years to modify the law of the jungle, was now to be subservient to the law of the laboratory, with innovations being pursued for their own sake regardless of their moral consequences. Instead the latter should be the determining factor, and our scientific development be guided by ethical considerations.

Many of the most brilliant – and most morally challenging – advances have been made in fields relating to birth. Judaism has always held that God and humanity are co-partners in the act of creating new lives. According to one opinion, modern medical skills sometimes seem to tip the balance of responsibility too far towards humanity and to be in danger of acting in lieu of God when one has no right to that role. It is a view that can be countered by pointing to the potential benefits that can arise, and in each instance the pitfalls of the one have to be balanced against the value of the other.

AIH, IVF and AID
A significant number of married couples cannot have a child by sexual intercourse and require medical help to achieve conception. One method is through artificial insemination, whereby the husband's seed is removed and implanted in the wife's womb. Critics of this claim that it is tampering with God's handiwork, but this can be dismissed by the argument that life has been entrusted to humanity to nurture and develop to the best; otherwise we would not be allowed to cure the simplest ailment. Some Orthodox authorities have opposed AIH (artificial insemination by the husband) on the grounds that the masturbation necessary to produce the male seed constitutes 'spillage' and wasting the seed which is prohibited by Jewish Law (Genesis 38.9-10). However, it is clear that in AIH the purpose of the act is not to prevent conception but to secure it. In Reform thinking, therefore, there is no objection to AIH for it fulfils both the desire of the couple to have a family and the biblical injunction to be fruitful and multiply (Genesis 1.28). For the same reasons there are also no reservations over IVF (in vitro fertilisation) – the process by which the egg of a woman who has difficulty conceiving is extracted and fertilised in a test tube with the sperm of her husband, and then transferred into the woman's womb to develop as normal.

A more difficult question arises when conception can only occur if the male seed is from a person other than the woman's husband. The assertion that AID (artificial insemination by a donor) is 'adultery without intercourse' is open to debate. It is true in the technical sense that a married woman is impregnated by a man to whom she is not married, but it does not necessarily amount to an emotional or physical relationship that breaks her marital vows. A further concern raised by Orthodoxy is that if the husband died it might be mistakenly thought that as the wife had a child by her husband, she did not have to undergo *chalitzah* – the ceremony which frees a childless widow from having to marry her deceased husband's brother – whereas in fact her husband was childless and so the ceremony does need to take place. As Reform regards *chalitzah* as an outdated concept that need not be maintained, it does not share this particular objection.

A more serious problem could be unintentional cases of incest in the cases of men and women who marry each other without realising that they are children of the same donor father. Such instances are likely to be extremely rare and should not by themselves be grounds for disallowing the technique. A much weightier consideration that is applicable in every case is the potentially harmful emotional consequences of AID: that the husband may feel no bond with a child with whom he has no biological connection; or that it alters the relationship between the husband and wife, and their perception of each other; or that if such children learn of the method of their conception, this may have a confusing effect on them; or that the children might seek to discover who is their actual father, to the hurt of their official father. It may be that instead of furthering family life AID could prove highly disruptive. The author suggests, therefore, that AID be avoided and that adoption is a preferable option for couples who cannot have children themselves. It puts the husband and wife in the same position emotionally and does not imbalance the relationship. It also serves to give a loving home to an already existing child whose parents are either unable or unwilling to provide for it. Nevertheless, if a child was to be conceived through AID and its mother was Jewish, then it would have Jewish status irrespective of the identity of the donor father. It would not be regarded as a *mamzer* by Reform as the concept of *mamzerut* is no longer recognised.

Surrogate Motherhood
Surrogate motherhood applies to a situation in which a woman is unable to nurture and carry a child in her womb for the normal duration of a pregnancy. A newly developed solution is for the seed and ovum of a husband and wife

to be extracted, fertilised in a test tube and then implanted into the womb of another woman. It, too, is fraught with practical problems: the fear that it become commercialised and that 'womb-leasing' turns a miraculous process into a business enterprise; the emotional effect on the carrying mother when the child is born and she has to give it to the 'real parents'; the trauma to all parties if she refuses to do so; the possibility that the child might be deformed or handicapped in some way and what happens if the commissioning couple refuse to accept it; the identity crisis that the child could suffer if it was to discover the circumstances of its birth; and the moral qualms if surrogacy was to be used not just by mothers incapable of carrying a foetus but by those who were unwilling to do so for reasons of convenience or career considerations. Nevertheless, it has to be recognised that there are instances in which a surrogate arrangement is the only method of child-bearing available and might prove successful.

Current British law states that surrogate motherhood agencies are illegal, the intention being that individuals may pursue such a course but it should not become a commercial activity. The author suggests that Jewish couples who cannot produce children of their own in any other way have the right to use a surrogate mother. However, it is vital that both partners are fully in agreement, and that they are aware of all the potential problems. It would be much more desirable if the surrogate mother is a member of the family, with whom both partners have a good relationship, and who would be able to maintain contact with the child. If there are difficulties in finding a suitable surrogate, it may be better to consider another course, such as adopting a child instead. The religious status of children born from surrogate mothers is not in doubt: it follows that of the mother from whose ovum it developed, not the mother who later incubated it for the rest of the pregnancy. In the biblical phraseology, it is the 'seed' that counts, not the temporary home that it enjoyed.

Embryology
As a result of some of the above techniques, doctors often find themselves with excess embryos that were originally created in case they were needed to replace an implantation that had failed to survive, but which are no longer required if the original implantation succeeded. The issue of whether these embryos can be used for experimentation has aroused much controversy, with forceful arguments being advanced by both sides. Many people are adamant that embryos – in other words, potential human beings – should not be

treated as laboratory spare-parts. For them it is morally wrong to experiment in this way and violates a fundamental principle: that we may not use humans as a means to an end but must respect the sanctity of life contained in each of them. The opposite view does not deny this, but claims that the benefits arising from experimentation over-ride such concerns. It is only by acquiring greater knowledge that we will be able to assist infertile couples to have children, or prevent genetic diseases being perpetuated down the generations, or manage to eradicate certain deformities. The nervousness that is rightly felt at entering such new territory does not necessarily mean it is forbidden ground. The same apprehension was felt initially about heart-transplants, whereas now they are accepted widely.

Much of the debate turns on when human life starts and at what stage the embryo acquires the human right to be protected from harm. At present British law permits research on living embryos under fourteen days old – at which point the brain and spine begin to form – after which they may not be kept alive. The traditional Jewish view that a foetus does not have the status of a full human being until birth (*Oholot* 7.6) means that destroying a foetus used for experiment is not akin to murder and automatically prohibited. Nevertheless, it is still a life in potential and so great care must be taken. There should be adequate safeguards as to the nature and length of experiments. Given these conditions, the author suggests that the good stemming from the knowledge arising from experimentation can justify the awesome nature of such a step.

2. WHAT IS THE REFORM ATTITUDE TO ABORTION AND BIRTH CONTROL?

Abortion

Abortion is a highly emotive issue both within the Jewish and non-Jewish world, with opinions ranging from those favouring abortion on demand to those seeking a total ban on the grounds that it is nothing less than murder. The traditional Jewish response has been to oppose abortion in principle yet permit it in specific circumstances. This attitude derives from the biblical incident when two men who were fighting injure a pregnant woman: if the woman dies, they are liable to the death penalty; if just the foetus dies, then they are merely given a fine (Exodus 21.22-3). The clear implication is that a foetus does not have the status of a living person. Although it should be protected and any maltreatment is punishable, fatal injury to it does not constitute murder. A passage in the *Mishnah* indicates that this remains the case until the head or greater part of the foetus has emerged from the mother's womb; thereafter it is considered a living being (*Oholot* 7.6). In a situation where the pregnancy endangered the mother, an abortion was deemed permissible as the mother's life took precedence over a life that only existed in potential. Thus the Jewish criterion for abortion was not how many weeks old was the foetus, but whether it presented a threat to the mother's health. In any conflict between the rights of the mother and the rights of the foetus, it is generally the former that prevail.

Subsequent Rabbinic decisions considered the extent to which saving the mother's health applied. Some authorities included concern for her mental health, as in cases where the difficulty of pregnancy or the burden of an extra child would endanger her sanity. The distress of the mother is also seen as grounds by some authorities to grant an abortion if the child is thought likely to be born physically deformed or mentally defective. Other authorities are more restrictive. British law permits abortion if it is agreed by two doctors that a woman's pregnancy causes risk to her life, or injury to the physical or mental health of either her or her family. Evidence of mental or physical abnormalities in the foetus would also justify abortion.

There is no definitive ruling within Reform on abortion, but there is a strong tendency to favour the liberal viewpoints of Jewish tradition; abortion is allowed in various circumstances where facilities are available for it to be carried out legally and safely. The right of an adult woman to make decisions about her own life and to have sovereignty over her own body are additional factors to be considered. Some Rabbis extend the principle of mental anguish and regard abortion as permissible "when the woman has serious emotional reservations about having the child"[1]. In the case of an unwanted child which may be unloved and uncared for, perhaps even abused, the quality of its life has to be taken into account. However, abortion as a form of contraception cannot be sanctioned.

A further concern is the role of the father in any decision. Whereas in traditional thinking it is purely the mother's physical and mental well-being that is the issue, in the Reform view it is advocated that the father's feeling

---

1 Barbara Borts, *Abortion – A Jewish Response*, p.6

should also be taken into account[1]. It is his child too, and he will be involved in the consequences of whatever decision is reached. Nevertheless the final word should still rest with the mother whose responsibility it would be to carry the foetus throughout the pregnancy and who would be the one most affected, physically and emotionally, by any abortion.

Birth Control
Jewish tradition has taken the injunction to "be fruitful and multiply" (Genesis 1.28) as proof that to have children is a duty. No limit was set on the number of children, and the minimum required to fulfil the command was considered to be a son and a daughter (*Yebamot* 6.6). Contraception was permitted if pregnancy might injure the health of the mother. The method of contraception used was dependent on whether it transgressed the ban on a male "spilling his seed", based on the condemnation of Onan in Genesis 38.9-10. Thus from an Orthodox perspective the pill, the diaphragm and spermicide are all permissible as they do not interfere with the sexual act. The same applies to the inter-uterine device (IUD), although its possible effects in causing infertility suggest that it should be used only by those not intending to have further children. Use of the condom is forbidden as it prevents the man's seed from entering the womb. Vasectomy is prohibited as it is regarded as akin to castration, which is prohibited in Jewish Law, although sterilisation for women is permitted (*Shabbat* 110b-111a).

In Reform thinking children are seen as a highly fulfilling part of marriage, as well as a means of continuing the traditions of Judaism. However, the decision to have children, and how many, is left entirely to the couple concerned. In addition to the *talmudic* attitude above, they must take into account social and economic factors as well as personal preferences. Some consider that the problems of the world population explosion require responsible families to limit the number of children they have; others feel that the depletion of world Jewry by a third in the Holocaust necessitates a high Jewish birth rate to replace those that were lost. The method of contraception is also regarded as a private matter for the husband and wife to agree upon. For most Reform Jews the criterion for deciding which type to use is not "spilling the seed" but the reliability and health aspect of the different options. Whatever method is chosen should be acceptable to both partners.

---

1 Idem

3. IS THERE A REFORM POLICY CONCERNING SMOKING?

Smoking has been common amongst inhabitants of Europe, including Jews, for four centuries and was not known to have any harmful effects until recently. Its widespread use even led to consideration of whether smoking required a blessing beforehand, although the verdict was negative on the grounds that although smoke was drawn into one's mouth, it was not consumed. Whilst there was some debate as to whether one should smoke on fast days, the only definite ban was smoking on the Sabbath because both a cigarette and pipe required lighting with a flame, which is one of the thirty-nine categories of work forbidden on the Sabbath according to Rabbinic interpretation. These grounds are not necessarily binding in the Reform view, as the traditional interpretation of Sabbath observance has been redefined according to a modern understanding of the nature of work (see VI.2). However, now that it has been medically proven that smoking is injurious to one's health, the issue of smoking is to be judged anew. The first consideration is whether individuals should do anything that is known to be detrimental to their health. It is clear that Judaism's teaching on the respect for life includes one's own life (hence the total opposition to suicide) and particularly one's physical well-being. Not only should one care for oneself but one should also not put oneself in danger (Genesis 9.5, *Baba Kamma* 8.6, 91b). To neglect one's health could be seen as a denial of the gift given to us by God. This applies to many other habits when done in excess – such as drinking alcohol – but smoking is injurious in itself, and even the 'light smoker' is liable to suffer from its effects.

Another consideration is the effect that smoking has on others. Current medical evidence suggests that non-smokers regularly in the presence of smokers are also liable to develop cancer through passively inhaling the smoke from cigarettes. In addition, non-smokers often feel nauseous and discomforted when in the same room as those smoking. The number of non-smokers is steadily increasing as a result of the growing awareness of the dangers of tobacco. Being concerned with the safety and comfort of others is a cardinal principle of Judaism (Leviticus 19.18) and applies to smoking as much as any other harmful activity. Equally relevant is the injunction not to endanger someone else through any action of one's own (Deuteronomy 22.8). This also questions the responsibility of parents who smoke. They establish a pattern of behaviour that their children may grow up to consider a model for themselves and choose to imitate. Parents who do not wish their children to smoke should not do so themselves.

Another aspect of smoking is that it is a potential fire hazard in view of the number of accidents that have occurred from smouldering ash on carpets and in waste bins. A synagogue is a public place where fire regulations must be of the highest standard so as to ensure the safety of all who enter the building; thus there is a strong case for limiting smoking to certain areas or banning it altogether. It can also be claimed that smoking is associated with a certain impropriety. Hence one does not smoke during solemn occasions, nor at a cemetery nor in a church. It can therefore be argued that smoking on synagogue premises is inappropriate per se, whether in the worship area or in any other room.

A mitigating factor is concern for the needs of those who are regular smokers and for whom a ban on smoking would cause distress. Their comfort and their freedom of choice must be respected too. Nevertheless, some might consider that it would render a service to smokers if they were encouraged to give up a habit which, however much it may be part of their lives, is ultimately against their best interests. It might also be said that this would not be an infringement of their rights as they are addicted to smoking and hence lack the ability to free themselves from it. This would seem to be confirmed by the number of people who have wanted to give up smoking but whose attempts have not been successful.

In view of the clear danger to personal health caused by smoking, the author suggests that it should be viewed as contrary to the values of Judaism and that it should be avoided. In other areas of Jewish tradition, Reform has had the courage to permit activities that were previously prohibited, on the grounds that the bans are no longer appropriate. It should therefore be equally forthright in opposing activities that are now deemed unsuitable, such as smoking. Current smokers should endeavour to give up, and members of their family should assist them. Many Reform synagogues already take a lead in discouraging smoking by banning it anywhere on their premises. The Sternberg Centre for Judaism – a public complex in which many people spend their working day – has adopted a policy of prohibiting smoking inside most buildings. However, in recognition of the hardship that this might cause some staff, a small number of private rooms have been set aside in which they may smoke. Smoking is permitted in the grounds of the Centre, although not in the school playground where it would be an undesirable influence on the children. Realistically, personal practice in the privacy of one's home will remain the decision of the individual or family concerned, but they are urged to give strong consideration to the supreme Jewish value of safeguarding one's own health and that of those around them.

4. WHAT IS THE REFORM RESPONSE TO AIDS?

The existence of AIDS (Acquired Immune Deficiency Syndrome) became widely known amongst the general public in the mid 1980s. It caused considerable disquiet, arousing fears that the population might be devastated by a modern version of the Black Death. People were appalled at its fatal effects, with no hope of a reprieve. They were also worried by the fact that so many who did not appear to suffer from it could nevertheless be carriers and develop the disease at any time, or pass it on to others. In some circles it was seen as Divine punishment for the sexual promiscuity associated with the 1960s and as an indication of the wrath of God. A high percentage of those with AIDS in Britain were either homosexuals who caught it from having several different sexual partners, or drug users who acquired it through sharing infected needles. However, the situation elsewhere was different: in the United States half of the victims were heterosexuals, with women being affected just as much as men. The likelihood is that the same pattern will eventually emerge in Britain, and that no section of the population will be unaffected; recent statistics seem to confirm such a trend. It is obvious that Jews who engage in multiple sexual liaisons or who use drugs intravenously are equally liable to contract the AIDS virus.

The response of Reform Rabbis has been to deal with all three aspects of AIDS – the causes, ways of avoiding it, and those who are victims of it. Many Rabbis have condemned the sexual adventurism that in several, though not all, cases led to contracting the virus. Some have advocated the formula of chastity before marriage and fidelity after marriage. Others have acknowledged the widespread practice of pre-marital sex but urged that it be limited to a permanent partner rather than be commonplace with casual acquaintances. These remarks have been addressed to both heterosexual and homosexual Jews, recognising that both exist and that the AIDS virus distinguishes between neither. The warnings apply also to those who are married couples, but have affairs with other people. Quite apart from the immorality involved, they endanger both themselves and their spouses.

Much public controversy accompanied the Government advertising campaign to combat the spread of AIDS. In particular it has been objected that its emphasis on 'safe sex' is misplaced and condones sexual permissiveness; it is argued that instead a 'moral revolution' should be called for and that sexual behaviour should be changed – a position echoed by the Orthodoxy. Much as many Reform Rabbis will agree with the idealism of this approach, they recognise the pragmatism of the 'safe sex' approach, basing themselves on the principle of *pikuach nefesh* ('the saving of life'): that emergency measures are justified when lives are in danger. This certainly applies to the potentially catastrophic effect of AIDS which could reach epidemic proportions. In these circumstances it is best to give advice on how to make sex safe even if it implies that contemporary mores can be maintained. It is equally important to provide sexual education for schoolchildren of around ten years and upwards for the practical reason that despite the legal age limit for sex and despite Jewish moral attitudes, it is better to arm children with the facts about AIDS than to leave them at risk. The needs of the hour must take precedence, although of course this should not preclude longer term education about the role of sex in a relationship, the significance of marriage and moral perspectives.

It should be noted that one of the major practical ways advised on how to avoid being infected with AIDS is to use a condom during sexual intercourse. According to Orthodox Judaism the condom is strictly forbidden, because it prevents male seed entering the womb and therefore constitutes the reprehensible act of 'spillage'. Reform thinking leaves the choice of contraception up to the couple concerned and thus has no intrinsic objection to its use (see X1.2). In the present situation this method seems especially appropriate, as the saving of life is so important that it takes precedence over almost all other laws.

Notwithstanding the above, there are many people who already have or will later develop AIDS and the question arises of how one should react to them. The Reform Rabbinate has taken a strong stand in pointing out that in many cases people have contracted AIDS through no fault of their own. They include those infected through blood transfusions, babies in the womb of women with AIDS who contract it through the placenta, and loyal spouses of partners who are promiscuous and who pass on the virus to them. In view of the many innocent victims of AIDS, it is clear that no credibility whatsoever can be given to the idea that it is Divine punishment. The Assembly of Rabbis has stated that "AIDS is a viral disease and we wholly reject the suggestion that it be understood as the wrath of God visited upon a particular group of sinners"[1]. The proper response to the innocent victims of AIDS is one of compassion and support. It applies equally to those who brought it upon themselves, for whilst one may condemn their initial folly, one must

---

1 Assembly of Rabbis, 16th December 1986

still be horrified at the severity and finality of their fate. Understanding and care should also be extended to the families of AIDS victims, for they not only witness their loved ones dying slowly and painfully, but may also be socially ostracised by friends who are frightened or disgusted by the situation. Moreover, such feelings may well be shared by the family themselves, compounding their pain and confusion. The Assembly of Rabbis has therefore called upon members of congregations to react with the same compassion to AIDS victims and their families as to all who suffer from disease and to exercise the *mitzvah* of *bikkur cholim* ('visiting the sick')[1].

5. WHAT IS THE REFORM ATTITUDE TO EUTHANASIA?

There are an increasing number of situations today in which people who previously might have died from accidents or illnesses can be kept alive thanks to the progress in medical techniques. Very often the individuals are able to resume the course of their life, even if it entails certain restrictions. At other times, though, no such return is possible; they are alive clinically but lack any quality of life. An example might be someone left in a permanent coma after a car crash, whose body depends on a life-support machine. Instances such as this beg the question of the extent to which efforts should be made to help them survive.

One response is to assert that life is sacred, however diminished in quality. It is the duty of those involved – the family and the medical profession – to assist the person in whatever way possible. All care necessary should be given and any pain should be controlled. Many people consider this the right and only course of action, and invest considerable physical and emotional energy to help those dependent on them.

Another response is to advocate euthanasia – defined as 'the action of inducing a gentle and easy death' – whereby it is decided to terminate the life of the person by administering drugs that cause death quickly and painlessly. Those in favour argue that one has a right to choose when and how one dies, particularly if circumstances render life unbearable. It is a notion that is fraught with difficulties: who are to be the judges of when a person is eligible for such 'mercy killing'? What criteria would be used in making the decision? How would one be sure that this is what the person concerned

---

1 Idem

wishes? What effect would it have on our attitude to life and the value of life? An alternative scenario is when individuals with their mental faculties intact, but whose bodies are paralysed, request the active termination of their life – voluntary euthanasia as opposed to that decided upon by others. Here, too, problems arise. How to be sure that the person is not acting under external pressure, or is not suffering from temporary depression? What degree of physical handicap or pain would justify voluntary euthanasia, and would requests be dependent on the approval of relatives or medical staff? Would the acceptability of voluntary euthanasia lead eventually to compulsory euthanasia being introduced for certain categories of people? Towering above such considerations are two Jewish principles that have always been recognised as cardinal: belief in the sanctity of life, and the conviction that the taking of life is a prerogative of God and not of human beings. It should also be noted that all forms of euthanasia are illegal in Britain. Reform therefore upholds the traditional position and, as a general principle, regards any termination of another person's life as murder, whether with or without their consent, including killing an already dying person. Cases in which euthanasia are performed by the individuals themselves, constitute suicide, which also contradicts Jewish ethics (see III.10).

Despite the opposition to euthanasia expressed above, it has to be admitted that there are some compelling arguments in support of it that cannot be dismissed out of hand. In certain instances of acute suffering a medically-administered death might appear to be a kindness, indeed a much more religious act than letting the agony continue. As euthanasia is illegal, there is no need to attempt the formidable exercise of formulating possible exceptions to a general prohibition; nevertheless, if the legal position were to change in this country (as happened recently in Holland) it would be appropriate to re-evaluate the Jewish attitude and to consider whether a new Jewish policy, or certain refinements to the existing one, would be justified.

A further response – which does fall within both Jewish and civil law – is to consider that the life of the person has degenerated to such an extent that whilst no active steps can be made to terminate it, one may desist from action that would prolong it. The various examples of this in *talmudic* literature (*Ketubot* 104a, *Avodah Zarah* 18a) indicate both that this has long been an issue and that such a solution was regarded as acceptable. Thus there are clear limits to the degree to which life must be maintained, and there is a distinction between taking life and not elongating it. In modern times this might include refraining from giving someone a blood transfusion, replacing a defective organ, or putting them on a life-support machine – the lack of which would lead to, but not directly cause, their death. This principle could also be extended to the case of the person already on a life-support machine, for it can be argued that the act of switching off does not kill the person but brings to an end efforts to prevent the onset of death. The option of refusing any further treatment applies to relatives of a critically ill person on whose behalf they have to make a decision. It should also be available to individuals to determine with regard to their own lives. Thus a mentally alert person whose body is failing should have the right to decide whether or not to continue medical treatment when the result may just be to preserve an intolerable and irreversible condition. Relatives may find this hard to accept and can certainly argue the point; however, unless they feel the person concerned is being pressurised into making such a decision, they should respect the person's wishes.

In any such situation a Reform Rabbi would be concerned not only with the legal and moral aspects but also with the emotional considerations for those involved. Discussion would include the distress they felt at the state of their relative (or the person's own feelings), the awesome responsibility involved in making a decision, and their ability to come to terms with the consequences. Giving pastoral support during and afterwards would be as important as helping the family reach a conclusion.

CHAPTER TWELVE

CONTEMPORARY ISSUES

*That which has been
is that which shall be,
And that which has been done
is that which shall be done
And there is nothing new
under the sun.*

Ecclesiastes 1.9

1. TO WHAT EXTENT SHOULD DIALOGUE WITH OTHER FAITHS BE ENCOURAGED?

There are some Jews who shun all forms of dialogue with other faiths on the grounds that it is an irrelevant issue which is a waste of time. They also warn of the danger that dialogue can lead to a lessening of one's own faith or even conversion.

In Reform synagogues the emphasis is on the positive value of dialogue. It is a condition of dialogue that neither party seeks to convert the other, and the purpose of the exchange is purely for the sharing of knowledge. The benefits of dialogue can be seen in three distinct areas, quite apart from the acquisition of knowledge itself. One is that greater understanding of each other's faiths can lead to mutual respect and in turn result in greater harmony between the individuals concerned. If these individuals also happen to be leaders of their communities, then the good relations can extend to different groups in society at large and promote inter-communal tolerance. As so many previous troubles have stemmed from religious rivalry and thrived on a mixture of ignorance and prejudice, the opportunity to reverse the trend and bridge the divide must be taken. Another benefit is that study of other faiths can shed much insight on one's own tradition. It throws the distinctive Jewish beliefs and practices into sharper relief, whilst it also indicates points of contact where two faiths have common sources. Thus the great similarity of many Jewish and Christian prayers is because both are based on passages independently extracted from the Bible. In addition, one can come to appreciate where one's faith has been influenced by another religion, such as the way Bachya ibn Pakuda's celebrated eleventh century pietistic work *Duties of the Heart* was strongly influenced by Muslim mysticism, or how the Friday night *kiddush* was taken by the Church and turned into the Eucharist. Such discoveries show how Judaism has often interacted with other faiths and been enriched in the process without losing its own identity.

A third benefit is that good works have arisen through inter-faith bodies such as The Council of Christians and Jews. Specifically dedicated to fighting 'the evils of prejudice, intolerance and discrimination between people of different religions', it has promoted local groups throughout the country and also organised frequent meetings between Christian and Jewish clergy at the highest level. Its powerful influence has been proven in many substantial matters that have wide-reaching influence, including the defence of Parliamentary legislation concerning Jewish dietary laws and publications on Christian-Jewish understanding. Most important of all, it helped prepare the ground for the Church of England's re-examination of its attitude towards Judaism in the light of the Holocaust, its recognition of past errors in Christian thinking and its declaration of the fraternal links with Jews. In recognition of the great progress made in recent decades and the increasing number of interfaith meetings, a special prayer has been composed for such occasions[1]:

> Lord of all creation, we stand in awe before You, impelled by visions of the harmony of man. We are children of many traditions – inheritors of shared wisdom and tragic misunderstandings, of proud hopes and humble successes. Now it is time for us to meet – in memory and truth, in courage and trust, in love and promise.
> In that which we share, let us see the common prayer of humanity; in that in which we differ, let us wonder at the freedom of man; in our unity and our differences, let us know the uniqueness that is God.
> May our faith in You bring us closer to each other.

A relatively new aspect of Jewish dialogue concerns Muslims. It is a difficult area because of the background of political enmity between Israel and the Arab world. However, it is clear that in previous centuries there were many occasions when Jews and Muslims co-existed happily, and that the Golden Age of Spanish Jewry was when the Iberian Peninsula was under Muslim control. It would be highly beneficial, therefore, to be able to show through religious dialogue with Muslims in Britain that the problems in the Middle East are limited to territorial and political causes, and that there is no reason *per se* why Jews and Muslims should not live in peace.

It must also be considered whether dialogue can be extended to other faiths as well. Christianity and Islam are both regarded as monotheistic faiths and therefore compatible with, although not the same as, Judaism. However, this does not apply to the Eastern religions which have now become more in evidence in the West, either through the migration of adherents or by gaining converts in Britain. The multiplicity of gods in Hinduism could be viewed as akin to idolatry in the eyes of Judaism, while the absence of God in Buddhism is equally alien to Jewish thought. Nevertheless, it has to be recognised that, unlike idolatry in biblical times, Buddhists and Hindus do not include abhorrent practices such as human sacrifice or sacred prostitutes, but teach a

---

1 *Forms of Prayer*, Vol I, p.297

deep reverence for life and seek to perfect man's spirituality. Moreover, they are the genuine beliefs of a sizeable minority within the general community and so understanding their faith is important if there is to be harmony in society. Relations with the Eastern religions may never be as close as those with Christianity and Islam where so much shared history and common strands exist, but dialogue with them should proceed 'for the sake of peace'.

Despite the positive attitude towards dialogue, it is not the practice to engage in joint worship with other faiths[1]. There is a clear difference between attending someone else's service or home ceremony as an interested spectator and participating in a common act of prayer carried out in the name of both faiths. The former promotes knowledge and goodwill; the latter blurs the distinctions between the faiths and muddles the different concepts that each one holds precious. Dialogue does not seek to unify differing religions, but to improve relations between them as they are.

2. WHAT IS THE REFORM POSITION ON BUSINESS ETHICS?

The way one conducts oneself in business is one of the litmus tests of one's Judaism. Jewish ethics offer clear guidelines as to how one should behave at work and are as fundamental to the faith as its dietary laws and Sabbath regulations. There is a mistaken view that associates Judaism primarily with home life and synagogue services, whereas in fact Judaism is concerned with all aspects of daily life. Its teachings apply seven days a week and it sees no distinction between religious life and ordinary affairs. The person who prays piously but acts unethically has transgressed Jewish Law and has rendered the prayers sterile.

Jewish tradition records a variety of laws affecting all aspects of business dealings, starting with the minimum standard expected, "You shall not steal, you shall not deal falsely, nor lie to one another" (Leviticus 19.11). Regarding customers, one is forbidden to give them short measure or defraud in appearances (Leviticus 19.35). This includes any attempt to conceal the true nature, value, origins, contents and quality of the goods for sale. One is also forbidden to overcharge, with the rule established in *talmudic* times that if the

---

1 Assembly of Rabbis, 6th December 1961

profit margin was more than one-sixth of the value of the article, then the sale is invalidated (*Baba Metzia* 30b). The percentage may be subject to debate, but the principle remains. Regarding competitors, it is considered as natural that one should want to do better than they, but one should not seek to put them out of business. The person who takes away someone's livelihood through unfair competition is compared to an adulterer – one who destroys the pattern of life that another person had established (*Sanhedrin* 81a). Regarding employees, wages should be paid on time (Leviticus 19.13), full compensation has to be given to anyone injured in the course of work, while there are strict laws concerning redundancy. It should be noted that there is no objection to profit itself, merely the stipulation that it has to be earned ethically.

These legal injunctions were reinforced by a series of homiletical sayings. It is pointed out that the promise that a person would enjoy length of days is only made in three instances – for honouring parents (Exodus 20.12), showing a kindness to animals (Deuteronomy 22.6-7) and being honest in business dealings (Deuteronomy 25.13-16). The Rabbis asserted that when a person dies, the first question that would be asked of him was whether he had acted with integrity in his business affairs (*Shabbat* 31a). Commenting on the need for exemplary behaviour in one's working life, a former Minister of the West London Synagogue wrote[1]:

> Deception in business is robbery. The tricks of the trade are not less dishonest because they are not punishable by the law of the land, or because the custom of the trade sanctions or condones them ... honesty and truthfulness are the first duty due from a man to his neighbour.

Strict ethical behaviour applies equally to customers. It is their duty not to waste the time of shopkeepers and to pay bills promptly. It is also out of keeping with Jewish ethics to consider it 'fair game' to cheat large corporations or official bodies on the grounds that 'they won't be affected by it' or by claiming that, like the taxman, 'they are uncaring and deserve being taken advantage of'. Ethics are indivisible. They cover both sides of the counter and range from returning any excess change one has been given, to honesty in multi-million pound transactions. The teaboy and the company

---

1 Morris Joseph, *Judaism As Creed and Life*, p.422

chairman should, if nothing else, at least have honesty in common.

The stress laid on daily ethics has manifested itself in recent revisions of the Reform liturgy for the High Holy Days. One of the confessions recited at *Yom Kippur* asks forgiveness[1]:

> For stealing telephone calls
> For paying our taxes by conjecture
> For petty theft and cheating
> For letting other people down
> For saying "who cares?"
> For not taking responsibility
> For pretending to be good
> For saying "who will ever know?"

While some found the introduction of such sentiments startlingly worldly, it was recognised that the more the prayer book corresponded to reality, the more likely it would be that prayers would be translated into action in the high street and city centre.

Pragmatic considerations also enter into the question. It is one of the unfortunate legacies of history that Jews have been associated with sharp business practices. It is a stereotype that is unjust to the vast majority of Jews in business, yet the slightest incident can rake it up and cast its shadow over all Jews. Jews may act as individuals but are judged as a community, and all Jews are responsible for the good name or opprobrium that they can bring upon Judaism. The Rabbis long ago declared that it is a greater sin to steal from a non-Jew than from a Jew because not only is stealing from anyone wrong, but in the former case it will also bring the Jewish faith into disrepute (*Tosefta* to *Baba Kamma* 10.15).

It has also been pointed out that good business ethics often make good business sense[2]. If one has a reputation for honest dealing, reliable goods and fair pricing, then one will attract customers and increase one's profitability. However, these should be regarded as bonuses rather than the justification for ethical standards. Honesty is a religious imperative and should be pursued not because it is useful but because it is right.

---

1 *Forms of Prayer*, Vol III, p.484
2 Trevor Chinn, 'Good Ethics Are Good Business', *Manna* (Autumn 1988) p.4

In order to emphasise the importance of business ethics, the 1988 Annual Conference of the RSGB passed a resolution declaring:

The teachings of Judaism call for ethical behaviour in all aspects of business dealing, whether it be between the directors of one company and another, between employer and employee, between professional and client, or shopkeeper and customer.

We call upon all members of Reform synagogues to be aware of their Jewish responsibilities in these matters. Morality is indivisible – it cannot be applied to one and not to another area of life, to the personal but not to the sphere of one's commercial or professional behaviour.

We urge that all synagogues should promote study of this area of Jewish teaching, offering in particular to those members in the world of business and the professions the guidance that Jewish law and teaching have to offer.

3. WHAT IS THE REFORM ATTITUDE TO HOMOSEXUALITY?

The Bible is adamantly opposed to homosexuality: "You shall not lie with a man as with a woman: it is an abomination" (Leviticus 18.22). The condemnation is repeated in even stronger terms in Leviticus 20.13 where the death penalty is laid down for all practitioners. Lesbianism is not mentioned in the Bible but first appears in the *Talmud* (*Shabbat* 65a, *Yebamot* 76a). Although it, too, is condemned, it is noticeable that no penalties are attached and the aversion to lesbianism seems much less strong, perhaps because the physical act is less pronounced and no spillage of seed is involved. This opposition to both homosexual and lesbian relationships formed the standard response of Judaism and was unchallenged until recent decades. It is maintained today in the Orthodox tradition which views homosexuality as an unnatural perversion. In Reform synagogues there is a willingness to re-examine the issue in the light of modern knowledge. (All subsequent references to homosexuality will apply to lesbianism too.) According to current medical understanding, homosexuality is very often a condition with which the person concerned is born. The majority of homosexuals have no choice in the matter and find it their natural state. An estimated 5%–10% of the general population is homosexual and there is no evidence to suggest that the Jewish population is any different. It would be wrong therefore to regard as sinful those whose homosexuality is a fact of nature; they are as they were born, and they can rephrase Genesis 1.27 as "male and female He created *me*".

It has to be recognised that however rational this approach, many heterosexuals still feel uncomfortable with the subject of homosexuality. It is partly the result of an innate antipathy to those markedly different from oneself and whose lifestyle is seen as undermining the normal pattern of procreation and family life. It is also based on a variety of unfounded prejudices, including the assumption that all homosexuals are child molesters. Whilst there is no doubt that some homosexuals have abused children, it is a generalisation that is as unjustified as accusing all heterosexual men of wanting to rape little girls. It is important therefore to distinguish between one's personal attitude to homosexuality and the rights of Jews who are homosexual. The legal position of homosexuality in Britain must also be taken into account. Whereas homosexuality was regarded previously as a criminal offence, punishable by prison sentence, since 1969 homosexual activity is legal between consenting adults in private. Lesbianism was not included in the original prohibitions concerning sexual behaviour (according to one theory because it was thought not to exist) and so has never been illegal.

It is important to recognise that the sexual preferences of individuals are only one aspect of their personality; this applies as much to homosexuals as it does to heterosexuals. It therefore cannot be the sole criterion by which a person is judged; indeed it is not anyone else's concern unless it causes hurt to others. Individuals should be valued according to their character, maturity, ethical conduct and involvement in Jewish life. It should be noted, although it may be deemed self-evident, that Jewish homosexuals feel as Jewish as do Jewish heterosexuals, having had a Jewish upbringing in a Jewish home and passing through the same educational system as did others. The only difference is that very often they feel isolated by the way in which the Jewish community is geared almost exclusively to married couples with children. They are also aware of the stigma attached to homosexuality both by Jewish tradition and by individual Jews today, and it can lead to them dropping out of communal life for fear of being rejected. Yet Jewish homosexuals and lesbians can be Jewish, have a strong Jewish identity and feel committed to Jewish life and practices. It is clear, therefore, that the traditional attitudes of Jewish Law are no longer appropriate in an age that recognises homosexuality as a natural state that cannot be altered. There is no reason why a Jew who is known to be a homosexual should not be a member of a synagogue and participate fully in communal activities. This would include having a *mitzvah* during services or occupying positions on Council. The only caveat would be that a homosexual who flaunted his sexuality and caused distress to others would not be made welcome – although this would of course apply equally to a heterosexual who behaved flagrantly in public in a sexually provocative way and disturbed communal life.

The Jewish attitude to the sexual acts of homosexuals should be to extend to them the permission that governs all sexual behaviour between consenting adults in private, and which has always applied to a wide range of practices between husband and wife in the intimacy of the marital relationship (*Nedarim* 20b). Conversely all infidelity, promiscuity or sexual exploitation, whether by heterosexuals or homosexuals, is to be condemned. Moreover, there should be an end to the double standards that exist whereby a person who breaks the seventh commandment and commits adultery can escape criticism whereas a homosexual who has a faithful relationship is viewed with horror.

The practice that has arisen in the United States of having separate homosexual synagogues is rejected. It makes the issue of one's sexual orientation the prime feature of one's identity and reinforces the prejudice that homosexuals are sufficiently different to be segregated from the rest of the community. Nevertheless, the special needs of Jewish homosexuals can be recognised, as are those of other groups in the Jewish community such as widows, one-parent families and divorcees. Thus specific activities may be arranged for them within the framework of the congregation, as happens in at least one Reform synagogue where there is a monthly meeting of the Jewish Gay and Lesbian Group. Another community has made a point of extending a special welcome to minorities within the Jewish world, including gays and lesbians, who feel alienated by established synagogues.

A related issue is the question of homosexual marriages. In Britain such unions are not recognised by civil law and have no legal validity, but this does not prevent there being a ceremony acknowledging the commitment of a couple to each other. The Jewish understanding of marriage is directed entirely to a heterosexual union and so a *chuppah* in its current form would not be appropriate. However, the author suggests that if a homosexual or lesbian couple decide to live together permanently, a special blessing could be devised for the occasion with appropriately written prayers; alternatively, the ceremony of fixing a *mezuzah* could be expanded, symbolising the establishment of a Jewish home and with the hope expressed that those living in it dwell together in harmony.

---

4. IS THERE A REFORM POLICY ON ECOLOGY?

Ecology in the sense of endeavouring to protect the planet from the harmful effects of human activity is a modern problem. In the past all efforts were directed towards 'subduing' the earth and asserting human mastery over it (Genesis 1.28). Now it is recognised that humanity has overreached itself and is endangering its own survival. In particular the widespread use of chemical products has polluted the water, land and air, and has harmed the ozone layer. The despoliation of natural resources, such as forests, has not only threatened many species of wildlife, but has upset the balance of the eco-system with potentially fatal results for the earth's atmosphere. In the 1980s the seriousness of the situation turned ecology from a fringe issue to a major item on the political agenda. The global nature of the problem means that any successful action will have to be taken by national governments and through international co-operation. However, from a Jewish standpoint such action is not only a political necessity but a religious command.

A variety of biblical and *talmudic* laws indicate that whilst the land was to be used for the benefit of humanity, it had to be treated responsibly. Thus any army besieging a city was prohibited from destroying fruit-bearing trees (Deuteronomy 20.19). From this arose the principle that all other instances of wasting resources were forbidden, including food (*Shabbat* 140b), water (*Yebamot* 11b) and all things that might be of use to others (*Baba Kamma* 91b). Safety standards were also enjoined. They ranged from disposal of domestic rubbish, for instance broken glass which should be buried in one's own land rather than scattered on the public domain (*Baba Kamma* 30a), to the effects of 'industrial' activity, for instance a threshing floor was prohibited within fifty cubits of the city limits lest chaff was carried by the wind and affected the health of city dwellers (*Baba Batra* 24b), while no furnaces were allowed in Jerusalem because of the fumes (*Baba Kamma* 82b).

Part of the philosophy behind such regulations is the view that the world does not belong to humanity but is the creation of God entrusted to humanity's stewardship. Despoiling the world is not only against our own self interest but a denial of God. Protecting it is one way of acknowledging God's creative power. It is a heavy responsibility that we have to take seriously. As the *Midrash* declares (Ecclesiastes *Rabbah* 7.13):

> In the hour when the Holy One, Blessed be He, created the first man,
> He took him and let him pass before all the trees of the Garden of Eden,
> And said to Him:
> See my works, how fine and excellent they are!
> Now all that I have created for you have I created.
> Think upon this, and do not corrupt and desolate My world;
> For if you do corrupt it, there is no-one to set it right after you.

Another aspect of Jewish philosophy is that we deal in the long-term not just in the present moment. There is a responsibility to the future and to the next generation. It is typified by Honi Ha'me'aggel (first century BCE) who was planting a sapling in his old age and was asked why he bothered doing so as he would never live long enough to enjoy its fruit. His reply serves as a message for our time too: "When I came into the world, I found it well stocked by those who had preceded me. I now plant for those who will come after me" (*Ta'anit* 23a).

It is important to note that intrinsic to both Jewish legal and homiletical literature was the notion that protection of the environment was the specific responsibility of each individual. It is something towards which everyone can and should make their own personal contribution. In a modern context, therefore, it is not just a task that is allocated to the government but is also the duty of every Jew in their own daily affairs. Whilst at first thought it may seem beyond the power of most people to have any effect on the environment, individuals can exercise a considerable range of options with a massive accumulative influence if they so choose, as will be seen below.

In response to both the concern expressed by Jewish tradition and the warnings of modern environmentalists, the RSGB has urged its synagogues to take an active interest in ecology and adopt particular measures to protect the environment. At the 1988 Annual Conference a resolution declared:

> This 47th Annual Conference, recognising the Rabbinic principle of *bal tashchit* ('do not destroy') calls upon all synagogues and their members to consider the principles of ecologically sound living and their application to our daily lives:

(a) A reverence for the Earth and all its creatures.
(b) Recognition of the inter-dependence of all life.
(c) Protection of the environment as a precondition of a healthy prosperous society.
(d) Recognition of the finite nature of the Earth's resources and our responsibility towards future generations.

A resolution at the 1990 Annual Conference urged members to recognise that "Care for the environment is not altruism but is essential to their own well-being". It urged them to take "every option available, both communally, privately and in business for environmentally responsible behaviour".

Several Reform synagogues have taken steps contributing towards a healthier world by measures such as collecting waste paper for recycling; using recycled paper for synagogue stationery, photocopying and toilet paper; asking cleaners to use environmentally-friendly cleaning materials (non-toxic); abolishing the use of non-biodegradable disposable cups and plates; taking empty coffee jars and wine bottles to a bottle bank; using free-range products for food cooked at synagogue functions and avoiding the use of pesticides in synagogue gardens. Whilst the small number of synagogues in the country means that such initiatives will have only a limited effect, they are an important statement of principle. They also offer a model for individuals to follow both at home and at work. As well as the above ideas, other suggestions are that one uses lead-free petrol, avoids aerosol cans containing chloro-fluoro-carbons (CFCs), buys organically grown produce whenever available, and that one plants saplings at *Tu Bi'Shevat*[1]. Each individual action counts and makes a difference; the combined effort of thousands of people makes an even bigger difference, and although we may not be able to complete the task by ourselves, that does not give us the right to desist from it (*Avot* 2.21).

5. SHOULD SYNAGOGUES BE INVOLVED IN POLITICAL OR SOCIAL ACTION?

There has been a tendency for many British Jews to regard synagogues as being occupied solely with internal Jewish affairs. They have become a sanctuary from the outside world, and wider issues are considered inappro-

---

1 For a fuller list see Borts, Chiat and Joseph, *Do Not Destroy My World*, Parts I and II

priate. According to this view, it is legitimate for synagogues to raise funds for the Jewish Welfare Board or to agitate on behalf of Soviet Jewry, but wrong for synagogues to be involved with pressure groups for better housing facilities locally, or to promote anti-apartheid campaigns. Individuals may throw themselves into political or social causes in a private capacity, but the community must be neutral in such areas and conserve its energy for specifically Jewish concerns.

It is a position that owes much to the British influence, but little to Jewish imperatives. It is based on the model of a distinction between Church and State in which religion should not concern itself with general issues but leave them to the politicians. It is an attitude also influenced by the long struggle by the Jewish community to be integrated into society, so that it is reluctant now to take corporate action and to stand out. It is feared that it would not only make the community open to attack by those who take an opposing view, but might also raise accusations of Jewish separatism.

If one delves into the Bible, however, a totally different scenario presents itself. The mission of the Prophets was primarily to protest against contemporary evils. They exposed the shortcomings of the political system, attacking the monarchy for its abuse of power (Isaiah 1.23). They decried the corruption of the religious hierarchy, condemning priests for their irreligion and hypocrisy (Isaiah 1.11-15). They railed against the malpractices of the business community, lambasting the way it cheated and grew rich at the expense of others (Amos 8.4-6). They criticised the neglect of human rights, castigating those who trampled on the weaker members of society (Amos 5.7,10-11). They reminded both the people and the leaders of Israel that the laws of Judaism apply as much to public affairs as they do to domestic life. Justice and righteousness have to take precedence over expediency and self-interest. Anything less was contravening the will of God. In Micah's paraphrase of the biblical teachings, "It has been told to you, mankind, what is good, and what the Lord requires of you: only to do justly, and to love mercy, and to walk humbly with your God" (6.8). For the Prophets there was no separation between spiritual and secular matters, and there was no area to which religious values did not extend. The same still holds true today.

There is little point in Judaism developing a responsible set of ethics if they are not applied to all aspects of life. Similarly there is no need for a vision of a Messianic world in which "nation shall not lift up sword against nation" (Micah 4.3) if one does not involve oneself in the affairs of the nation. The moral foundations of Judaism must speak to all situations and a failure to do so challenges the very purpose of the faith. Synagogues do not necessarily have a monopoly on ethical sensitivities, but neither do political circles, and the former might well have as good a perspective as the latter. The command to "let justice roll down like water and righteousness like an everlasting stream" (Amos 5.24) cannot be limited to synagogue council meetings but is a direct prescription for political and social action generally. Indeed it may be claimed that it was one of the contributions of early Reform Judaism to rediscover and stress the voice of the Prophets. Despite being read out in synagogue as part of the weekly *haftarah* portion every Sabbath, they sometimes became lost amongst the emphasis on ritual practices and *halachic* arguments that had grown up over the centuries. Yet the words of Isaiah and Amos are as much part of Judaism as those of Rashi and Maimonides. Jewish causes should not be ignored, but there is every reason for synagogues today to try to put into practice the great prophetic cries for social justice wherever the need arises.

In keeping with the dictates of prophetic Judaism, many Reform synagogues have committees concerned with general issues within society so as to make a distinctively Jewish contribution, ranging from local charities to the Third World, from promoting disarmament to combating racism. The RSGB Social Issues Group often acts as a central resource supplying background information and campaign ideas. Its members have also played a role in initiating specific groups such as Jews Against Apartheid, Jewish Support for the Homeless, JONAH (Jews Organised for a Nuclear Arms Halt) and *Tzedek* (Jewish Action for a Just World). The fact that some of these interests may be identified at times with certain political groups is seen as coincidental to the pursuit of Jewish ideals. The activities are undertaken for religious reasons even though it is inevitable that they may sometimes cross political boundaries. There will also be many instances where there is a common goal but different opinions as to the best method of achieving it. Thus Jewish teaching would be horrified at the thought of the global destruction possible in a nuclear war and would urge its prevention. However, individuals will differ as to whether unilateral or multilateral disarmament is the way most likely to achieve it. Nevertheless these differences do not absolve the community from its responsibility to raise such issues and from formulating a Jewish response where possible. In recent years the Annual Conference of the RSGB has passed resolutions on a variety of pressing social and political problems, urging all synagogues to be concerned with them as part of their religious duty. Amongst the topics covered were:

Apartheid[1]
Conference congratulates the South African Government on the steps taken thus far to reduce racial discrimination in the Republic. It welcomes the stated intentions to repeal the remaining discriminatory legislation so as ultimately to abolish apartheid ... remembering the words of the prophet Amos, "Are you not as the children of the Ethiopians unto me says the Lord?" (Amos 9.7) ... Calls upon individual members and constituent synagogues to support Jews Against Apartheid and other anti-apartheid organisations working to achieve equality before the law for all South Africa's citizens, and in general to involve themselves in working to eradicate the evils of racism and prejudice from society.

Arms Trade[1]
Conference, mindful of the prophet Micah's vision of a universal peace when nations "Shall hammer their swords into ploughshares and their spears into pruning hooks" and when "Nation shall not lift up sword against nation" (Micah 4.3-4) ... Notes that 87% of weapons in the Third World were supplied by the five permanent members of the UN Security Council and draws attention to the appalling dangers created by the international arms trade terrifyingly demonstrated by the Gulf War and its aftermath ... Urges Her Majesty's Government to cease exporting weapons to unstable and irresponsible regimes and those that have a poor record in human rights and demonstrate a low regard for human life ... It calls upon the Government to work for a reduction in the international arms trade and to exercise its powers and influence to redirect resources of the arms industry and its sophisticated technology towards output beneficial to humanity ... Calls upon individuals and congregations to educate themselves on this issue, to lobby MPs and MEPs urging them to press for reduction in the arms trade, and to lend their support to organisations working on these issues.

Homelessness[1]
Conference, mindful of Jewish teaching to "Share your food with the hungry and bring the homeless into your home" (Isaiah 58.7) and to "Let your house be open wide and the poor be members of your household" (*Avot* 1.5) ... Recognises the problem of homelessness – the lack of those

---

1 RSGB Annual Conference 1991

basic housing facilities available to the majority of our fellow citizens – as an affront to the dignity of the individual and a threat to the well-being of society; it deplores a situation which denies the concept of a community based upon social justice ... Believes that in large measure this desperate and increasing problem in our society results directly from economic and social policies of recent years eg changes in benefit systems, high interest rates, the closing of mental hospitals ... Welcomes all attempts made by Her Majesty's Government to supply adequate shelter and living accommodation to the homeless, but believes that a much greater percentage of the national budget must be applied to the elimination of this evil. It therefore urges the Government to invest money in permanent housing rather than in temporary bed and breakfast accommodation; to invest in future generations by providing day care facilities for homeless families; to make adequate provision in the community, when closing down mental hospitals, for the needs of those suffering from nervous and mental disorders. It calls upon individuals and congregations to support the work of charitable housing associations located in their communities, to run study programmes, *tzedakah* projects and youth activities which will raise the awareness among their members of the problems of the homeless.

Human Rights[1]
Conference, mindful of Jewish teaching that, "All human beings are created in the image of God" (Genesis 1.27) and that "You may not stand idly by the blood of your neighbour" (Leviticus 19.16), and aware that the Universal Declaration of Human Rights of 1948 recognises that "The inherent dignity and ... the equal and inalienable rights of all members of the human family is the foundation of freedom, justice and peace in the world" ... Calls upon Her Majesty's Government to do everything in its power to protect the rights of individuals and exert its influence in the United Nations and in all other international family of forums towards achieving the purposes of the Declaration of Human Rights ... Urges the Government when establishing diplomatic relations with other states to take note of and have regard to their record on Human Rights ... In the light of recent evidence of serious miscarriages of justice with their tragic conscquences on the lives of those wrongly convicted, calls for the

---

[1] RSGB Annual Conference 1991

independent review of the criminal justice system ... Calls upon RSGB synagogues and their members to inform themselves of human rights issues and to support organisations with proven records of working to achieve human dignity and justice wherever these values, which are central to Judaism, are disregarded.

Racism[2]
Conference, mindful of Jewish teaching that all humans are created in the image of God (Genesis 1.26) and that we should "Know the heart of the stranger for we were strangers in the land of Egypt" (Exodus 23.9) ... Unequivocably condemns racism and discrimination in any form and wherever it is to be found ... Expresses concern that many aspects of the implementation of the immigration laws and responses to requests for political asylum appear arbitrary, discriminatory and contrary to natural justice ... Calls upon Her Majesty's Government to review immigration procedures and work towards restoring the reputation of this country as a place of security for refugees; review current racial equality legislation with a view to strengthening local and national monitoring bodies; review the criminal justice system in order that racism can be eradicated from its institutions; investigate the possibility of introducing legislation to inhibit and prohibit group libel ... Calls upon constituent synagogues to conduct education programmes with children, young people and adults in order to increase knowledge of Jewish teaching that all human beings and all races are created equal and to increase awareness of the extent of racism in the United Kingdom; take practical action by uniting with other groups locally (eg other faiths, Community Relations Councils) to build community links to monitor local race and community relations and to campaign against injustice where necessary.

World Poverty and Hunger[2]
Conference expresses profound concern at the continuing extent of world hunger and poverty ... Notes that Jewish tradition enjoins us to give direct assistance to those in need for their immediate requirements, to work in partnership to help them become self-reliant and self-supporting and to work for long-term change to eradicate the causes of poverty; recent doubts about the objectivity of certain organisations in certain

---

2 RSGB Annual Conference 1990

circumstances should not prevent us from responding to the wider need ... Calls upon Her Majesty's Government and the European Community to increase their provision for overseas aid to meet the UN target of 0.7% of gross national product and to target a far greater proportion through Non-Governmental Organisations where these have proved to be effective agencies for ensuring real long-term development for the poorest people ... Calls upon constituent synagogues and associated bodies to help combat world hunger by direct participation in national education and fund-raising programmes run within the Jewish community; creating links with a specific overseas community or institution (eg school, clinic) or undertaking a particular project.

6. MAY JEWS BECOME FREEMASONS?

The Order of Freemasons has frequently caused controversy. When it was formed in the early 1700s, it was associated with free-thinkers and anti-clerics, and was often accused of fermenting revolutionary tendencies. In the 1980s the Methodists denounced the movement as incompatible with Christian belief and forbade Methodists to be members of the Order (a position already taken by the Roman Catholic Church in 1738), while the Church of England also expressed reservations.

From a Jewish perspective the fact that Freemasonry is a secret society is not objectionable in itself. It may well be distasteful to some people and give rise to accusations of elitism and self-interest, but Jews have every right to join a private association providing its beliefs and practices do not oppose the tenets of Judaism and are not harmful to either members or non-members. Freemasonry does not consider itself to be a religion, or a substitute for religion. It demands of its members belief in a Supreme Being – known as "the Great Architect of the Universe" – but provides no system of faith of its own. Indeed discussion of religion is forbidden at Masonic meetings, which not only avoids friction between those of different faiths but also prevents any Masonic dogma from developing. It is expected that Masons continue to subscribe to their own particular faith and without imposing any additional layers of belief. The prayers that do take place at its meetings are merely part of the ritual procedures and are not intended as a form of worship. Their rituals, too, are purely ceremonial and lack any religious significance. It seems clear that whilst the Masonic rites may appear bizarre to many outsiders, they do not contravene Jewish theology.

The practical effects of Freemasonry seem to be beneficial. As well as providing fraternal meetings for fellow Masons, they promote many welfare activities and have established a network of hospitals, libraries and old age homes. Although primarily intended for their own membership, they also extend to the general public. Its three pillars – brotherly love, honesty and charity – are in keeping with Jewish teaching. The only caveat would be if loyalty between fellow Masons meant that one broke the law of the land or transgressed Jewish ethics. Such behaviour would be unacceptable and justify condemnation. However, there is no objection to mutual help providing it does not cross these boundaries.

It should be noted in passing that much of Freemasonry is based on biblical texts and in particular on the building of Solomon's Temple which is recorded in the first Book of Kings. Thus the ranks of Freemasons supposedly correspond to those amongst the builders of ancient Israel – Apprentice, Mason and Master Mason; Hebrew is occasionally present in Masonic rituals as the names of Solomon's builders are used as code words; the Shield of David features as a symbol in some Masonic rituals. The Jewish connections are not necessarily historical – for instance the Shield of David was not associated with Solomon's Temple – although they engender a positive attitude to the Israelites of old. Freemasons have also generally shown much tolerance to Jews, whether as a result of this biblical affinity or because of their free-thinking origins. Thus Jews were admitted to Masonic lodges from the earliest years of the Order, and at a time when many other avenues – universities, parliament, local office – were closed to them. Indeed the high involvement of Jews led to German anti-semitic literature claiming that part of the blame for Germany's defeat in the First World War was due to a sinister alliance of Jews and Freemasons! Accusations of a Jewish Masonic plot to dominate the world also appeared in various editions of the Protocols of Zion. There was, of course, no truth in such assertions, but they illustrate the prejudice and ignorance surrounding Masons as much as that concerning Jews. The Jewish organisation *B'nai Brith* is closely modelled upon Freemasonry, being a specifically Jewish fraternal order, based on the same principle and with its own system of lodges, special rituals and regalia, and with members calling each other Brother and Sister.

The author suggests, therefore, that the tenets and activities of Freemasonry are not in conflict with Judaism and that there is no bar to Jews becoming Masons. The recent opposition to Freemasons expressed by the Churches reflects a Christian emphasis on doctrinal matters that is not matched in Judaism. The Order can be seen as a social and charitable body whose rituals amount to harmless pageantry and whose secrecy is regrettable but of little consequence. Participation by Jews is purely a matter for personal decision.

7. WHAT IS THE REFORM ATTITUDE TO YOGA, NEW AGE AND OTHER MODERN TRENDS?

There has been an enormous interest in alternatives to the Judeo-Christian heritage in the West since the First World War. Jews, too, have been part of this trend, motivated both by dissatisfaction with Judaism as they see it and attraction to particular aspects of other paths. These include Eastern religions, new cults, secular philosophies and the occult. In many cases they are incompatible with Judaism, involving a completely different set of beliefs that either contradict Jewish tenets or that introduce alien ideas. Jews who adopt such approaches have effectively left the Jewish religion. Their departure is not only a cause for regret but also a challenge. It highlights the failure of Judaism as taught to answer the spiritual needs of certain individuals within it. Sometimes it is a matter of presentation: spirituality, self-examination, personal growth, communal sharing, awareness of nature and inner peace are elements that are often admired in other religions but unseen in Judaism. Yet they all exist within Judaism, albeit little expressed and overshadowed by other characteristics. A number of Reform synagogues have made great efforts in recent years to bring to the fore such features – by changes within the service that allow greater freedom of self-expression and more spontaneity; by establishing *chavurot* that cater for smaller, more intimate groups engaged in prayer and study; and by running workshops on creative spirituality that respond to personal needs and aspirations.

There are other trends that are not necessarily at variance with Judaism and can be engaged in alongside one's Jewish beliefs. In the case of yoga much depends on the approach taken. If it is treated as an alternative religion, as it is amongst some devotees, with its own all-inclusive set of beliefs and practices, then it is difficult to reconcile with Judaism. However, in its general format today it has been divested of any religious association and for most people it is seen purely as a secular activity, as a useful discipline that encourages bodily and mental fitness. As a method of relaxation, coping with stress and positive thinking, it can be welcomed. There is nothing un-Jewish about physical exercise, while the act of meditation is no stranger to the liturgy or to Jewish mystical strands. The value of silence and reflection is well attested in Jewish thought, being regarded as a source of wisdom as well as a means of healing troubled spirits (*Megillah* 18a, *Avot* 1.17, *Zohar* 173a). Indeed, it has long been a tradition that one should spend time every night reflecting upon the events of the day, and thereby restore one's sense of inner calm before retiring.

Another aspect of yoga is casting aside outer images and mundane distractions; instead, one should be in touch with one's higher self and concentrate on more spiritual aspects. This coincides with *Chasidic* teachings on the need to transcend selfish desires, empty the mind of egoistical concerns, and realise the divine spark within one. The use of mantras is a technical device to help achieve this through intense concentration, and have also been employed in Jewish mystical traditions. The only caveat regarding yoga is that the mantras used should not have any religious symbolism to them, while the timing of one's yoga activity should not conflict with Jewish services or home celebrations.

Transcendental Meditation (TM) has similarities to yoga but is separate from it. It is not compatible with Judaism because it purports to be a complete belief system that has no need for other faiths, including Judaism. Moreover, it sees meditation not just as a beneficial exercise but as a way of achieving enlightenment through self-realisation. There is no God, just one's own inner godliness. For Judaism this is a denial of God and the substitution of self-worship. It conflicts with the Jewish view that the goal of prayer and contemplation is communion with God, the highest power of all. There is also concern over the stature accorded to its central figure, the Maharishi, as there is over other gurus in similar cults. The complete hold that they have over their followers verges on the idolatrous. Judaism itself knows of many charismatic personalities, but excessive hero-worship has always been discouraged. The fact that Moses' name is hardly mentioned in the *Haggadah* is no accident but part of this policy. Indeed this has been one of several reasons why the Reform Movement has declined to establish a Reform Chief Rabbi, and why it regards as unhealthy the unquestioning adulation accorded to some *Chasidic* leaders.

Another recent trend has been the New Age movement – a mixture of astrology, the occult, meditation, psychology, mysticism and alternative healing arts – that purports to herald the dawn of a completely new era in human existence. It does not have a clearly defined belief system, but it is characterised by an emphasis on individual freedom, giving full reign to one's inner being and exploring one's own personal divinity. New Age thinkers reject monotheist religions, and considers them not only old-fashioned but also positively harmful; Judaism is regarded as being particularly at fault for inventing the idea of God and for imposing a moral code, both of which are considered unnatural and constricting. Instead, it is held that there is an energy force in the universe, while there are no moral absolutes other than what feels right at a given time. In Jewish eyes this is merely a new form of paganism (a title to which New Age does not object) with the ego replacing God and with personal whim ousting social responsibility. In a world that is God-centred, freedom and duty are intertwined, balancing each other and allowing self-development alongside care for others. In the classic formulation by Hillel "If I am not for myself, who is for me? But if I am only for myself, what am I? And if not now, when?" (*Avot* 1.14). A me-centred world abrogates communal caring, dismembers the structure of society and can result in the rights of many individuals (particularly weaker members of society) being endangered rather than enhanced. Equally worrying is the extreme intolerance displayed by some of the groups associated with New Age, whose laudable aims can turn into horrific policies. Thus it has been suggested that the desire to control world population might mean allowing famines to take their 'natural' course unaided; thus the hope that all nations live in togetherness might entail dismantling those who are incompatible with their surroundings, notably Israel.

It should be noted that 'New Age' has become a fashionable term for many other developments that are not necessarily connected with the philosophical roots of the New Age movement. However, this blurring of distinctions can be counter-productive in that it gives an acceptable image to a pagan cult; members of Reform synagogues are urged to be wary of inadvertently condoning it. Of course it must be admitted that some of the ideas of New Age are appealing and worthwhile, such as emphasis on ecological harmony, healthy diet, spiritual growth and self-exploration. They may not be original to New Age but have been given prominence by it. These features must be separated from the unacceptable aspects of the movement. Indeed, they can be found within Jewish teaching, although they have been neglected and allowed almost to disappear from sight. They should be re-emphasised and taken up by synagogues; and Jews on the fringes of the community seeking a more spiritual and meaningful approach to life should be encouraged to pursue such concerns within a Jewish framework.

THIS IS REFORM

The following is a personal summary of some of the main tenets of Reform Judaism. It is offered as a useful précis, but with the caveat that any such generalisation inevitably omits or simplifies aspects of a large and complex subject.

Reform
traces its roots to Abraham's response to the call of God and tries to fulfil the covenant established by him for his descendants.

Reform
sees the revelation at Mount Sinai as crucial, providing the impetus for Jewish life ever since.

Reform
considers that the *Torah* contains the word of God, although interpreted and written down by human beings.

Reform
holds that God's revelation did not end at Sinai but continues, and that it is the duty of each generation to understand the will of God in its own time.

Reform
values the legacy of the Prophetic books and sees them as a source of inspiration for Jewish belief and conduct.

Reform
regards Rabbinic Law as a vital part of Judaism, albeit human in origin and subject to amendment.

Reform
recognises that change has always been part of Judaism and must continue to be applied where appropriate to keep it vibrant.

Reform
accepts that, alongside tradition, the dictates of reason, conscience and the expanding frontiers of science are important influences on our religious decisions.

Reform
holds that being religious does not necessarily mean one is always certain about one's beliefs, but that one is engaged in a religious search.

Reform
offers general guidelines for Jewish living which allow for individual choice within certain parameters and in the context of communal consensus.

Reform
holds that the glory of Judaism lies in its ethical teachings and that they should always be evident in our daily conduct.

Reform
believes that laws should be intelligible, prayer should be comprehensible, rituals should be meaningful, women should be equal, and our neighbours should be loved as ourselves.

Reform
believes that handing on the faith and practice of Judaism positively to the next generation is a key obligation upon all Jews.

Reform
regards itself as one of many valid expressions of Judaism, all of which seek to fulfil Jewish tradition according to their own understanding.

Reform
regards Judaism as one of many paths to God, sharing several basic tenets with other faiths, but with its own distinctive identity.

Reform
considers that Israel is an important part of Jewish life today, although Judaism itself transcends territorial limitations.

Reform
regards all Jews as fellow-Jews, with common bonds and a special responsibility for each other.

Reform
recognises that we are also part of the larger family of humanity, and that we should work for the greater good of all around us.

Reform
believes that all who inhabit the earth have a duty to treat it with care so that future generations will not suffer because of us.

Reform
has a vision of a Messianic Age when the world is at peace with itself, and towards which everyone can contribute.

APPENDIX ONE

REFORM GUIDELINES
from Chapter I Section 3

The following is a summary of the guidelines for the development of Reform *halachah* in Rabbi A M Bayfield's *God's Demands and Israel's Needs*.

1. The assumption that tradition should be followed unless there are very good reasons for departing from it.

2. The arrangement of principles into a hierarchy in which one principle may override another. Thus the principle that the Sabbath should be a day of joy can justify switching on lights on the Sabbath even though it is forbidden according to Orthodox interpretation of the rule not to create a fire on the Sabbath.

3. The acceptance that individual responses may vary within the broad performance of a *mitzvah*. Thus some will observe *kashrut* by abstaining from forbidden foods, others by not mixing milk and meat, and others by becoming vegetarian.

4. The awareness that the observances officially kept in synagogue can have an important educational role and should be used as a bridge between tradition and the individual. Thus although *havdalah* is normally a home ceremony, if it is performed in synagogue before a Saturday night function it maintains an option that otherwise may be lost to many individuals.

5. The evaluation of a custom should not be based on its original purpose but on its present value. Thus the fact that the *ner tamid* (eternal light) represents the *menorah*, which provided permanent light for the Temple (Exodus 27.20), is of little consequence besides its contemporary significance as the eternal presence of God.

6. General philosophy is not enough and practical details must be provided for everyday situations. Thus it needs to be stated whether, for instance, "you shall not steal" applies to using the office telephone for personal calls.

7. Alongside the set procedures in status matters, discretion must have an important

place so as to prevent deserving cases being rejected because general rules cannot take every eventuality into account.

8. A readiness to differ from tradition when appropriate and to avoid the syndrome of regarding the past as wonderful and the present as contemptible. Respect and humility are necessary, but we have as much authority to legislate for our times as previous generations did for theirs.

9. Common sense is another vital criterion, which would prevent instances of good intentions leading to ridiculous conclusions. Thus the rule that a married woman should cover her hair so as not to attract the attention of other men results in many wearing a *sheitel* (wig) that makes her more beautiful than did her natural hair.

10. The process of establishing a Reform position should not be limited to Rabbis but include discussion and study with the general community, so that there is no gulf between Rabbis and congregants and to encourage a greater sense of individual commitment.

APPENDIX TWO

KASHRUT
from Chapter V Section 2

The policy established for the students' kitchen at the Leo Baeck College consists of traditional *halachic* standards interpreted liberally. It is quoted here not as a definitive Reform statement but as one example of the public observance of *kashrut* at a Reform institution.

1. Both milk products and meat products may be used.

2. All meat products should be *kosher*. Products containing animal fat should be avoided, although it should be noted that whilst they remain cold they cause no problems for other people.

3. Separate pots and pans, plates and cutlery should be maintained for milk products and meat products.

4. Although it is not strictly necessary, it may be convenient to have separate dishcloths and cleaning materials.

5. To avoid confusion it may well be easiest to keep pots, pans, plates, etc in separate cupboards and mark them whenever possible.

6. Separate tablecloths are not necessary.

7. Only glass plates, cups, etc are used (which are more easily rendered *kosher* if a mistake occurs).

8. To avoid doubt over what has happened in the past, kitchens should be made *kosher* from the point at which these rules are adopted:
    (a) The empty oven should be heated up;
    (b) Cooking utensils should be passed through a fire;
    (c) The fridge should be cleaned;
    (d) All plates and cutlery (including two piece cutlery, wooden spoons, etc) should be washed in boiling water.

9. Milk and meat products may be placed in the same fridge but it is advisable to use separate shelves; two fridges might simplify the practicalities even though this is not *halachically* necessary.

10. Prepared food may be brought in from outside provided that no *terefah* products are included, and milk and meat are separated; particular care should be given to products containing animal fats, eg certain biscuits.

11. It is very important that goodwill is relied upon and that accidental infringements are dealt with sensibly and liberally.

BIBLIOGRAPHY

The following list includes sources quoted in the book as well as other publications relating to Reform Judaism in Britain. Those marked with an asterisk are published by the RSGB or other institutions located at the Sternberg Centre for Judaism, London.

UNPUBLISHED DOCUMENTS
Current Procedures and Practices of the Rabbinic Court of the Reform
    Synagogues of Great Britain (1985)
Assembly of Rabbis Revised Constitution (1981)
Minutes of the Assembly of Rabbis

BOOKS

*Blue, Lionel & **Forms of Prayer for Jewish Worship**
Magonet, Jonathan (eds) Volume I (Daily, Sabbath and Occasional Prayers) (1977)

*Blue, Lionel & **Forms of Prayer for Jewish Worship**
Magonet, Jonathan (eds) Volume III (Prayers for High Holy Days) (1985)

*Blue, Lionel & **Forms of Prayer for Jewish Worship**
Magonet, Jonathan (eds) Shavuot – Introductory Format (1988)

Cooper, Howard (ed) **Soul Searching: Studies in Judaism and Psychotherapy** (SCM Press, 1988)

Joseph, Morris **Judaism as Creed and Life** – Fourth Edition (Routledge & Kegan Paul, 1958)

*Marmur, Dow (ed) **A Genuine Search** (1979)

*Marmur, Dow (ed) **Reform Judaism** (1973)

Singer, Simeon (ed) **The Authorised Daily Prayer Book** (United Synagogue 1962)

BOOKLETS

*Bayfield, A M	**God's Demands and Israel's Needs** (Guidelines for the Development of Reform Halacha) (1981)
*Borts, Barbara	**Abortion – A Jewish Response** (1984)
*Borts, Barbara & Chiat Sheila & Joseph Vicky	**Do Not Destroy My World** Parts I and II (1989)
*Borts, Barbara & Eimer, Dee & others	**Women and Tallit** (1988)
*de Lange, Elaine	**Women in Reform Judaism** (1974)
*Golby, Amanda	**Conversion to Judaism** (1991)
*Golby, Amanda	**Women in Reform Judaism** (1991)
*Greengross, Wendy	**Jewish and Homosexual** (1982)
*Ish-Horowicz, Moshe	**Halakhah – Orthodoxy and Reform** (1988)
*Kershen, Anne J (ed)	**150 Years of Progressive Judaism in Britain** (1990)
*Leigh, Michael	**Aspects of Kashrut** (1973)
*Magonet, Jonathan	**The New Reform Prayer Book** (1977)
*Marmur, Dow	**Intermarriage** (1973)
*Marmur, Dow	**The Jewish Family Today and Tomorrow** (1983)
*Marmur, Dow	**Remember The Sabbath Day** (Guidelines for the Celebration and Observance of Shabbat) (1983)
*Roodyn, Donald Bernard	**Alternative Kashrut: Judaism, Vegetarianism and the Factory Farm** (1976)
*Romain, Jonathan	**Calendar of Torah and Haftarah Readings** (1990)
*Romain, Jonathan	**How To Grow** (1985)
*Rothschild, Walter	**Cremation** (1991)

*RSGB	**Funeral Service** (1974)
*Solomons, Stanley	**Brit Milah** (1988)
*Tabick, Larry & Bulka, Colin & Miller, Steve	**The Plight of the Homeless – A Jewish Response** (1989)
Waterman, Stanley & Kosmin, Barry	**British Jewry in the Eighties** (Board of Deputies, 1986)

CURRENT PERIODICALS
***European Judaism**

***Inform** (Newsletter of the RSGB)

***Manna** (Journal of the Sternberg Centre for Judaism)

***New Ideas in Progressive Jewish Education**

Amongst many articles of note in the above periodicals, particular attention is drawn to the theological essay on 'Progressive Judaism' by Rabbi A M Bayfield in the Spring 1990 edition of **Manna**.

HEBREW TEXTS
Some of the Rabbinic texts quoted can be found in English translation:

Mishnah	Translated by Herbert Danby (Oxford University Press, 1933)
Talmud (Babylonian)	Translation edited by Isadore Epstein (Soncino, 1935)

GLOSSARY

The literal meaning of each word is given in brackets. Hebrew words in the explanation are translated if they do not appear elsewhere in the glossary.

Adar
Hebrew month occurring around March; *Purim* is on the 14th *Adar*.
Agunah (**a chained woman**)
Woman unable to remarry in synagogue because the bonds of her existing marriage have not been severed.
Aleinu (**it is our duty**)
Prayer concerning the duties of Israel, occurring towards the end of all daily, Sabbath and festival services.
Aliyah; **plural:** *Aliyot* (**going up**)
The honour of being called to recite the blessings over the *Torah* during a service; it can also mean emigration to Israel.
Amidah (**standing**)
Central prayer in all daily, Sabbath and festival services; also known as the *Shmoneh Esreh* (the eighteen benedictions) and the *Tefillah* (the prayer).
Arba kanfot (**four corners**)
Garment with *tzitzit* on each of its four corners, worn in fulfilment of the command in Numbers 15.39; also known as *tallit katan*.
Ashkenazi (**biblical place name**)
Term now used for Jews originating from Central and Eastern Europe.
Bal tashchit (**do not destroy**)
The command in Deuteronomy 20.19 not to destroy trees unnecessarily.
Bar/batmitzvah (**son/daughter of the commandment**)
Ceremony for boys and girls aged thirteen in which they are called to read from the *Torah* in acknowledgement of the beginnings of Jewish adulthood.
Barchu (**bless**)
Prayer in all daily, Sabbath and festival services calling the worshippers to bless God.

Bat chayil **(daughter of worth)**
: Group ceremony in Orthodox synagogues for girls aged twelve, involving prayers and readings in acknowledgement of their Jewish adulthood.

Bedeken **(covering)**
: Ceremony immediately prior to a wedding in which the groom places the veil on the bride to ensure there is no mistake as to her identity, as happened in the case of Jacob in Genesis 29.25.

Beth Din **(court of law)**
: Rabbinic court, nowadays primarily concerned with supervising status cases, such as conversion, adoption and divorce.

Bikkur cholim **(visiting the sick)**
: The meritorious act of visiting anyone who is ill.

Bimah **(raised position)**
: Platform upon which is the reading desk in synagogue.

Birkat ha'mazon **(blessing over meals)**
: Thanksgiving for food.

Bittul b'shishim **(cancelled by a sixtieth)**
: Ruling that a piece of non-*kosher* food that is mixed accidentally with some *kosher* food does not render it unfit providing that it is less than one sixtieth of the volume.

Brit milah **(covenant of circumcision)**
: Ceremony in which a boy's foreskin is removed when he is eight days old in fulfilment of Genesis 17.10.

Chad gadya **(one little kid)**
: Song at the end of the Passover meal about the fate of a kid, usually interpreted as a symbol for Israel.

Chai **(living)**
: Pendant bearing the Hebrew word *chai* as a token of Jewish identity.

Chalitzah **(removing a shoe)**
: Ceremony in which a man signals his refusal to marry his late brother's childless widow, based on Deuteronomy 25.9.

Challah; plural: *challot* **(bread)**
: Plaited loaf used at the Sabbath, as a symbol of the sustenance God gave the Israelites whilst in the wilderness.

Chametz **(leaven)**
: Food that contains leaven and therefore which may not be eaten during the festival of Passover, based on Exodus 12.15.

Chanukah **(dedication)**
  Festival that usually occurs in December celebrating the re-dedication of the Temple by the Maccabees in 167 BCE and the survival of the Jewish faith despite attempts to destroy it by the Assyrians.
Chanukat ha'bayit **(dedication of one's home)**
  Ceremony of affixing a *mezuzah* to one's new home.
Chanukiah
  Nine-branched candelabra used at *Chanukah*
Chasidim; **adjective:** *Chasidic* **(pious ones)**
  Jewish sect founded in Eastern Europe in the late eighteenth century as a revivalist movement, now part of the ultra-Orthodox establishment.
Chavurah; **plural:** *chavurot* **(group)**
  Small association of like-minded individuals who meet together for prayer, study and Jewish celebrations.
Chazan; **plural:** *chazanim* **(cantor)**
  Trained singer who leads congregational prayers.
Chevra Kaddisha **(holy brotherhood)**
  Burial society that carries out the washing and shrouding of a Jewish corpse.
Chumash **(five)**
  The printed edition of the Five Books of Moses.
Chuppah **(canopy)**
  Cloth draped over four poles, under which a bride and groom stand during their wedding ceremony.
Churban **(destruction)**
  A reference to the Holocaust, in which six million Jews were murdered; also known as the *Shoah*.
Cohen **(priest)**
  A descendant of the high priest Aaron, and still having a priestly role in Orthodox synagogues today.
Dayanim **(judges)**
  Full-time judges who sit on a *Beth Din* and administer Jewish Law in the cases brought before it.
Diaspora **(dispersion)**
  Any land in which Jews live outside of Israel.
Dreidl **(spinning top)**
  Children's toy used at the festival of *Chanukah*, with four Hebrew letters on its side standing for 'A Great Miracle Happened There'.

Duchaning (**blessing**)
: Blessing given by priests in Orthodox synagogues on Sabbath or festivals, using the text of Numbers 6.24-6.

Edim (**witnesses**)
: Two adult witnesses are required to sign a *ketubah* according to Jewish Law, although Orthodoxy permits only men to be witnesses.

Elul
: Hebrew month prior to *Rosh Hashanah*, characterised by spiritual preparations for the oncoming New Year.

Eretz Yisrael
: The land of Israel.

Eshet chayil (**a woman of worth**)
: Poem recited by men on Friday evening in praise of their wives, taken from Proverbs 31.

Get; plural: *gittin* (**bill of divorce**)
: Document certifying the religious divorce of a couple.

Haftarah (**conclusion**)
: Reading from the Prophets that supplements the *Torah* portion at Sabbath and festival services.

Haggadah (**narration**)
: Book read at the Passover meal which recounts the Exodus from Egypt.

Halachah; adjective: *halachic* (**the path**)
: Jewish Law as derived from the Bible and Rabbinic literature.

Havdalah (**separation**)
: Ceremony that concludes the Sabbath, and marks the beginning of the working week; also performed at the close of festivals.

Kaddish (**sanctification**)
: Prayer at the end of daily, Sabbath and festival services in praise of God; has come to be regarded as a memorial prayer, with names of the deceased often mentioned beforehand.

Kapparot (**expiation**)
: The act of swinging a live cock, or some coins, over a person's head before *Yom Kippur* to deflect punishment for any sins one has committed.

Kashrut (**appropriate food**)
: The dietary laws concerning forbidden and permitted foods.

Kavvanah (concentration)
: The act of concentrating on the meaning of prayers that one is reciting rather than saying them by rote.

Kedushah (holiness)
: The third paragraph of the *Amidah*.

Kehillot (congregation)
: A Jewish community.

Keriah (cutting)
: The act of tearing a piece of clothing worn by a mourner shortly before a funeral.

Ketubah (document)
: The marriage contract signed by a bride and groom, and read out at the wedding ceremony.

Kiddush (sanctification)
: Blessings over bread and wine made before Sabbath and festival meals.

Kippah (covering)
: Head covering that is either worn continuously or just during prayer.

Kittel (gown)
: White robe worn at the High Holy Days, by a groom at his marriage, and by the leader of a *seder*.

K'lal Yisrael (the unity of Israel)
: The notion that all Jews are bound to each other as part of the same people, whatever their religious, cultural or geographical differences.

Kol Nidrei (all vows)
: Name given to the service on the eve of *Yom Kippur*, taken from the opening words of the prayer that starts the service.

Kosher (fit)
: Food that is permissible for Jews to eat according to the dietary laws.

Knesset (gathering)
: The parliament of the State of Israel.

Kvatter (godfather)
: Person who hands a baby boy to a *mohel* for circumcision.

Kvatterin (godmother)
: Person who brings a baby boy from his mother into the room where he will be circumcised.

Lag ba'Omer (33rd day of the counting of the *Omer*)
: Minor festival traditionally associated with happy events during an otherwise mournful period; often chosen as a date for weddings.

Lulav (palm)
: Used generally to refer to the palm, willow and myrtle branches that are bound together and waved at *Sukkot*.

Maccabee
: Family who led the Jewish revolt against the Assyrians, leading to the rededication of the Temple in 167 BCE.

Machzor (cycle)
: The festival prayer book.

Maftir (concluding)
: The last of the seven portions into which the weekly *Torah* reading is divided according to the annual cycle.

Magen David (shield of David)
: Jewish symbol, now part of the flag of Israel.

Mamzer; plural: *mamzerim* (illegitimate person)
: A person born of an incestuous or adulterous relationship.

Mamzerut (illegitimacy)
: The condition of being a *mamzer*.

Mazeltov (good luck)
: Term of congratulations.

Menorah (candelabra)
: Seven-branched candlestick that was used in the Temple.

Mezuzah (doorpost)
: Container with the first two paragraphs of the *Shema* inside attached to the front door of one's home and other rooms.

Mikveh (gathering of water)
: Ritual bath used privately by those converting to Judaism, by women following their menstrual period, or by a bride and groom before their wedding.

Minhag (custom)
: A practice that has evolved and may vary according to locality.

Minyan (quorum)
: The presence of ten adult males which, traditionally, is required in order for certain prayers to be said publicly.

Mi-sheberach (may He who blesses)
: Blessing given after performing a *mitzvah* in a synagogue service.

Mishnah; adjective: *mishnaic* (learning)
: Rabbinic commentary on the Bible completed around 200 CE.

Mitzvah; plural: *mitzvot* (command)
: One of the 613 commandments; also a good deed; also an honour in a synagogue service.

Mizrach (east)
: Plaque on the eastern wall of a house, indicating the direction of Jerusalem.

Mohel; plural: *mohalim* (circumciser)
: Person who performs a circumcision.

Ner Tamid (eternal light)
: Light above the ark in synagogue that is always on, reminiscent of the *menorah* in the Temple; now often also regarded as a reminder of the eternal presence of God.

Niddah (menstruous woman)
: Woman who is in the midst of her menstrual cycle; traditionally banned from all physical contact with any man, including her husband.

Nisan
: Hebrew month occurring around April; Passover is on 15th *Nisan*.

Omer, Counting of the (a measure)
: The forty-nine day period between *Pesach* and *Shavuot*; originally offerings from the barley harvest were brought each day to a Temple and counted.

Parashah (portion)
: A section from the weekly reading of the *Torah*.

Pesach (Passover)
: Festival celebrating the Exodus from Egypt.

Pidyon ha'ben (redemption of the first born)
: Ceremony in which traditionally a first born boy is presented to a priest and then redeemed by his father.

Pikuach nefesh (saving of life)
: The ruling that all prohibitions (excluding idolatry, incest and murder) may be ignored in order to preserve human life.

Prosbul (before the assembly)
: Legal formula to override the ban on claiming debts after the Sabbatical Year; enacted by Hillel in the first century.

Purim (lots)
: Festival celebrating the deliverance of the Jews of Persia from Haman's attempts to kill them

***Rosh Hashanah* (Head of the Year)**
: The Jewish New Year.

***Sandek* (companion of the father)**
: Person who holds a baby boy whilst it is being circumcised.

***Sanhedrin* (council)**
: Assembly of 71 elders that met in Jerusalem and was the supreme legislative body in ancient Israel.

***Seder*; plural: *Sedarim* (order)**
: The service surrounding the Passover meal.

***Selichot* (supplications)**
: Penitential prayers recited shortly before the New Year.

***Semichah* (laying of hands)**
: Ordination ceremony for Rabbis.

***Sephardi* (biblical place name)**
: Term now used for Jews originating from the Spanish peninsula and the Mediterranean.

***Shabbat* (Sabbath)**
: The day of rest, beginning at sunset on Friday evening.

Shabbateanism
: Seventeenth century movement that considered Shabbetai Zvi to be the Messiah; it was discredited after his conversion to Islam, although some adherents maintained their belief.

***Shalom Aleichem* (peace be with you)**
: Song on Friday evening to welcome the Sabbath.

***Shatnes* (mixed fabric)**
: Clothing that contains a mixture of wool and linen, banned according to Leviticus 19.19.

***Shavuot* (weeks)**
: Festival celebrating the revelation at Mount Sinai.

***Shechitah* (slaughter)**
: Jewish method of killing animals for food as quickly and painlessly as possible.

***Sheitel* (wig)**
: Wig worn by some Orthodox women upon marriage as a sign of modesty.

***Sheloshim* (thirty)**
: The first month of mourning after the loss of a close relative.

Shema (hear)
Quotation from Deuteronomy 6.4-9, ll.13-21 and Numbers 15.37-41 recited in all morning and evening services.

Shemini Atzeret (eighth day of assembly)
The additional eighth day of *Sukkot* in the Orthodox calendar, but combined with *Simchat Torah* by the Reform.

Sheva brachot (seven blessings)
Blessings recited at a marriage ceremony.

Shivah (seven)
The first week of mourning after the loss of a close relative.

Shnoddering (offering)
The custom in some circles of encouraging those given an honour in the synagogue service to make a donation to synagogue funds and announcing the amount publicly.

Shomer (guard)
Person who supervises the production of *kosher* food.

Shofar (horn)
The horn of a *kosher* animal, often a ram, used at the New Year and Day of Atonement.

Shul
Yiddish term for synagogue.

Shulchan Aruch (the prepared table)
Sixteenth century work by Joseph Caro summarising the main practices of Jewish Law; it became recognised as a definitive statement and served to standardise divergent customs.

Siddur (order)
Prayer book

Simchat Torah (rejoicing of the law)
Festival immediately after *Sukkot* marking the end of the cycle of readings from the Pentateuch, by reciting the last chapter of Deuteronomy and immediately starting a new cycle of readings with the first chapter of Genesis.

Siyyum (conclusion)
Celebration held after completing the study of a tractate from the *Talmud*.

Sofer; plural: *soferim* (scribe)
Person responsible for writing the Hebrew text of ritual objects such as a *Torah*, *mezuzah* and *tefillin*.

***Sukkot* (Tabernacles)**
Festival commemorating the wanderings of the Israelites in the wilderness, and the time of the fruit harvest.
***Taharah* (purification)**
Ritual washing of a dead body.
***Tallit* (gown)**
Prayer shawl.
***Tallit katan* (small gown)**
Undergarment with *tzitzit* on each of the four corners; also known as *arba kanfot*.
***Talmud* (learning)**
Rabbinic commentary on the *Mishnah*; repository of Jewish Law completed around 500 CE.
***Tashlich* (casting)**
Ceremony at *Rosh Hashanah* of symbolically casting one's sins into a river or the sea.
***Tefillin* (prayer boxes)**
Leather boxes containing the *Shema* worn on one's head and arm in conformity with Deuteronomy 6.8.
***Terefah* (torn)**
Generally used to refer to food that is not fit for consumption by Jews.
***Tevilah* (immersion)**
Immersion in a *mikveh* or river, generally by a proselyte for conversion, or by a woman at the end of her menstrual period.
***Tichel* (covering)**
Headscarf worn by some Orthodox women upon marriage.
***Tikkun Leil Shavuot* (study for the night of *Shavuot*)**
All night study session on the eve of *Shavuot*, paralleling the preparation made by the Israelites in anticipation of the revelation at Mount Sinai.
***Tikkun olam* (repairing the world)**
Restoring the world to the state of harmony that existed in the Garden of Eden.
***Tishah B'Av* (ninth of *Av*)**
Fast day commemorating the destruction of the First and Second Temples in Jerusalem, and other tragedies in Jewish history.
***Torah* (teaching)**
The five books of Moses; also used to refer to the entirety of Jewish teaching.

Tropp (**melody**)
   The cantillation by which the weekly *Torah* portion is sung in some synagogues.
Tu Bi'Shevat (**fifteenth of** *Shevat*)
   The New Year for Trees; the time at which saplings are planted and existing trees are tithed.
Tzedakah (**righteousness**)
   Charity.
Tzitzit (**fringes**)
   The fringes on the four corners of a *tallit*.
Unetaneh tokef (**we declare how profound**)
   Prayer at the beginning of the *Rosh Hashanah* additional service on the theme of the supreme power of God.
Vachers (**watchers**)
   Individuals who watch over the dead body before it is buried, reciting psalms.
Yahrzeit (**time of year**)
   The anniversary of a person's death.
Yeshivah (**academy**)
   Institution for Jewish studies, primarily concentrating on the *Talmud*.
Yigdal (**may He be magnified**)
   Song at the end of Sabbath and festival evening services, summarising Maimonides' Thirteen Principles of Faith.
Yihud (**togetherness**)
   The time a bride and groom spend alone together immediately after their marriage; originally the time of consummation.
Yizkor (**may He remember**)
   Memorial service for those who have died, held on *Yom Kippur* and at other times.
Yom Ha'atzma'ut (**day of independence**)
   Israel Independence Day.
Yom Kippur (**day of atonement**)
   Day spent in prayer, repentance and fasting.
Yom Ha'Shoah (**day of destruction**)
   Fast day commemorating the victims of the Holocaust.
Zemirot (**songs**)
   Melodies particularly associated with Sabbath table songs.

INDEX

The Glossary starting on page 255 provides explanations of Hebrew terms.

abortion 211-13
adoption 174, 175, 176, 183, 209
adultery 48, 189-90, 191, 229
after-life 36-7, 79-80
agunah 89, 186, 195
AID 209
AIDS 216-18
AIH 208
Akiva school 20, 165
Aleinu 20, 79, 87, 88
aliyah 20, 202, 204
Amidah:
    development 78
    language of 86, 87
    Reform changes 21, 79, 88
    relationship with God in 30
    resurrection reference 36, 88
animals, treatment of, 112, 113, 225
anti-semitism 19, 201
apartheid 235
apostasy 156, 170-1, 180
Aramaic 80, 86
arba kanfot 92-3, 125
arms trade 235
artificial insemination 208-9

Artzenu 203-4
Ashkenazi:
    child naming 42
    liturgy 81
    Reform history 5
    tallit style 93
Assembly of Rabbis:
    establishment of guidelines 10, 174
    membership 18
Association of Reform and Liberal *Mohalim* 14, 40
Association of Synagogues in Great Britain 24
astrology 38, 241
authority:
    Oral Law 6
    Reform Rabbis 18, 53, 159
    Torah 3, 6, 244
autopsy 56-7

baby blessing 41-2, 73
baptism 156, 178, *see also* 'Jews for Jesus'
Barchu 87, 102
barmitzvah:
    adult men 47
    ceremony 43-7, 89, 157

non-Jewish father's role 73
photography 105
bat chayil 8, 47
batmitzvah:
   adult women 47, 91
   ceremony 44-7, 89
   non-Jewish father's role 73
   photography 105
   tallit present 94
bat Torah ceremony 46
bedeken 51
Ben Gurion, David 205
ben Torah ceremony 46
best man 51, 74
Beth Din, Reform:
   adoptions role 174, 175, 176, 183
   conversions role 15, 174-6, 179-83, 187-8
   divorce role 184-9
   establishment 7, 174
   mamzerut 190
   membership 18, 174
   Orthodox attitude to 53, 187, 193-4
   status decisions 18, 53, 156, 174-6
Bevis Marks 5
birth 40
birth control 213
blessings over food 114
B'nai Brith 239
body, donating to science 58
books 119, *see also* prayer book
Bradford Reform Synagogue 200
bridesmaids 51, 74
brit milah 40
Buddhism 223
burial 24, 67-9, *see also* funerals
business ethics 224-7, 233

candlesticks 118
car travel 4, 9, 136-7
Centre for Jewish Education 14
Chad gadya 86
chai sign 125
chalitzah 47, 89, 209
chametz 145-6
chanting 99
Chanukah 48, 99, 126, 160
chanukiah 118
charity 46, 110, 119, 143, 161-3
Chasidism 21, 23, 81, 125, 241
chazan 102
chevra kaddisha 56
children:
   adoption 183, 209
   conversion of 179, 181-3
   naming 42, 70
   of mixed-faith marriage 169-70
   see also baby blessing, bar/batmitzvah, education
choirs 19, 101-2
Christianity 24, 178, 222-4, 238, 239
Christmas 125-6
chuppah 50, 51-2, 180, 184, 229
Church of England 223
cigarettes 214-15
circumcision:
   adopted children 183
   ceremony 40-1
   converts 178, 181
   non-Jewish children 43
   non-Jewish father's role 73
civic duty 127
clothing:
   arba kanfot 92, 125
   distinctive Jewish 125
   funerals 59

general 96-7
head-covering 6, 96, 125
kittel 52, 143
Rabbinic 21, 143
ritual 92
shatnes 3, 95
tallit 12, 21, 92, 93-5
tefillin 20, 90, 92, 95
weddings 52
Yom Kippur 143-4
cohen:
    funerals 60, 191, 193
    marriage 48, 90, 191-3
    pidyon ha'ben 42-3, 191-3
    Reform attitude 191-3
condoms 213, 217
conduct 110, 244
Conservative movement 187
contraception 212, 213, 217
conversion:
    Beth Din role 174-6, 179-83, 187-8
    children 179, 181-3
    course requirements 15, 178
    learning difficulties 175
    Liberal-Reform differences 15
    mikveh 9, 15, 116, 117, 178, *see also tevilah*
    mixed-faith marriages 168
    Orthodox attitude 20, 187-8, 196
    Reform attitude 176-81
    status of converts 179, 190
    traditional approach 176-7
    see also 'Jews for Jesus'
Council of Christians and Jews 222
Council of Reform and Liberal Rabbis 14
covenant 2, 244

cremation 24, 67-9

Day of Atonement *see Yom Kippur*
death 56-8, 186, *see also* after-life, euthanasia, funerals, hospices, mourning customs, resurrection
death penalty 6, 24, 79, 195
dietary laws *see kashrut*
divorce:
    Beth Din role 174-6, 184-9
    Liberal-Reform differences 15
    Orthodox attitude to Reform 15, 20, 187-9
    rate 122
    Reform procedure 15, 20, 184-7
    re-marriage 48, 122
    see also get
dreidls 160
dress *see* clothing

ecology 230-2, 245
education, Jewish:
    at home 163-4
    importance of study 108-9
    Jewish day schools 165-6
    Rabbi's role 16
    religion school 164-5, 167-8, 179, 181-2
    schools 126, 166
    synagogue 164
electricity, use on *Shabbat* 137
embryology 210-11
employment on *Shabbat* 135
environmental concerns 230-2
Esther, Fast of 150
ethics 110, 224-7, 233-4, 244

euthanasia 218-20
expulsion of Jews (from England and Spain) 150

faith 30-1
family life, Jewish 120-3
fast days 4, 149-51
Feinstein, Moshe 196
fertilisation techniques 208-9
festivals:
    permitted activities 142
    second days 147-9
first born, redemption of (*pidyon ha'ben*) 42-3, 191, 192, 193
foetus, status of 211-13
food *see kashrut*
Freemasons 238-40
free-will 35, 38
Friends of Progressive Judaism in Israel 14, 203
fund-raising 160-1
funerals:
    clothing 59
    cremation 24, 67-9
    donations 62
    flowers 61
    'Jews for Jesus' 172
    minyan 61, 104
    non-Jewish spouse 74-5
    service 59-61
    stillborn children 70
    suicides 72
    timing 58-9
    see also mourning customs

gambling 160-1

Gedaliah, Fast of 150
Germany:
    Orthodox-Reform relationship 197
    Reform origins 5, 23-4
get:
    Beth Din role 184-6
    Israeli position 189
    Liberal policy 15
    Orthodox policy 185-6, 188-9, 195, 196
    Reform policy 15, 20, 184-6, 188-9
    re-marriage 47, 185-7
ghettos 5
God, Reform beliefs 28-31, 156-7
good deeds 110
grace after meals 86, 90
Green issues 230-2
guilt, collective 34
gurus 241

Haftarah:
    bar/batmitzvah readings 44
    blessings 20, 102
    readings 99-100
Haggadah 3, 146, 241
halachah:
    Beth Din role 174
    development 6, 24
    Reform attitudes 7, 8-12, 21, 28, 187
    Reform guidelines 248-9
havdalah 90, 118, 132-3, 248
head-covering 6, 12, 96, 125
Hebrew, attitudes to:
    Liberal 12, 13

Reform 24, 86-8
  teaching 164, 165
High Holy Day prayer book (*machzor*)
  21, 84-6, 153
Hinduism 223
Holocaust:
  commemoration 151-3
  cremation objections 68
  effect on Christian thinking 223
  effect on Reform thinking 19, 32, 200
  Memorial Service 81, 152-3
  perceptions of God's role 30, 35
  Tishah B'Av 150, 151-2
  Yom Ha'Shoah 152
home, Jewish 117-20
homelessness 22, 235-6
homosexuality 22, 227-30
horoscopes 38
hospices 54-6
hospitality 117, 132
human rights 21, 206, 233, 236-7, 245
hunger 237-8

illness *see* hospices
incest 189-90, 209
Initiation Society 40
insanity 185-6
insemination, artificial 208-9
interest payment 24, 195
inter-faith relations 8, 177, 222-4
in vitro fertilisation (IVF) 208
Islam 222-4
Israel, State of:
  borders 205-6
  citizenship 188, 204
  Law of Return 188, 204

Messianic Age 33
Reform attitude 20
Reform Movement in 203-4
status of Reform converts 188
status of Reform divorces 188-9
support for 203
uncritical support 204-5
Yom Ha'atzma'ut 81, 201
Zionism 200-2
IVF 208

Jerusalem Platform 201
Jewish Burial Society 56
Jewish education *see* education
Jewish family life 120-3
Jewish Gay and Lesbian Group 229
Jewish home 117-20
Jewish Religious Union 12
Jewish status *see* status
Jewish Support for the Homeless 234
Jewish Welfare Board 233
Jews Against Apartheid 234
'Jews for Jesus' 170-2
Joint Israel Appeal (JIA) 161, 203
JONAH 234
Judaism, Reform-Orthodox position
  22-5
Judea 206

Kaddish:
  at cremations 69
  Holocaust memorial service 153
  language 80, 86
  minyan for 102, 104
  Reform practice 17, 22-3, 80
  yahrzeit 66-7

kapparot 143
Karaites 195
kashrut:
    Leo Baeck College policy 252
    Liberal approach 15
    personal observance 11, 111-13, 125, 248
    Reform approach 15, 111, 125, 194, 248
    synagogue functions 12, 21, 114
    wine 115
Kedushah 102
ketubah:
    cancelling 184
    illustrated 52, 119
    names on 42
    parents' 47
    text 50
    witnesses 51, 90
kiddush 90, 114, 118, 131, 138-40
kippah 96
kitchen, *kosher* 119
k'lal Yisrael 20, 194-5
Kol Nidrei:
    appeals 161-3
    prayer 21, 86
kosher see kashrut, kitchen, *Pesach*
Kristallnacht 153
kvatter 40, 73
kvatterin 40

language of prayer book:
    inclusive 21, 28, 88-9
    vernacular 5, 12, 80, 86-8
Law of Return 188, 204
learning 108-9
Leo Baeck College 14, 18, 158, 251

lesbianism 227-30
Levites 192
Liberal Movement:
    history 12-13
    relationship with Reform 13-16, 187
life, respect for 3, 57, 214, 218
life-support machines 218, 220
loans during Sabbatical year 6, 195
Lotan, kibbutz 201
lulav 144

machzor 21, 84-6, 153
magen David 125
Maimonides 13, 28, 95, 234
mamzer:
    definition 189-90
    marriage 48, 190, 194, 195
    Orthodox view 186, 189-90, 194, 196
    Reform approach 9, 48, 186, 190-1, 195
Marks, David 6
marriage:
    homosexual 229-30
    in Israel 188, 189
    living together before 122-3
    mixed-faith 18, 22, 167-70, 181
    Orthodox attitude to Reform 52-3
    Orthodox-Reform 194, 196
    polygamy 6, 24, 190
    reciprocal vows 4, 50
    relationship 121-2
    validity 52-3
    weddings 47-52, 73-4, 104-5, 150-1
    see also divorce, *ketubah*

Marriage Act (1949) 53, 167
meditation 241
membership of a synagogue 156-8
Messiah 31-3, 79, 170-1
Messianic Age 32-3, 36, 79, 95, 171, 245
mezuzah 117-18
mikveh 9, 48, 115-17, see also conversion
minyan 61, 89, 102-4
miscarriage 70-1
mixed-faith marriage see marriage
mizrach 119
Montagu, Lily 12
Montefiore, Claude 12
moral commands, Reform attitude 4, see also business ethics, political action, social action
mourning customs:
　after *shivah* 64-5
　at time of death 62
　miscarriage 71
　non-Jewish spouse 74-5
　shivah 62-4
　stillbirth 4, 10, 69-70
　stone-setting 65-6
　suicide 72
　yahrzeit 66-7
murder 211, 219
music 3, 8, 19, 24, 100-2

naming children 42, 70
nationalism, Jewish 19, 201, 204
ner tamid 101, 248
New Age 241-2
non-Jewish:
　children 43

choristers 101
employees on *Shabbat* 136
relatives at ceremonies 72-5
see also status
nuclear issue 21, 234

Omer period 48, 152
organ playing 3, 8, 12, 19, 21, 100-2
organs, donating and transplanting 58
Orthodox Judaism:
　attitude to Liberal Movement 13
　attitude to Reform conversions 187-8
　attitude to Reform divorces 188-9
　attitude to Reform marriages 52-3
　Reform comparison 22-5

paganism 242
Pesach (Passover)
　fast of the firstborn 150
　food 113, 145
　length 147-8
　observance 145-6
　plate 118
Pharisees 23, 36
photographs of ceremonies 104-5
pidyon ha'ben ceremony 42, 191, 192, 193
political action 21-2, 232-4
polygamy 6, 24
postmortem 56-7
poverty 21, 237-8
prayer 31, 109-10, 241, 245
prayer book:
　development 20, 78-83
　Forms of Prayer 78

274 FAITH AND PRACTICE

High Holy Day Services 20-1, 84-6, 153
Holocaust reminders 153
language 5, 12, 21, 28, 86-9, *see also* Hebrew
Liberal-Reform differences 13
Reform changes 20-1
pregnancy 70, 211-13
priesthood 4, 192-3
Prophets 21, 233-4, 244
proselytes:
    bar/batmitzvah 47
    family deaths 75
    status 179, 190, 192
    traditional attitudes to 176-7
    see also conversion
Protocols of Zion 239
Pro-Zion 14, 203
punishment 2-3, 33, 35-6, 37
Purim:
    Fast of Esther 150
    Liberal attitude 13
    weddings 48

Rabbinic:
    Judaism 23, 36
    Law 6, 244
    Literature 6, 81, 133
Rabbis:
    authority 18, 53, 159
    role 8, 16-19, 49, 249
    training 14, 17, 18
    women 13, 21, 89, 158-60
racism 237
Rashi 234
Reform Movement, history 5-8
Reform Synagogues of Great Britain (RSGB):

Beth Din 174, 176
    ecology policy 231-2
    Israel policies 205-6
    Pro-Zion 203
    shechitah policy 112
    Social Issues Group 234
    Sternberg Centre 116, 174
    ULPS comparison 12, 14-15
    Zionism 201-2
refugees (1930s) 7
Reinhart, Harold 7, 175
religion school 164-5, 167-8, 179, 181-2
resurrection of the dead 24, 36, 68, 79-80
revelation 2, 3, 11, 28, 30, 244
reward and punishment 33, 35-6, 37
ritual:
    clothing 92
    objects 118
    observances, Reform attitude 4, 20-1, 245
robbery 225-6, 248
Rosh Hashanah:
    Liberal-Reform differences 15
    observance 142-3, 147
    Reform changes 21
    second day 148, 149

Sabbath:
    beginning 138
    celebration alone 139-40
    Day 132-3
    definition of work 9, 133-6
    ending 139
    Eve 131-2
    evening service times 138-9

hobbies 136
housework 136
money handling 135
observance 3, 10, 130
preparation 130-1
travel 4, 9, 24, 136-7
use of electricity 11, 134, 137, 248
see also services
sacrifices 3, 9, 24, 79, 192
Sadducees 23, 36
'safe sex' 216
Samaria 206
Samaritan community 195
sandek 41, 73
Sanhedrin 6
Satmar Chasidim 200
schools:
    assembly 166
    choice of 126
    Jewish day 165-6
    religious education classes 166
seances 37
seder, communal 8, 146
Selichot service 20, 85
Sephardi:
    child naming 42
    liturgy 81
    Reform history 5
    tallit style 93
sermons 8
services:
    length 5, 6, 79
    Liberal 12-13
    minyan for 103-4
    music 3, 8, 12, 19, 21, 24, 100-2
    non-Jews attending 72-3
    Reform changes 20-1
    Reform-Orthodox comparison 22
    Reform variation 19
    Sabbath (second century) 6
    see also funerals, prayer book, weddings *and* festivals by name
sexual behaviour:
    AIDS 216-18
    homosexuality 227-30
    pre-marital 123, 216
Shabbat see Sabbath
Shabbateanism 23
shatnes 95
Shavuot 46, 99, 144, 147, 148
shechitah 112
sheitel 96, 249
sheloshim 64, 65
Shema 86, 87
Shemini Atzeret 144, 149
Sheva brachot 50, 51, 104
shivah:
    minyan 103-4
    observance 62-4
    stillborn children 69, 70
    suicides 72
shofar 4, 142
Shulchan Aruch 7, 11
siddur 13
Simchat Torah:
    Liberal attitude 13
    Reform celebration 98, 144-5, 148-9
    scroll carrying 12, 89, 145
Sinai 2, 28, 30, 147, 244
single parent families 122
Six Day War 201
smoking 214-15
social action 232-4
society, Jewish relationship with 123-7

276 FAITH AND PRACTICE

soul, immortality of 36-7
Soviet Jewry 8, 204, 233
spiritualism 37-8
status, Jewish:
    AID 209
    babies 43
    Beth Din role 18, 156, 174-6, 193
    'Jews for Jesus' 172
    Liberal-Reform differences 14-15
    mixed-faith marriages 169-70
    non-Jewish relatives 72-5
    Orthodox-Reform differences 193-7
    Reform conversions 187-8
    Reform divorces 188-9
    Reform marriages 52-3
    Reform policies 20, 193-7, 248
    surrogate motherhood 210
    synagogue membership 156
stealing 225-6, 248
sterilisation 213
Sternberg Centre for Judaism 116, 153, 170, 215
stillborn children 4, 10, 69-70
stone-setting 65-6, 72
Strauss, Joseph 200
study 108-9
suffering 33-6
suicide 72, 214, 219
sukkah 90, 144
Sukkot 98, 99, 144, 148-9
superstitions 62, 118, *see also* spiritualism
surrogate motherhood 209-10
synagogue:
    fund-raising 160-1
    kashrut 11, 21, 114
    membership 156-8, 169, 172

religion school 164-5, 167-8
seating arrangements 12, 91

taharah 56
tallit 12, 21, 92, 93-5
Talmud:
    early Reform attitude 6
    on conversion 177
    on funerals 61
    on *kashrut* 112
    on language 86
    on prolonging life 219
    on role of women 90, 93, 159
    present Reform attitude 21
    Sabbath work guidelines 133-5
tashlich 142-3
tefillin 20, 90, 92, 95
telephone, use on *Shabbat* 11, 137
Temple:
    destruction 60, 149-50
    Freemasonry 239
    menorah 248
    music 100-1
    rebuilding 32, 192
    services 79, 144
tevilah:
    for children 181, 183
    'Jews for Jesus' 172
    Liberal policy 15
    Reform policy 15, 20, 178, 194
    see also conversion
theft 225-6, 248
Thirteen Principles 13, 28
Tikkun olam 32
Tishah B'Av 48, 99, 101, 149-50, 151-2
tombstones 65

Torah:
   authorship 5, 244
   bar/batmitzvah ceremony 44-5, 157
   blessings 102
   early Reform theology 6
   minyan for reading 103
   readings 97-9
   role 2-3
   scrolls 89, 145, 153
   Shavuot 147
   translations 86
   triennial cycle 97, 99
tradition, Reform attitude 3-4, 245, 248
Transcendental Meditation (TM) 241
transplants, organ 57-8
Tu Bi'Shevat 232
Tzedek 234
tzitzit 92-3

Unetaneh tokef 21
Union of Liberal and Progressive Synagogues (ULPS) 12, 14-15
United States:
   AIDS 216
   Orthodox-Reform relationship 23, 196, 197
   Reform Movement 8, 23

vachers 57
vasectomy 213
video recording of ceremonies 104-5

wall coverings 119
Warsaw Ghetto Uprising 152
weddings 47-52, 73-4, 104-5, 150-1
   see also marriage
West London Synagogue:
   courts 174
   history 5, 12
   influence 7
   marriage legislation 53
   membership restrictions 158
Westminster Synagogue 153
wine, *kosher* 115
women:
   clothing 96-7
   family role 121
   funerals 60-1
   halachic status 7
   head-covering 96, 249
   inclusive language 21, 28, 88-9
   mikveh 115-17
   prayers 79
   Rabbis 13, 21, 89, 158-60
   Reform role 4, 9, 89-92, 245
   ritual wear 92
   tallit wearing 93-4
   wife's vows 3
   see also batmitzvah, mikveh
world poverty and hunger 237-8
World Union for Progressive Judaism 14, 201
World Zionist Organisation 20, 201

Yahel, kibbutz 201
yahrzeit 66-7, 72, 75, 153
Yiddish 20
Yigdal 13
Yizkor service 67, 84, 144
yoga 240-1
Yom Ha'atzma'ut 81, 146, 201, 205
Yom Ha'Shoah 152

Yom Kippur:
  Biblical mention 149
  confessions 226
  health 17
  Kol Nidrei appeals 161-3
  observance 143-4
  services 84-5, 153
  sin offering 160

Zionism 20, 200-2